MW01025745

Sartre and the Phenomenology of Education

Sartre and the Phenomenology of Education

Education for Resistance

Cameron Bassiri

LEXINGTON BOOKS
Lanham • Boulder • New York • London

Published by Lexington Books
An imprint of The Rowman & Littlefield Publishing Group, Inc.
4501 Forbes Boulevard, Suite 200, Lanham, Maryland 20706
www.rowman.com

86-90 Paul Street, London EC2A 4NE

British Library Cataloguing in Publication Information Available

Library of Congress Cataloging-in-Publication Data

Names: Bassiri, Cameron, author.
Title: Sartre and the phenomenology of education : education for resistance / Cameron Bassiri.
Description: Lanham : Lexington Books, [2024] | Includes bibliographical references and index.
Identifiers: LCCN 2023040463 (print) | LCCN 2023040464 (ebook) | ISBN 9781666905175 (cloth) | ISBN 9781666905182 (ebook)
Subjects: LCSH: Sartre, Jean-Paul, 1905-1980--Knowledge and learning--Education. | Education--Philosophy. | Phenomenology.
Classification: LCC B2430.S34 A5 2024 (print) | LCC B2430.S34 (ebook) | DDC 142/.7--dc23/eng/20231016
LC record available at https://lccn.loc.gov/2023040463
LC ebook record available at https://lccn.loc.gov/2023040464

∞™ The paper used in this publication meets the minimum requirements of American National Standard for Information Sciences—Permanence of Paper for Printed Library Materials, ANSI/NISO Z39.48-1992.

For my parents and my sister

Contents

Acknowledgments ix

Introduction: Sartre's Phenomenology of Education 1

PART I: COMMITTED EDUCATION 13

Chapter 1: Education as Praxis 15

Chapter 2: The Temporality of Committed Education 45

Chapter 3: Literature and the Culture of the Imaginary 71

PART II: INSTITUTIONALIZED EDUCATION 101

Chapter 4: Education as Assimilation 103

Chapter 5: The Temporality of Institutionalized Education 133

Chapter 6: Institutionalized Culture as Perpetual Depersonalization 159

Conclusion: Biography and Prophecy 189

Bibliography 203

Index 209

About the Author 221

Acknowledgments

This book is the completion of a train of thought that began several years ago. As I developed and completed this project, I was fortunate enough to work with a number of colleagues, and I would like to take the opportunity to thank them here. To begin, I would like to thank Matt Senie. He read the first complete draft of the book, certain of the revisions, and made several helpful suggestions to improve its overall quality. I would also like to thank Topher Vanek and Meghan Flatley. They were both involved with the project from its early stages and provided invaluable help with my research. Moreover, as the bulk of this research was done during the Pandemic, I am especially grateful for the time we spent discussing the project over Zoom. I would also like to thank Ian Gardner, who helped with research, particularly regarding John Stuart Mill and the theme of education, in the late stages of the project. I would also like to thank Carly Johnson and Andrew Wagner. They both read late drafts of some of the chapters of the book, were available for discussion in the months leading up to its completion, and made valuable comments as I continued to revise and polish the text. They also designed the cover for this book, which, both for its quality and appropriateness for its theme, I am especially thankful. Finally, I would like to thank my parents and my sister. As has always been the case, they have supported me in my pursuit of philosophy and shown an interest in my projects. This book is dedicated to them.

Introduction

Sartre's Phenomenology of Education

This book is an attempt to provide a Sartrean, phenomenological account of education on the basis of a close and careful reading of texts that span the entirety of Sartre's career. The theme of education was a perennial concern in Sartre's thinking and continued to develop with the different phases and orientations of his work. For example, in his early essay on Husserl's concept of intentionality, he is critical of "assimilation," "digestive" theories of knowledge, and the inherited tradition of French academic philosophy (Sartre 2010, 41).[1] And later, in his study of Flaubert, he devotes substantial portions of the text to discussions of the school system in mid-nineteenth-century France to demonstrate the importance of education for the process of Flaubert's personalization.[2] Finally, and perhaps most explicitly, in his later interviews and lectures he provides several accounts of the intellectual, their role in universities, and his own experiences as a student (Sartre 1947, 29).[3] In order to accomplish the task of establishing a comprehensive, Sartrean phenomenology of education, however, I have had to be selective with the texts from the respective periods of Sartre's philosophical thinking, primarily working through volume 1 of the *Critique of Dialectical Reason*, while also making use of the relevant texts from his early and later thought.[4] Through a close reading of such texts, I intend to show both the extent to which Sartre was sensitive to education as a historical, cultural, and philosophical issue, and that implicit, promising, and original phenomenological analyses of two orientations toward education can be articulated on their basis.[5]

The theme of education, despite its centrality for an understanding of the possibility and limits of Sartre's thought, has been largely ignored. And although there is a small literature on this topic, the importance of education for core Sartrean themes, in particular with certain of his guiding concerns in the *Critique*, has not been sufficiently appreciated.[6] This is particularly significant because the central concerns motivating the *Critique*, in particular the relation between the individual and the group and the logic and variety of group forms, naturally lend themselves to the theme of education, to the relation between students and teachers, the students to one another, and of educational groups as such. Through an account and development of the theme of education in Sartre's thought, this book serves as a reconceptualization and extension of core Sartrean concepts, such as the look, the third, as well as reflection, temporality, and the imagination. Finally, the task of providing a Sartrean phenomenology of education involves a renewed reflection on the relation between existentialism and Marxism and argues for the unique integration of subjectivity and alterity in Sartre's theory of groups through an educational hermeneutic of volume 1 of the *Critique*.

In order to demonstrate the importance of the *Critique* for a phenomenological analysis of education, I will show that the logic of the theory of groups corresponds to the logic of education, and that there are two principal forms of education to be extrapolated from the *Critique*, one that manifests its freedom and creativity, the other its ossature and alienation. In so doing, I will provide an account of a genuinely Sartrean approach to education, one which corresponds to the chapter on "The Organization" and which I have termed "Committed Education," as well as its complementary opposite, a degraded, ossified approach to education, which corresponds to "The Institution" and which I have termed "Institutionalized Education."[7] I have chosen these two group forms for a number of reasons. The Organization is the first moment of concretion in the *Critique* and contains the necessary structure, differentiation, and distribution of functions and responsibility for an established system of education to be possible. The previous group forms, namely, the group in fusion and the sworn group, do not have the internal complexity to sustain a formal system of education. This is not to say, however, that education is completely absent, nor that learning does not occur, but rather that the conditions for a *permanent* educational structure that serves as an integral component of the group is not yet possible.

The group in fusion forms itself spontaneously on the basis of an "apocalyptic moment," storms the Bastille, engages in violence to overthrow the king, and so forth (Sartre 2004a, 357). However, it is not capable of sustaining itself in such a form permanently or indefinitely. It addresses the needs of the present moment, but the relation between the members, their articulation of space, the manner in which they live time, and so forth, cannot sustain themselves in revolutionary form. This is witnessed in the text itself. Once the tasks of the group in fusion are achieved, and the revolutionary moment settles, a pledge becomes necessary for the group members to maintain cohesion, to continue to address the external threats of the government, but to now also address the internal threat of the group's dissolution. In the latter case, if an oath is not sworn, members may abandon the group, attempt to overtake it, and so forth, and the group risks dissolving into seriality or becoming a hierarchical and oppressive group. Sartre writes: "The group becomes the common objective in everyone: its *permanence* must be secured" (Sartre 2004a, 416). And again: "This reciprocity is *mediated*: I give my pledge to all the third parties, as forming the group of which I am a member, and it is the group which enables everyone to guarantee the statute of permanence to everyone" (Sartre 2004a, 421). As of yet, the group is still largely determined by the need to preserve its unity, to ensure loyalty to the group, to maintain its results, and has not yet determined itself, that is, *reflectively* grasped and "acted on itself" in order for the systematic education of its members to be of primary concern (Sartre 2004a, 445).

These two group forms, though not essential chronologically or logically to the formation of the organized group, can nevertheless serve as stages directed toward its formation. As Sartre writes: "The dialectic—as a formal law of movement—remains silent on questions of priority. There is actually no *a priori* ground for supposing that seriality is an earlier statute than the group, although it is true that the group constitutes itself in and against it" (Sartre 2004a, 678). There is, therefore, no *a priori necessity* that an Organization emerge on the basis of the statutory group, and not, for example, immediately out of the group in fusion. What is clear, however, is that the internal complexity of the organized group is the first stage in the *Critique* both in which a sustainable educational form becomes possible, but also in which it is appropriate to establish such a formal system of education. The Organization, as "the action on itself of the pledged group," further differentiates itself, is defined as "a distribution of tasks" and therefore determines roles and responsibilities, functions, and so forth, that are not only necessary for the group to maintain its cohesion as organized, but that make possible the unique "distribution of tasks," and relations among group members that comprise the possibility, as well as a system, of education (Sartre 2004a, 445–46). Sartre, as mentioned earlier, does not include an explicit account of education in "The Organization" or elsewhere in the *Critique*, and I will thus define "a system of education" in as broad a manner as possible, as the transmission of knowledge of one individual or sub-group within the Organization to another individual, group, or groups, such that "the common objective" of the group is capable of being realized, the unity of the group is preserved, and the development and future of the group are further guaranteed by the necessary education of the group members (Sartre 2004a, 459).

In the Institution, a degraded Organization, such a system of education and common objective are fundamentally altered. This group form will therefore show what education looks like in an oppressive, alienated, and rigidly hierarchical group which is guided by either a single institution or a single individual. Sartre writes: "The institution will produce its agents (organizers and organized) by giving them institutional determinations in advance, and institutionalized agents will then reciprocally identify themselves, in their relations of directed alterity, with the practical system of institutional relations" (Sartre 2004a, 607). This group, as an alienated form of the Organization, naturally lends itself to a discussion of education in groups which alter the essential characteristics of the organized group. As a result, it shows the fragility of organized educational forms, and the danger of their possible regression into oppressive, coercive, hierarchical systems of education that impose education on the group members. In this respect, the transmission of knowledge becomes limiting, alienating, and oppressive, and the system of education is meant to "produce" passive, obedient, "assimilated" group members (Sartre 2004a, 607; Sartre 1947, 29).

In order to guide the development of this book, I will draw a parallel between Sartre's conception of writing, the author, and their public, and the theme of education, the teacher, and the students. To further guide this book as a whole, I will modify certain of the fundamental questions from *What Is Literature?* namely, "What is Writing?" "Why Write?" and "For Whom Does One Write?" and reinterpret them to read: "What is education?" or, more specifically, "What is a Sartrean phenomenology of education?" "Why educate?" and "For whom does one educate?" (Sartre 1988, 25, 48, 70). Furthermore, these questions, following the two forms of education listed above, lead to two different responses, one of which emphasizes and promotes freedom, spontaneity, and creativity, the other passivity, obedience, and "assimilation" (Sartre 1947, 29). Moreover, in *What Is Literature?* Sartre writes: "Thus, whether he is an essayist, a pamphleteer, a satirist, or a novelist, whether he speaks only of individual passions or whether he attacks the social order, the writer, a free man addressing free men, has only one subject—freedom" (Sartre 1988, 68). And later:

> One does not write for slaves. The art of prose is bound up with the only régime in which prose has meaning, democracy. When one is threatened, the other is too. And it is not enough to defend them with the pen. A day comes when the pen is forced to stop, and the writer must then take up arms. Thus, however you might have come to it, whatever the opinions you might have professed, literature throws you into battle. Writing is a certain way of wanting freedom, once you have begun, you are committed, willy-nilly. (Sartre 1988, 67)

Both of these statements lend themselves to educational reinterpretation. They anticipate the role and responsibility of the teacher in committed education, but also, by way of contrast, indicate the potential alteration of these characteristics of the teacher in institutionalized education. Thus, situated and reinterpreted within the horizon of an educational hermeneutic of the *Critique*, each educational group form responds to the questions and claims of *What Is Literature?* with the aim of maintaining its form and pursuing its respective ends.

There is an additional element required to adequately situate the task of this book and show exactly why education necessarily takes these two forms. As is well known, in *Search for a Method,* Sartre states that "Marxism is the philosophy of our time" (Sartre 1968, 30). One consequence of this statement is that philosophy, literature, cultural products, and so forth, are all created within the historical context described and addressed by Marx. He further writes: "We cannot go beyond it [Marxism] because we have not gone beyond the circumstances which engendered it" (Sartre 1968, 30). As a result, the theme of education and, therefore, any attempt to provide a phenomenology of education, will also have to inhere within the context of Marxist thought. Thus, to slightly modify the above quotation with regard to my task, "Marxism is the horizon of the education of our time," and conditions and limits any approach to education as such, as well as pedagogical techniques, educational aims, and so forth, I will say here then, as further responses to the questions from *What Is Literature?* and situated within the context of Marxist thought, that committed education, a genuine Sartrean approach to education, *is a form of resistance.* And its complementary opposite, institutionalized education, *has the aim of educating to serve the sovereign, in either an individual, institution, or culture.* The aims of committed education as resistance, and of sovereign education as passive acceptance and assimilation, it follows, necessarily occur, in truth could only occur, within this context and must be understood within it. Committed education is therefore a necessary response to such circumstances, while remaining a genuine, educational group on its own terms. Its contradictory opposite, institutionalized education, as inherently and necessarily oppressive, harmonizes with such conditions, makes use of them as necessary in order for the instruction, obedience, and passivity of the group members and the subordinate components of the group to continue.[8]

Moreover, in the *Critique*, Sartre claims that need and scarcity are fundamental elements of "our history," and therefore that any historical understanding up to the present must incorporate them in its account (Sartre 2004a, 123). He writes: "It is worth pointing out that this univocal relation of surrounding materiality to individuals is expressed *in our History* in a particular and contingent form since the whole of human development, at least up to now, has been a bitter struggle against *scarcity*" (Sartre 2004a, 123). It is, however, possible that other histories which are not rooted in need and scarcity are possible, and they would have to be understood accordingly. He writes: "It is indeed logically possible to conceive of other organisms on other planets having a relation to their environment other than scarcity" (Sartre 2004a, 123). With regard to education, then, it is clear that it too occurs in a context of need and scarcity, is conditioned by them, and fashions itself in relation to them. Thus, in order for a properly Sartrean account of education to be developed, it must be rooted in the facts of need and scarcity, though it is also possible that different educational forms would correspond to histories that do not struggle with scarcity.

The discussions thus far have been concerned with grounding the theme of education in Sartre's texts, providing an account of its conditions and group forms, but did not sufficiently focus on the group members and their relation to the group. In order to do so, it is necessary to incorporate a theme from Sartre's study of Flaubert, namely, personalization.[9] This theme, I will argue, is implicit in Sartre's theory of groups, further explains why they freely develop and ossify but, above all, will complement the analyses in the *Critique* by further explaining exactly why certain group forms produce corresponding group members. In so interpreting the theme of personalization, I have limited my use of it to those aspects which are essential to the theme of education. In *The Family Idiot*, Sartre defines personalization in the following way: "In any event, personalization in the individual is nothing more than the surpassing and preservation (assumption and inner negation) at the core of a project to totalize what the world has made—and continues to make—of us" (Sartre 1987, 7).[10] This "progressive" element of Sartre's method, which I am reading into the "regressive" character of the *Critique*, makes possible an account of the personalizing effect that particular forms of education have on group members. Moreover, education, as a basis for the future of the group members and the group itself, is continuously integrated, and the process of educational personalization continues in the development of the group.[11] Sartre writes: "For this reason, the other name of this totalization which is endlessly detotalized and retotalized is *personalization*" (Sartre 1987, 6). Moreover, and continuing to build on the singularity of personalization in the account of Flaubert, through the education of its members, and their functioning as a whole, *the groups themselves are personalized*, that is, they develop certain structures, customs and traditions, cultures, and so forth. Furthermore, personalization, understood as an "endless" process of "detotalization and retotalization," raises the question of the *educational effects* on the future of the group (Sartre 1987, 6). Reinterpreted within the horizon of education, personalization opens the problem both of the constitution of group members and the continued constitution of the group by the educated group members.

The theme of personalization, as witnessed by Sartre's analysis of Flaubert, but also in other texts and interviews, is intrinsically linked to the theme of the imagination. With regard to the Flaubert project, he stated in an interview with Michel Contat and Michel Rybalka: "I believe the greatest difficulty was introducing the idea of the imaginary as the central determining factor in a person."[12] In order, then, to see the manner in which a group educates its members, personalizes them in so doing, and prepares them to be full group members, it is necessary to understand the proper relation between personalization and the imagination. To be personalized through education within a group, it follows, is to be educated with the explicit aim of *being able to imagine.* And, regarding the relation between subjectivity, freedom, and the imagination, Sartre writes in *The Imaginary*: "We may therefore conclude that imagination is not an empirical power added to consciousness, but is the whole of consciousness as it realizes its freedom" (Sartre 2004b, 186). I will argue that there is an internal connection between the concept of personalization and the capacity of subjectivity to imagine, and further that there is a form of personalization and imagination proper to each group form. Within committed education, *in order to be fully personalized, group members must be able to imagine.* And the aims of education, in a genuine, committed, educational group, are to *educate the group members to imagine.* Through its production of images and its self-derealization, the committed imagination, as a form of resistance, allows the group to continue to modify itself while maintaining its organized form. In an oppressive, institutionalized group, on the other hand, the process of personalization is in truth a process of depersonalization, and the aims of its education are simply *to educate to perceive and accept the established order as it is and to imagine in order to serve and sustain the institutionalized interests of the group.*

By integrating the concepts of personalization, education, and the imagination, I will show that groups succeed and fail by virtue of the form of the imagination present in them. Group failures are *failures of the imagination.* And such failures further explain the degradation of an initially free, organized group into an oppressive, institutionalized group, which can involve relapsing into seriality, regression into a prior group form, or continued alienation. On this basis, I will argue, in building on Sartre's aim of providing the structures of history in the *Critique*, that the imagination *undergirds, directs, and orients dialectical reason.* The dialectical rationality and intelligibility of group action relies on a particular understanding and role of the imagination in dialectical reason.[13] Part of the "structure of group *praxis*," that is, involves the presence and use of the imagination, and the *praxis* of each individual, as well as the group as a whole as comprised of particular group members, can only be comprehensively understood with the incorporation of the imagination (Sartre 2004a, 348). There is, therefore, a primacy of the imagination within the *Critique* regarding the intelligibility of the action of groups, in the case of the Organization for the free development and creativity of a genuine, educational group. Through education the group becomes a *communis imaginans* with the perpetual educational task of modifying itself, revising its educational forms, and adapting itself to new circumstances. There is a need for images in groups, for "poets," for the production of images in order for the group to educate itself, to interpret and relate to itself, and ultimately to freely develop itself to maintain itself in a modified form.[14] As such, this particular production of images has the aim of maintaining the freedom, truth, and "common objective" of the group (Sartre 2004a, 459). Education to resist through the imagination is concerned both with the potential threat that the group poses to itself as well as properly responding to need, scarcity, and the practico-inert.

It follows from what has just been discussed that if the dialectic develops freely through the creative imagination in committed education, it is limited, stunted, or constrained, in the repressed imagination of the Institution. And this is exactly what happens in the Institution regarding the theme of education. As the first transformation of the Institution, Sartre writes: "The institution, as such, has a considerable force of inertia because it posits itself, in and through its inert-being as essentiality and defines men as the inessential means of its perpetuation" (Sartre 2004a 600–601). Moreover, as Sartre notes later, the inertia of the Institution makes a claim to the future of the group members. Previous generations perpetuate the "prefabricated inertia" of the group by condemning the subsequent generations to a rigid destiny (Sartre 2004a, 606). Thus, the development of the dialectic in the Institution is only in the direction of further alienation, degradation, and depersonalization. The Institution educates its members to passively accept the institutional order of the group, and to imagine with the aim of producing new ways of preserving the institutionalized sovereign and hierarchy. There is, it follows, an internal differentiation within institutionalized education itself, namely, education to passively accept through perception and to passively accept and modify through the imagination to maintain the institutionalized order. Moreover, and as the second transformation of the Institution, this particular group form involves a sovereign, a leader, an individual who imposes their will on the orientation of the group as a whole. Through their "power," such an individual guides the life, and in this case, the education of the group (Sartre 2004a, 607). As a result, the lack and distortion of the imagination in institutions constricts its movement, confines it to a single, inertial process, and depersonalizes both the group members and the group, inscribing them with an imposed institutional character.

There is, within the dialectic of education itself, between committed and institutionalized education, a conflict of the imaginary, of forms of the imagination, a conflict analogous to the "conflict of rationalities" Sartre discusses in the *Critique* (Sartre 2004a, 802). Rather than a contradiction between "the dialectical movement of human *praxis* and the atomizing rationality of positivism," there is a conflict between the free and creative imagination of committed education with the repressed and "reproductive" imagination of institutionalized education (Sartre 2004a, 802). The "pull" of the dialectic, its tension and "direction," is in part due to the presence, limits, and use of the imagination in educational forms within the groups that they serve to compose, orient, and guide. Dialectical reason, in this sense, rests on the imagination, and one of the forms of tension between groups is that between their respective appreciation of the imagination, which, when extended to the continuous modification of groups, is also a conflict of the possibility of the imagined future with the perceived actuality of the present. The conflict is therefore between the creative imagination that undergirds the free development of the dialectic and the repressed imagination, which alienates it to a repetitive, inertial process, whose capacity is limited by the interests of the sovereign and serves the established order.

NOTES

1. The French text from the article on Husserl reads: "«Il la mangeait des yeux.» Cette phrase et beaucoup d'autres signes marquent assez l'illusion commune au realism et à l'idéalisme, selon laquelle connaître, c'est manger. La philosophie française, après cent ans d'académisme, en est encore là" (Sartre 1947, 29). A little later in the same paragraph, he writes: "Les puissantes arêtes du monde étaient rongées par ces diligentes diastases: assimilation, unification, identification" (Sartre 1947, 29).

2. With regard to the Flaubert study, in the English translation, see "School Years" in Sartre (1989, 3–352) and in the French, see "Le Collége" in Sartre (1971b, 1107–464). Also see Pucciani's discussions and quotations from Sartre regarding the importance of a system of education in Pucciani (1981, 499–500). For a more recent account of Sartre's views on education, with a particular emphasis on his account of Flaubert as an instance of the impact of education on subjectivity, see Gordon and Gordon (1997, 66–81).

3. For two later accounts of the intellectual, see Sartre (1974, 228–85) and Sartre (1974, 286–98). For a critique of the educational system in France, see Sartre (1974, 62–63). In discussing "the subject of the philosophy paper in Rouen-Le Havre," Sartre states: "There is no relationship, no contact whatever between these young people and their teachers. Bourgeois culture in France is destroying itself" (Sartre 1974, 63). And with regard to his own experiences, the following exchange from the interview entitled "The Purposes of Writing," though brief, is telling: "Sartre: I wanted to write novels and plays a long time before I knew what philosophy was. I still want to; I've wanted to my whole life. Chapsal: *Since School?* Sartre: Even before that. I found philosophy at school so boring that I was convinced it was just a waste of time. My attitude owed something perhaps to the way the subject was taught in those days" (Sartre 1974, 12).

4. In a late interview, Sartre provided an account of himself as a teacher and his approach to teaching. Of particular significance is the following claim: "I thought that teaching consisted not in making an adult speak in front of young people but in having

discussions with them starting from concrete problems. When they said, 'This guy is an idiot: he says this, but I have experienced something else,' I had to explain to them that one could conceive of the matter differently" (Rybalka, Pucciani, Gruenheck 1981, 47). For the complete account, in which he discusses boxing with his students and allowing them to smoke in class, see Rybalka, Pucciani, Gruenheck (1981, 47). Over the course of this text, I will simply write "the *Critique*" when referring to volume 1 of the *Critique of Dialectical Reason.*

5. For an account of the university culture, his first reaction to reading Marx, as well as what he and his contemporaries desired from philosophy and education, see Sartre (1968, 17–21).

6. For early, classic accounts of existentialist theories of education, see Kneller (1958, 114–48), Freire (1992, 57–74), Morris (1966, 99–133), and Barnes (1967, 281–317). For a more recent account see Detmer (2005, 78–90) and Gordon (2016, 71–88). Barnes has also discussed Sartre's views on education in her commentary on *The Family Idiot.* In particular, see Barnes (1981, 124–25). Most relevant to my purposes here are the following claims: "In fact, the school was a model of a serialized institution in all of its worst aspects. Here as in his discussion of the history of the school, Sartre, quite evidently, is directing his remarks also at contemporary education and specifically at the events leading up to and following the French students' revolt in 1968. He introduces his discussion by quoting one of the graffiti from that later event. 'Anybody who puts a grade on a paper is an asshole [*un con*]' 2:1121)" (Barnes 1981, 124–25). The English translation of the graffiti can be found in Sartre (1989, 17). For statements from Sartre regarding the relation between education and May 1969, see Sartre (1974, 61–63, 297–98). For a further account of Sartre's role in May 1968, its importance for Sartre's thinking on education, and its relation to the *Critique*, see Poster (1975, 389–98).

7. There are other ways of pedagogically interpreting these two groups, as well as other group forms in the *Critique.* However, as I will argue, these are the two fundamental forms of education to be developed through a close reading of the *Critique.* It should not, however, be thought that there are not forms of education "between" these two groups, or that these two groups alone exhaust the possibilities of a phenomenological account of educational groups in Sartre.

8. There is here a further, significant parallel with Sartre's views on the relation between literature and metaphysics in his essay "On *The Sound and the Fury*: Time in the work of Faulkner." He there writes: "A fictional technique always relates back to the novelist's metaphysics" (Sartre 1955, 84). Moreover, and worth noting in regard to my task here and the continuity of Sartre's thought from an early emphasis on metaphysics to a later emphasis on the conditions of a particular history, in the final paragraph of this article, Sartre states: "Why have Faulkner and so many other writers chosen this particular absurdity which is so un-novelistic and so untrue? I think we should have to look for the reason in the social conditions of our present life. Faulkner's despair seems to me to precede his metaphysics. . . . We are living in a time of impossible revolutions, and Faulkner uses his extraordinary art to describe our suffocation and a world dying of old age" (Sartre 1955, 93).

9. See Flynn (2014, 396–401). Moreover, regarding the relation between the "new" concept of personalization and earlier Sartrean concepts, see Flynn (2014, 397).

10. For Sartre's initial comments on personalization in *The Family Idiot*, see Sartre (1987, 3–5).

11. It is important to note a difference between what I am developing here and Sartre's aims in the Flaubert project. I am arguing for the integration of the members into the group through the process of education. In principle, it is possible for the prior education of the group member to "swerve away," to take unexpected turns in the life of the educated group member, etc. (Sartre 1987, 7). However, I am not incorporating the "nonassimilable" into my account (Sartre 1987, 6). Central though it is for Sartre in his understanding of Flaubert, it is not essential to accounting for the educational importance of personalization. Thus, on my account, education can be "detotalized and retotalized," "surpassed," etc., but it will not result in the concept of "the *person*," such that "they are always the *surpassed* result of the whole mass of totalizing operations by which we continuously try to assimilate the nonassimilable" (Sartre 1987, 6).

12. See Contat and Rybalka (1977, 119).

13. These claims should not be misinterpreted as serving as an equivalent to Heidegger's view in *Kant and the Problem of Metaphysics* that "the transcendental imagination is the root of sensibility and understanding" (Heidegger 1997, 98). Rather, the ability to imagine, on the basis of the education received, serves as a constituent element of individual *praxis* and collective action. In so doing, it both helps determine and make intelligible the manner in which dialectical reason unfolds across various group forms and why it does so.

14. For a classical critique of images and "poets," see Plato (1968, 598a–601b). I will discuss the problem of false images, of "imitation," in groups when addressing institutionalized education (Plato 1968, 598a). As I will argue, such a critique of images is appropriate to a repressive educational system.

PART I

Committed Education

Chapter 1

Education as Praxis

The chapter titled "The Organization" is the first moment of concretion in volume 1 of the *Critique of Dialectical Reason* and the point in the text in which a system of education becomes possible.[1] After the revolutionary action of the group in fusion and the settled differentiation and pledge of the statutory group, it is necessary for the group both to maintain its unity and to continue to develop its internal complexity in order to achieve the "common objective" and adapt to new circumstances (Sartre 2004a, 416).[2] In its initial characterization, it is defined as "the action on itself of the statutory group" (Sartre 2004a, 445). As such, it is the first moment of sustained reflection of the group on itself in the *Critique*. And it is precisely through this reflection that the group is able to consider its history, structures, its "concrete objectives" and the means necessary to attain them (Sartre 2004a, 416). Moreover, it is through such reflection that the problem of the education of the group can present itself, and that the question of the type of education, its different forms and methods, and in general a system of education, becomes possible and integrated into the functioning of the group. Neither prior group form possessed the internal coherence, permanent structures, or reflection necessary to consider the question of how to educate its members, what an appropriate form of education would look like, and how the group itself would be capable of providing such an education for its members at all. Both previous group forms are occupied by immediate aims—revolutionary action and internal cohesion, respectively—and as a result are not yet at a stage where the more distant, or mediate, ends can be considered clearly and the means to their realization established. The Organization, however, as an *internal and immediate reflection* of the statutory group on itself, and therefore as a *mediate reflection* on its history as the group in fusion, has the necessary foundation to establish a system of education and to connect the education of the group members to the future of the group. As a result, with the shift in the logic of groups to reflection, there is a shift from immediacy to mediation, from spontaneous action and pledged unity to the group questioning itself as a group of a certain sort and in so doing thematizing its future as a concern which is intrinsically linked to its education.

This early account of the Organization as a form of self-reflection is interwoven with an additional concern of Sartre's *Critique* as a whole, namely, the intelligibility of collective action. Furthermore, it is in the particular action made possible in the Organization by virtue of the presence of reflection that the Organization is further differentiated from the previous group forms and that education can be conceived of as a unique form of *praxis*. In this regard, the reflection and further, internal articulation of the Organization demonstrate its advancement over the *"non-differentiated praxis"* of the group in fusion and the pledge, the relations founded on it, and the corresponding *praxis* of the statutory group (Sartre 2004a, 416, 445). In addition to its advanced structure, the Organization introduces a new form of *praxis* into group action, one that was not possible until this group form had been achieved and which will further develop "the translucid (but abstract) *praxis* of the individual, and the rudimentary *praxis* of [the group in fusion]—translation modified" (Sartre 2004a, 445). By conceiving of education as itself a form of *praxis* and the collective action of the organized group as informed by education, it becomes clear that the question as to the nature of the *praxis* of the Organization, of its development of the *praxis* of the individual and that of the group, requires an account of the theme of education to be adequately answered.

In order to comprehensively account for the reflective constitution of the group through education and its significance for group members, an additional element needs to be taken into account, namely, personalization. This element is implicit in the Organization in particular, but more generally in the theory of groups as a whole in the *Critique,* though it is not fully developed or expressed until *The Family Idiot.*[3] In educating its members, the Organization also *personalizes* them. And in the Flaubert text, personalization is defined in the following manner: "personalization in the individual is nothing more than the surpassing and preservation (assumption and inner negation) at the core of a project to totalize what the world has made—and continues to make—of us" (Sartre 1987, 7).[4] I will slightly modify this definition, and claim first that personalization is the perennial totalization by the group member of what the group as a whole has made of them. Secondly, the totalizing project of the group member is not only an "assumption and inner negation," but an extension and further development of what the group has made of them through education (Sartre 1987, 7). That is to say that in the context of the Organization, it is the particular form of education that makes possible a particular form of totalization and that the personal identity of the group member, their role in the group as a group member as well as their fundamental life-choice are informed, conditioned, and cultivated through the system of education in the group. The Organization, therefore, through its internal reflection on itself, provides a basis for both individual and collective identity through its system of education. In this regard, education is understood as an additional "action of the group on itself," as a unique form of reflection that continues to clarify the group to itself, develop it as needed, and makes possible the necessary, future reflection of educated group members (Sartre 2004a, 445). As such, education is the schema through which the group relates to and understands itself, and contributes to the intelligibility of its collective action.[5]

THE TASK OF EDUCATION

After having introduced the reflective character of the Organization and its differentiation from the two previous group forms, Sartre notes a two-fold sense in the very term "organization." He writes: "The word 'organisation' refers both to the internal action by which a group defines its structures and the group itself as a structured activity in the practical field, either on worked matter or other groups" (Sartre 2004a, 446). An organized group, then, is one in which the group reflects on and modifies itself, its structures, and its functioning, and in so doing works on material objects and establishes relations with other groups. Its immanent reflection is therefore linked to its transcendent relations. One consequence for the theme of education is that the Organization educates its group members in accordance with the internal needs of the group, but also concerning the group's relations to the natural world and other groups. Education itself, therefore, has a corresponding two-fold character insofar as it has the responsibility of preparing the group members for full membership in the group, while also recognizing the consequences education will have for the transcendent action of the group. Thus, education is an act of the group on itself, a systematic reflection of the group on itself, which also possesses an external orientation toward materiality and the other groups with which it comes into contact.

This duality within the reflective action of the Organization leads Sartre to further characterize it as "a distribution of tasks" (Sartre 2004a, 446). In order to attain the goals of the group, both short- and long-term, and for the "system of relations, and relations between relations" to become concrete and intelligible, it is necessary for the Organization to build on the differentiation established through the pledge of the statutory group for the individual and the group as a whole to have a more determinate character (Sartre 2004a, 445). The reflective determination of this particular group form thus involves distributing tasks, responsibilities, functions, and assigning members an identity on the basis of the task they have been assigned. The group will accordingly "produce" the group members it needs on the basis of the current circumstances and the "common objective," that is, "the common interest, common danger, common need assigning a common aim" (Sartre 2004a, 446–47). Moreover, as a condition of possibility for the "distribution of tasks," Sartre notes a prior "distribution, that is to say, the creation within the group of *specialized apparatuses*" (Sartre 2004a, 447). And though these apparatuses are confined to an abstract phase of the *praxis* of the group, one wherein the precise goals of the group have not yet been clearly articulated, they contribute to the future realization of its concrete ends. The "distribution of tasks" throughout the group, administered through its particular apparatuses, makes possible both the establishment and fulfillment of the tasks necessary for the group (Sartre 2004a, 446).

In order to illustrate this point, Sartre uses the example of a soccer club.[6] Within such an organized group, there is a certain order and hierarchy, a system of recruitment and training, and the manner in which the club is able to distribute tasks to its various members depends upon the apparatuses and sub-groups which assign such tasks. Each member of the club, whether the coach, players, and so on, has a particular function within the club and their personal identity is connected to this function. Moreover, these functions are "predetermined," or sketched in advance, such that the individual is meant to actively take up and fulfill the task precisely as the club had previously defined it (Sartre 2004a, 450). The club makes a *demand* on its group members that they live up to their predetermined functions, that, in the case of the soccer club, the players train, are healthy, perform during the games, and so on. Sartre writes: "The team in which he has been *signified* by this function is then obliged to raise him to a (physical and technical) level at which he will be capable of performing the actions which the group requires" (Sartre 2004a, 450). And reciprocally, the members of the group demand that the club make possible the fulfillment of their functions, as well as that the other group members live up to the club's expectations. Sartre writes: "as a function of the group, he will require his fellow team members not to deflect him from his duty, or even help him to carry it out, and if necessary to force him to do so" (Sartre 2004a, 451). In addition to the reciprocity of tasks and responsibilities within such an organized group, there is also a tension, a constant demand or burden that contributes to the functioning and development of the group. Each group member, in other words, has the duty to fulfill their function and the right to demand that others fulfill theirs, which, according to Sartre, constitutes "a *power*" that the various group members have over one another (Sartre 2004a, 451).

At this point, the fundamental difference between the task of education and the other tasks in the organized group begins to present itself. As I have just shown, tasks are distributed on the basis of the needs of the group in order to attain certain ends. Sartre writes: "In the normal exercise of organized activity, *function* is a positive definition of the common individual: either the group as a whole or some already differentiated 'organ' *assigns* it to him. It is a determination of individual *praxis:* an individual belongs to the group insofar as he carries out a certain task and *only that task"* (Sartre 2004a, 449). While particular apparatuses assign particular functions to particular individuals, *education is a task of the group as a whole.* It is not confined to any single apparatus, sub-group, or period in the group's history, but is a constant task of the group as a whole that is assigned to all members as members of this particular group. Education, however, is a unique task precisely because it affects all of the members of the group, and the education obtained at one age, or in one context, or in one generation, continues to affect, guide, and orient the group members and the group itself. All of the group members, at different moments in their life in the group either are, have been, or will be, educated by the group. Furthermore, the group members are educated in accordance with the present standards and aims of the group. And the system of education, which may itself be comprised of "systems" or apparatuses corresponding to the level of education, the subject, and so on, is determined in light of the past of the group, with attention to the present, and an open, yet partly sketched future.

The educational apparatus formally educates for a determined period of time, which can itself depend on the interests of the students, the needs of the group, and so on, but regardless of such differences, it *continues to educate* after this period has ended by making possible the future of the individual in the group. It is, in this respect, *a perennial task.* And as such, it is an incomplete task, one which continually serves as a point of departure for the group members as they continue to fulfill their functions within the group. The knowledge obtained through education is not simply "applied" in various fields, but also reflected on, continuously understood and relearned, as the group members carry out their tasks. And what makes it unique is the special sense in which it is both a beginning for the group, a point of entrance for the group members, and a responsibility which continues after the period of formal education has ended. The group provides the resources for the education of its members, but assigns education as a particular task, function, and responsibility that permeates the whole of the group. Moreover, following the logic of the soccer club discussed above, the group members themselves place a demand on the group to be educated. This demand, which is in truth a demand to be able to fulfill their functions and role in the life of the group, can be directed at the group itself, a situation, or a teacher. This demand is also a demand each member makes on all the other members of the group. Furthermore, this demand too is constant. It applies to the period of formal education and the continued, subsequent development within the group.

The task of education has a second quality which further differentiates it from other tasks in the group. Although Sartre does not discuss an explicit hierarchy of tasks and functions, or an order within the Organization which can be determined a priori, education serves as a condition of possibility of the fulfillment of all other tasks and functions, and therefore is a transcendental condition for the unity and future of the group. And with an established system of education, which is itself revised and reflected on as part of the reflection of the Organization, the group will determine what needs to be taught, how subjects should be taught, and so on. However, and this emphatically differentiates the task of education from other tasks, *without a form of education appropriate to the group, the other tasks and functions cannot be fulfilled and are not capable of being "distributed*" (Sartre 2004a, 446, my emphasis). All other specialized tasks and functions, it follows, are dependent on this original task, this *arch-task,* which, as an origin, is also continuously present as a condition of possibility of the structure and future of the group. In this sense, education is "a second pledge," but one which is unique insofar as it makes possible life as a particular group member with a particular role in the group (Sartre 2004a, 485).[7]

What, however, one may ask, does such a perennial task look like after the period of formal education? How is it that the task of education can continue to permeate the whole of the group, such that the knowledge obtained is present in the tasks and functions of the educated group members? A comparison with Sartre's concept of literature from *What is Literature?* will help respond to these questions. First, it is important to note the range of what Sartre considers committed literature. He writes: "To be sure, the book is the noblest, most ancient of forms; to be sure, we will always have to return to it. But there is a *literary* art of radio, film, editorial work, and reporting" (Sartre 1988, 267). And again: "We must learn to speak in images, to transpose the ideas of our books into these new languages. Our job is to reveal to the public its own needs and, little by little, to form it so that it *needs to read*" (Sartre 1988, 217). The author, in committed literature, whose ultimate end is freedom, has a responsibility to the readers and the public to contribute to the overcoming of various, present forms of oppression and alienation. Reading, moreover, is defined as "a pact of generosity between author and reader. Each one trusts the other; each one counts on the other, demands of the other as much as he demands of himself" (Sartre 1988, 61). Literature itself, then, as oriented toward freedom, places a task, in truth a burden, on both the author and the reader, such that in freely engaging one another, they continue to unveil the contradictions of the present to be overcome in the future. The author has an individual task that permeates the group insofar as they have the obligation to articulate the present to the group, its concerns and contradictions, their possible solutions, a possible future orientation, and so on. Correspondingly, the reading public has an obligation to engage with the author, the forms and images of literature, to make demands on literature, and to then act on the basis of the knowledge obtained through literary text.

Following the logic of our earlier discussions regarding the soccer club as well as the "specialized apparatuses" that serve as a foundation for particular tasks and relations, it is clear that committed literature, which is itself a *literary group*, depends upon a system of education (Sartre 2004a, 447). Furthermore, education as I am describing it here, and will develop it throughout this chapter, is itself "a literary art" that "speaks in images" (Sartre 1988, 217, 267). In order for literature to have a meaningful presence within the group, and in order for it to fulfill its function of appealing to the freedom of the reader, articulating the present, and so on, a system of education must already have been in place to make literature in the group not only possible, but actual in the relation between author and reader. The designated apparatuses, at given stages, and with the suitable and necessary methods, techniques, and so on, need to have made literature both a value and accessible to the group such that the public can *continuously* learn from it and engage with it as a project whose end is freedom. This particular form of education, then, what I have termed committed education, is a condition of possibility for committed literature. If it is to be both possible and actual, a distribution of educational tasks must already have been decided upon and put into practice in order for the writer to be able to appeal to the freedom of the reader and for the reader to demand the revelatory *praxis* of the writer. As a result, education, a single task of the group, carried out through various apparatuses within the group, extends throughout the group as a whole regarding its past, present, and future, and makes it possible for authors and readers to continuously carry out their individual tasks and to act collectively through the images of literature (Sartre 2004a, 447). Education, in all of its forms, is a task that undergirds and makes possible all other tasks, functions, and responsibilities. As such, it is differentiated from the other, specific tasks in the group which have specific, fixed ends, insofar as its task is the education of the group as a whole, both during a fixed period in the life of the group members and in their future as educated, reflective, full group members.

THE PERSONALIZATION OF THE TEACHER

After having provided an account of education as an arch-task, it is necessary to show the manner in which the group prepares the teacher to fulfill their pedagogical role. Such preparation, which involves educationally situating the teacher in the present of the group through the appropriate knowledge of the past and anticipation of the future, is a further form of Sartre's concept of personalization. The teacher in this form of education, what I am terming "the committed teacher," is temporally and epistemologically personalized throughout this process. I will integrate the concept of personalization into the Organization and, along with certain of the features of Sartre's existential psychoanalysis, demonstrate the role it plays in fashioning an imaginative, empathetic, thoughtful teacher. Together, these concepts will serve as a basis for what it means to be such a teacher, or, in slightly different terms, to make committed teaching one's life project. Such educational personalization will also focus on the knowledge, ignorance, and imagination of the teacher, and will be general and open in order to appreciate the freedom and individuality of the teacher. It will not, then, be an overly determined or detailed analysis, but is meant to guide, to serve as a point of departure, and to demand the appropriate interpretation relative to the specific subject and academic content. As such, I am primarily concerned with explaining *the concept, role, and orientation* of the committed teacher in the Organization and situating them in this group form.

To begin, it is necessary to discuss the perspective of the group on the individual who is going to be a teacher, such that it can properly personalize them. What is the group's understanding of such an individual? First, and as the basis for the teacher's subsequent ability to engage in committed teaching, what can be understood as a primary transcendental condition, the teacher is recognized as "a being which is what it is not, and is not what it is" (Sartre 1984, 116). This claim has to be understood on a few different levels. First, the group understands the teacher in both their facticity and transcendence, past and future, a freedom which in their irreducibility lives and transcends their situation in the group. Secondly, though a group member, the group recognizes that they are more than their role in the group, more than the teacher they will become, irreducible to the primary manifestation they will have in the group. In recognizing this dual character of the individual, the group can begin the process of preparing them to teach. Thus, the group is *empathetically oriented* toward the individual in such a manner that, while providing a common basis for all teachers, the necessary pedagogical techniques, and knowledge of the subject matter, it recognizes that these will uniquely relate to the past of the individual, help fashion their present, and accommodate their future. The groups's orientation toward the teacher is therefore "completely flexible and adapts itself to the slightest observable changes in the subject. Its concern is to understand what is *individual*" (Sartre 1984, 732). The process of personalization, in this regard, is in truth a plurality of personalizations specific to the individuals in the process.

Moreover, with the necessary understanding of the transcendence of the teacher, and that the group is personalizing the individual for its own future, the process of personalization itself is presented and carried out as *to-be-surpassed.* An essential element of this process, therefore, is that of the group understanding itself as a certain kind of group, one that is guided, incarnated, and changed through its education. Without such a corresponding understanding of itself, the bounds of the group would serve to unduly limit the teacher both in their preparation for, and subsequent act of, teaching. As an additional result, the group would continue to limit itself. On a collective level, then, the group further understands itself as "what it is not and not what it is" in order to allow the appropriate form of teaching to be possible, and for it to have the impact on the group it was designed to have (Sartre 1984, 116). A restriction on both the individual and the group, rooted in a false understanding or distortion of either, would result in a state of affairs in which the teacher would not be adequately prepared to teach and in which the group would not be receptive to the changes such teaching could bring about in the students and the group.

The personalization of an educator in committed education involves an education that both produces the kind of teacher that the group needs while also recognizing and appreciating their subjectivity. The group is itself tasked with the responsibility of personalizing the teacher as a teacher in order to fulfill their function. In this regard, the group provides a specific manner in which the teacher "assumes and negates" the group, its history, as well as the previous forms and methods of education within the group (Sartre 1987, 7). This form of personalization instills the necessary knowledge of the group for the teacher to be able to fulfill their task and function, but does so by making possible spontaneity, creativity, and a particular attitude on the part of the teacher. The group, in recognizing its own limitations, appreciates itself as a condition of possibility, but one which is meant to create a possibility which is only a sketch, in many ways unforeseen, and therefore a condition which is uncertain about the very possibility it is tasked with creating. Paradoxically, the process of personalization is a process wherein the group produces the kind of teacher it needs but does so precisely by recognizing the limitations of its own pedagogical abilities and responsibilities. It makes possible the dual, tense relation in the teacher as being both an inheritance and a negation of the group. The teacher is a unique incarnation of the group as its assumption through their knowledge and its negation in their development of such knowledge, their own style of presenting it, and the manner in which they relate it to the life of the students and the group.

Regarding the history and material conditions of the group, the educational apparatuses have the task of personalizing the teacher by teaching them the conditions within which such teaching currently takes place, has done so historically, and, to a certain extent, will continue to do so. This involves, in light of the education of the group, its particular educational history, its past and present systems of education, the previous issues the system faced, and changes in curricula. From this point of view, concerning its present form, as well as the level of education and subject that the teacher has chosen to teach, the group will provide the teacher with the past life of the group both before and after the teacher has lived it. Obviously, in many senses the group has not lived the life of the teacher, nor will the teacher ever fully live the life of the past of the group or of the future of the students before them. However, in instilling the necessary, and, it is important to note, necessarily limited knowledge of the group for the teacher, the group allows the teacher to have epistemologically lived the necessary life of the group to be able to then teach the students, and to have produced a teacher who will subsequently live a life not yet lived by the group in its collective and educational history. The future of the group *is still the life of the group*, but as of yet it is an open, not-yet-lived through, not-yet-personalized life which the teacher has the task of realizing. The group, then, on the one hand, has lived the life of the teacher before them in order to make their future life in the group as a teacher possible, and on the other hand has not done so, has not, in this sense, lived its own life, insofar as the group is incarnated in the teacher who will continue, develop, and, as needed, even interrupt the past life of the group in its future through their teaching.

In providing the essential principles and techniques for future teaching, the group indicates the future life of the teacher, outlines it, and makes it familiar and intelligible. It therefore also indicates and anticipates its own present, its realization in a future state, but only to a minimal extent. It educationally temporalizes the individual in preparing them and temporalizes itself in advance insofar as it makes possible the future act of teaching in the present but not as a mere repetition of the present. It accordingly interprets the future of the teacher as *its own* present which it is not yet but necessarily will be. The group, in this peculiar sense, personalizes the teacher through instilling knowledge, pedagogical techniques, and so on, and, in so doing, never fully lives its own life, never fully coincides with itself, insofar as it is making possible its not-yet-lived-life through the future life of the teacher and the students. The group will accordingly emphasize past curricula, the relation between them and previous historical situations in the group, why they were necessary, and so on. And to the necessary extent, the group will show the teacher how it responded and continues to respond to such conditions. In this respect, the personalization process ensures that the teacher has lived the necessary life of the group in order to then present it to the students as part of their personalization process and future in the group.

This historical grounding in the education of the group is complemented by the pedagogical freedom that the group makes possible. While the process of fashioning future educators necessarily involves meeting particular criteria, understanding how to develop curricula, lesson plans, and so on, one of the central elements of the personalization of the teacher is its *incomplete, indeterminate, and creative character.* The different elements of teaching, such as the presentation of content in the classroom, the nature of assignments, context, and so on, are themselves taught in such a way that the teacher, in the process of personalization, internalizes them *on their own terms*, or, perhaps better, *makes them their own*, in such a way that they serve as a point of departure, as guidelines, if only as suggestions, for how the teacher ought to teach in the future. In this respect, Sartre's account of the training of the players of a soccer club is especially illuminating. Each plays a particular position, with a designated role, responsibility, set of skills and techniques, and the team cultivates the required abilities of each position through its training. However, the individual player also develops "*an individual style* [my emphasis]" (Catalano 1986, 187). In this sense, though playing the same position, two halfbacks, center forwards, and so on, on two different teams, can play the "same" position, but do so entirely differently. The training therefore serves as a point of departure and sets various limits to how the position is to be played. However, within the established range of the position, the player is free to develop and modify as necessary what was taught to fulfill the aims of the group. Similarly, in preparing the teacher, the necessary techniques, information, and so on, are given, but with the explicit understanding that they will not *exhaustively* personalize the teacher. It will be the responsibility of the teacher to build on and extend them through their own, unique style of teaching.

The personalization of the teacher is incomplete for a second reason as well. As much as the group prepares the teacher to teach a certain subject, to interact with students, there are always unpredictable, unforeseen elements in the culture of a given classroom. Thus, depending on the individual class, the relation established between the teacher and students, as well as the other elements that comprise the historical moment of the group, there will be unique and unexpected aspects of teaching and the classroom experience which require modification on the part of the teacher. The personalization begins with preparation for "an educational class as such," or "a group of students as such," but cannot take into account every nuance that will present itself in a particular classroom.[8] As a result, even while teachers may themselves teach classes as part of their preparation, the very act of teaching itself, in truth, *the very nature of education itself,* is defined by an intrinsic uncertainty and unpredictability. The group does not need an educator who has been educated "all the way down," who has been instilled with certain, necessarily fixed educational standards and practices, but rather a teacher defined by spontaneity, the ability to adapt to the culture of a given class and to constantly revise their pedagogy in order to appropriately teach the "same" class or subject throughout the life of the group. Through such initial personalization, the group provides the resources for teachers to *continuously personalize* themselves by reflecting on their pedagogy and their experience in the classroom.

In personalizing the teacher by recognizing their subjectivity, the group enacts "a creative imperative," while also instilling such an imperative in the teacher (Sartre 2004a, 450). Sartre writes: "Function is both negative and positive: in the practical movement, *a prohibition* (do not do *anything else*) is perceived as a positive determination, as a *creative imperative*: do *precisely that*" (Sartre 2004a, 450). In the case of committed personalization, such an imperative takes the form of preparation that is a point of departure for future, spontaneous, and unique teaching. In order to accomplish this last goal, *the group will personalize the teacher by appealing to and cultivating their imagination.*[9] The group will emphasize the imaginative development of curricula on the part of the teacher, of assignments, discussion in the classroom, and so on. It will therefore create the space for the teacher to imagine on the basis of the current teaching methods presented and the history of education in the group. In this sense, through the recognition of its own limitations, the group creates the space for the *pedagogical imagination.* In truth, both knowledge and the recognition of what it does not know are foundations for the teacher's imagination. The knowledge instilled, for example, demands its own imaginative fulfillment through the appropriate, creative, situated presentation of it. However, the previously appreciated incompleteness of the personalization of the teacher is necessary insofar as it makes possible the independent and appropriate imaginative acts of the teacher in dialogue with the students.

The imagination founded in knowledge and its limits also extends the relation between perception and the imagination in Sartre's thought.[10] In the personalization of the teacher, the group encourages the teacher to derealize its prior educational reality. It recognizes the importance of the imaginative surpassing of the educational given, and therefore encourages the "assumption and inner negation" of the prior educational reality through the imagination and the use of whatever works of art, novels, media, and so on, are necessary for the teacher to teach a particular subject in the most appropriate way possible for the class and its culture (Sartre 1987, 7). Just as Sartre claimed in *What is Literature?* that the author must learn to speak in images, to write in the various forms of technology, so must the committed teacher learn to teach in images in accordance with the same media available. Regardless of the subject, for example, the teacher will be encouraged to include works of art, relevant historical aspects of the material, and so on. And again, this process of cultivating the imagination will vary with the particular circumstances of the group, its history, the teacher, the level of education, and so on. The emphasis is on the teacher's imaginative use of all of the resources available in order to appeal to the imagination of the students in the act of teaching. Therefore, to slightly paraphrase Kierkegaard, as important as it is to emphasize the "what" in teaching, the content of the subject, and lesson, it is equally important to emphasize the "how" in teaching, the manner in which the teacher teaches, which in this case involves the use of appropriate images to cultivate the imagination of the students (Kierkegaard 1946, 213).

As an additional, necessary moment of this process, the teacher is also personalized with a respect for the object of knowledge, the nature of the subject-matter, and the intrinsic requirements it possesses. In this sense, and in extending the concept of empathy discussed above, the teacher is personalized to *empathize with the object of knowledge* in order to approach it in the right way, find the appropriate imaginative ways of presenting it, and properly situate it within the culture of the classroom. As a complement to this, the group will also cultivate an empathetic relation to each student in their singularity, as comprised of facticity and transcendence, of connecting with the material in a unique, individual way. Thus, the group will personalize the teacher to be "flexible" in their approach to the object as well as the reception of the class to the academic content (Sartre 1984, 732). The group, then, as a complement to allowing the teacher to develop their own pedagogy, instills an appreciation for the object which will appear in and through such pedagogy. The group, therefore, will instill an appreciation for allowing the object of education to appear on its own terms, with the accompanying recognition that the manner of appearance of the object is intrinsically connected to the appropriate, imaginative presentation of the object. The educational object will accordingly be allowed to appear as an identity across a multiplicity of educational, imaginative acts which situate the object in its unique individuality in an academic setting.

In encouraging the imagination of the teacher and providing them with the grounding in the history of the group and its educational forms, the group prepares the teacher to be both an incarnation of the imaginary and a model of resistance through the imagination. The teacher is personalized to become an "imaginary teacher," and as such promotes the use of the imagination in teaching. In this case, unlike that of Flaubert, the teachers becomes imaginative in order to further embed themselves in the real, to situate themselves in the group, and to meaningfully engage with their students. The orientation of the imagination, in this case, is the diametrical opposite of that found in Flaubert, insofar as it is not a flight from reality, but an orientation toward it, a creative, derealizing dimension of the teacher *which allows the real to appear as real* because it has been given the proper expression. Therefore, in imaginatively modifying curricula and assignments, and therewith resisting the ossification and alienation of the group as well as the imposition of conflicting values and pedagogies from other groups, the teacher is personalized as a model of the appropriate orientation toward the imaginary in education and the lives of the students.[11] And as noted above, the use of the imagination will vary according to the style of the teacher, the age of the students, and the historical context. In a more general sense, *the style of the teacher is their imagination and unique production of images*. This particular, educational form of resistance in the group will be present in the pedagogy of the committed teacher and the imaginative presentation of content to the students.

THE COMMITTED TEACHER

My analysis of education as a unique task within the organized group and the personalization of the teacher leads to the question of the nature of teaching itself in such a group. In order to provide an adequate account of committed teaching, it is necessary to extend and modify two central concepts from the *Critique*, namely, the third and reciprocity. First, on the basis of the personalization of the committed teacher just discussed, I will show that the function of the teacher extends Sartre's concept of the third and develops it into what I have termed "the educational third." On the one hand, the teacher is a third as are all other group members. On the other hand, the teacher's role as a third is unique both with regard to the students, the other group members, and the generations within the group.[12] Their regulative function as a totalizing third will be seen to possess a unique, multidimensional status. Secondly, my account of committed teaching will also involve a renewed reflection on Sartre's account of reciprocity. He writes: "a ternary relation, as the mediation of man amongst men, is the basis on which reciprocity becomes aware of itself as a reciprocal connection" (Sartre 2004a, 109). This awareness, I will show, is developed in relation to the knowledge and ignorance in the group achieved through the dialogue between the teacher and the students. Moreover, Sartre writes: "Thus reciprocity, though completely opposed to alienation and reification, does not save men from them. Reciprocal ternary relations are the basis of *all* relations between men, whatever form they may subsequently take" (Sartre 2004a, 111). In this and the next section I will show the unique role that education plays both in the establishment of reciprocal relations and as one instance of them. Thus, I will draw out certain implications of such a notion of reciprocity in the organized group as it maintains itself and develops as needed through education.

To begin, one may ask, what kind of third is the committed teacher? How are they able to fulfill their unique, pedagogical task? Following the internal logic of the development of groups, the teacher emerges through the self-reflection of the pledged group once it has reached a particular level of sophistication. The teacher is therefore a result of such reflection but also, as noted earlier, an additional reflective component within the functioning of the Organization as a whole. The role of the teacher is understood and created with regard to the character of the newly formed organized group, its history, and the recognition that education is necessary for its continued unification and the realization of "the common objective" (Sartre 2004a, 416). The teacher also plays a further foundational role. As part of the arch-task of education, the totalizing activity of the teacher immediately affects all of the students, and, with different degrees of mediation, the other group members as well. Their individual *praxis* makes possible all other tasks and functions. As necessarily resulting from the previous two group forms and an act of reflection, as well as being viewed as necessary to the articulation and life of the group, the teacher is a mediated-mediating transcendental ground for the continuation of the group. As education, in general, is an arch-task, so is the function of the teacher an *arch-function,* one which is originary, constant, and a condition of possibility for both present and future tasks and functions.

As such a transcendental third, the teacher mediates between the past and present of the group, its history, its structures, and its reflective, self-understanding. And this mediating function, this individual-collective, historical temporalization, involves its own particular blend of immanence and transcendence, or, to use Sartre's phrase, "a transcendence-immanence tension" (Sartre 2004a, 374). First, as emerging out of the reflection of the statutory group on itself, the teacher has an *immediate* transcendence-immanence tension with the prior group, and a *mediate* transcendence-immanence tension with the group in fusion. As a moment of the reflection of the prior group on itself, the teacher is an immanent, continuous part of the history of the formation of groups within the Organization. However, as reflective, the teacher is also at a distance from the organized group and its history. The teacher, in fact, in the language of *Being and Nothingness,* serves as the "ideal distance" between the group as reflecting and the group as reflected on, is a form of the tension between reflected and reflecting, and ultimately between the identity and difference of the group (Sartre 1984, 123). The teacher, however, as a moment of the reflection of the group on itself, as preserving the tension between the reflecting and the reflected-on, is an additional term through which the reflecting is able to reflect on itself and therefore also take itself as the reflected-on. It is through the teacher, then, that the group can reflect on itself, and in so doing preserve its identity in the duality of itself as the unity of the reflected and the reflecting. As such, the teacher is a unique individual who, in their own pedagogical tension, makes possible and lives in and through the tension of the group as it reflectively articulates itself in its past and present through education.

The teacher, furthermore, is one moment of the group's "presence to itself," its relation to itself in its past and present, and a manner of articulating itself in the present moment (Sartre 1984, 124). In their very status within the group, the teacher is immanent to it while maintaining the necessary distance from it in order to understand and articulate it through their educational *praxis*. They are, in this sense, in several forms of the group at once, in several generations, a *present* group member that incarnates and signifies the *history* of the group. They are a member of their own past generation, the prior form of the group, but participate in the present generation and guide it through their teaching. Thus, they are a present third of a past generation who is tasked with educating the present and future generations of the group. As an inheritance of the past, the teacher is a particular memory, a collective memory, a sign of the past of the group that made their present role as well as the present reality itself possible. Their pedagogical task is therefore a multilayered task comprised of educating the group while also serving as an embodiment of the past for the group. In their totalizing activity as an educational third, the teacher establishes educational reciprocity between the organized group's temporally prior stages in order for the two preceding group forms to have a meaningful educational presence in the Organization. As a third, the teacher "looks at" the previous two group forms and integrates them in their teaching while also serving as their temporal sign. Although the Organization as a whole is the reflection of the statutory group on itself, within this reflection, the teacher totalizes the relations of the previous groups to the Organization and in so doing academically incorporates them and their members into the present of the organized group.

There is an additional feature to the immanence-transcendence tension characteristic of the teacher. First, as a group member with an assigned function, identical in this respect to all other group members, the teacher is immanent to the order, functioning, and aims of the group. However, on the basis of their knowledge, the teacher is also transcendent to the group in order to continue to make it possible. Their knowledge places them at a distance from the immanence of the educational process in order to structure, develop, and guide it. Their individual reflective act puts them at the distance necessary to grasp the functioning of the group and its past and communicate the material of the particular subject to the students. Their epistemological status and role, paradoxically, place them inside and outside the group, a transcendent presence in the immanence of education. Furthermore, the teacher is transcendent to the other tasks insofar as their task and function serve as the condition of possibility for all of the others. Not only do they transcend the group through *praxis*, but their very task ascribes them a transcendence that fundamentally differentiates their task from all others.

In addition to the transcendence accomplished through knowledge, the teacher has the individual freedom and responsibility to teach content which is consistent with their personalization and the demands of the group, but which is also irreducible to them. In this regard, the life lived by the teacher becomes a basis for the life of the group in both its present and future forms. As a result, not only is the teacher "more than their function" insofar as they do not fully coincide with it, and develop it as a free *praxis*, but the group recognizes the teacher as "more than their function," that is, as an individual with their own creativity and style of teaching, and therefore does not expect the teacher as a free *praxis* to *be* a teacher.[13] Through content specific to each subject, age, and so on, the teacher contributes to the fashioning of the idea the group has of itself, and the manner in which the students relate to and understand themselves both as students and as group members. The teacher is responsible for creating, within the classroom, and as an extension of the present of the group, an image of the classroom, its culture, and the content taught, and "that image is valid for all and for our whole era" (Sartre 2007, 24). This image, pedagogically understood, is an image of what it means to be a student, to relate properly to the material, and to engage collectively in a dialogue concerned with truth. In being "valid for all and for our whole era," the image of the class within the group immediately bears upon the particular group of students and the teacher, and mediately, with increasing degrees of mediation, to the other students and the other group members (Sartre 2007, 24).

Moreover, the form of teaching, though informed by a process of personalization and the present moment, is "invented" (Sartre 2007, 46). As such, it is in part defined by the ultimate end of the freedom of the students and the group, but is also spontaneous, unexpected, and possibly a challenge to the group. As one incarnation of knowledge, the teacher fashions a present image of the group, both regarding what it is and what it should be and contributes to the creation of such a group through their decision of the particular content to teach. Although rooted in the demands of the Organization and its system of personalization, the teacher is *individually responsible* for a particular knowledge and ignorance of the students. From this point of view, the teacher "conditions" both the ignorance and knowledge of the students, but does so in order for them to attain the necessary knowledge, freedom, and use of the imagination (Sartre 1992, 28).[14] The task of the teacher, it follows, is further complicated by this responsibility, insofar as the choice of what is taught is both a choice of the kind of students and eventual group members who will be produced through education as well as the future character of the group. Of course, there is a context for the choice of the teacher, involving the age of the students, the subject-matter, and the academic expectations, but within the given class and subject, the texts chosen, the authors read, the relations established between the content and the group, will all contribute to what it means to have studied a particular subject, to have read a particular author, and so on. In so doing, the teacher establishes a knowledge and ignorance of the students which will continue throughout their education and into their future lives.

On the basis of the analysis of the teacher as a kind of third and their choice of knowledge and ignorance, it is now possible to turn to the act of committed teaching in detail. In order to fully articulate and comprehend the approach and orientation of the committed teacher in the classroom, an initial comparison with existential psychoanalysis is necessary. In a late interview, while discussing the importance of empathy in understanding another person in general, and for his project of an existential psychoanalysis of Flaubert in particular, Sartre states that empathy is "the attitude necessary for understanding a man," and is, by extension, "the attitude necessary" for the committed teacher to understand the students individually and collectively in the educational process (Contat and Rybalka 1977, 113).[15] Through such an empathetic attitude, the committed teacher is present to the class collectively and each student individually, and has the responsibility of inventing an imaginative pedagogy which speaks to both the collective and individual dimensions of the classroom. The task of the teacher, then, is ultimately a multidimensional task insofar as the fulfillment of the act of teaching necessarily involves a plurality of relations to the students. And as teaching is a process which occurs across a given unit, semester, and so on, the teacher requires the empathy and flexibility to adapt their pedagogy as necessary in light of the development of the culture of the class as a whole and the individual students. The empathetic orientation of the teacher is a further form of "the look" appropriate to the committed educator, in truth it is a necessary, foundational look which is twofold in its significance. It is both an academic recognition of the individuality of the student, and a recognition of the community of students as a genuine community. It is an individual-collective look, a perception of a group of subjects in their subjectivity, which helps constitute the genuine, necessary, empathetic relation for dialogue in education.[16]

In light of this account of the existential orientation of the teacher and the claim that the imagination is an aim of committed education that serves as a form of resistance, the following two questions present themselves: First, how does the teacher implement the imagination in teaching? And secondly, how do the students imaginatively respond to the content presented? In order to respond to these two questions, I will provide an account of the pedagogical imaginary, beginning with the role of the imagination in teaching, and then turning to the imaginative response of the students. The teacher cultivates the imagination of the students with an incomplete presentation of the material that requires the use of the imagination for its fulfillment. And there is no necessary or a priori method for this imaginative exchange. Texts, films, music, and so on, can all be used as needed in order for the imagination of the students to be stimulated in such a way that the perceptual content is grasped, imaginatively considered, and completed by an imagining act that attains knowledge. The content presented is held in a certain suspense, presented but concealed in order for the students to engage with it as necessary. This educational suspension involves an extension of Husserl's concepts of both the phenomenological and eidetic reductions, and the implementation of what I am terming the *imaginative reduction.*[17] This reduction, moreover, is empirical, intersubjective, and incomplete, and ultimately a process of "directed creation" initiated by the teacher and completed by the students (Sartre 1988, 53).[18] In the presentation of content, the teacher brackets the material through such an epoché, presents it in a form of neutrality and incompleteness, and demands that the students respond appropriately to the suspended content. In order to attain the status of a particular reality present to the students in the form of knowledge, the content requires imaginative suspension such that the students can look at it "purely," that is, imaginatively, in such a way that they will recognize what is lacking and provide the necessary fulfillment through an imaginative act. The partially empty and fulfilled intention of the teacher in the presentation of content is ultimately fulfilled through the initially empty intentions of the students. There is, to slightly modify Aristotle, neither teaching nor learning without images (Aristotle 1984b, 685).

The teacher, as a transcendence-immanence tension, is an educational third whose unique task of suspending content regulates the relations among the students as thirds to them, the other students, and the content taught. And this imaginative reduction comprised of a plurality of interpretations is an extension of the empathy discussed above. The students, too, are inside and outside the reduction. They are brought into it through the teacher, and they dwell in the reduction through their individual and collective use of the imagination. It is, therefore, on the basis of the student as a kind of *homme imaginaire*, as an individual who has freely chosen to take the necessary aesthetic, imaginative stance toward themselves and education in entering the educational epoché, that collective imagining and dialogue become possible. The knowledge, derealized and neutralized through its presentation to the students, draws the students into the particular epoché of the given subject-matter, and once obtained, is internalized and made their own by the students. The students then leave the educational space to reenter it with the next epoché, which corresponds to the next lesson, unit, and so on. The students, it follows, begin outside the epoché due to the *lack of knowledge*, imaginatively move within it to attain knowledge, and return outside the epoché once they have personalized such knowledge. The teacher then returns to their own educational transcendence as they prepare the next epoché, the next reduction, and the continued cultivation of the imagination. The students, on the other hand, begin outside the process because of their lack of knowledge, enter into it in order to attain knowledge, and then return outside the process as they prepare for the next epoché and reduction. Such an educational process is therefore a constant play of immanences and transcendences, of imaginative and conceptual spatializations, and of the effecting and completing of epochés and reductions through the use of the imagination.

A further feature of the imaginative reduction, which I have discussed to an extent, is that it is an *empirical reduction.* It can, therefore, be modified in accordance with the subject being taught, the age of the students, the general culture of the classroom, and so on. The act of suspension is therefore a universal pedagogical act which allows the material to be grasped purely on its own terms, as in need of imaginative fulfillment, and without any prior assumptions or preconceived notions about the material on the part of the students.[19] However, it does not bracket out the entirety of the natural attitude, and in so doing continues to stand on the ground of the world. It is continuously informed by the material taught, the knowledge obtained, and the development of the culture of the class throughout a given period of time. The knowledge of the students, therefore, serves as a condition for the development of the imaginative suspension effected by the teacher insofar as the imaginative presentation of content, as empirical and capable of being modified as needed, develops in accordance with the knowledge of the class. As a result, content which was previously bracketed and incompletely presented, once fulfilled through the appropriate imaginative acts of the students, becomes a posited reality which is integrated into the subsequent imaginative reduction of the next stages of the lesson, the subsequent content that required the prior knowledge of the principles of the subject being taught, and so on. And although informed by previous content and building on the achieved knowledge, the imaginative reduction is a perpetual beginning and a way to keep the content new. It is informed by prior knowledge, but irreducible to it insofar as it continues to incorporate and reincorporate it into the subsequent lessons in various, imaginative ways. The content, in other words, is not only originally new because it has not yet been learned, but also because it takes on a different character throughout the educational process in its relation to the newly presented content.

The imaginative suspension, the attempt to present content without previous assumptions or associations and as constantly new, is further defined as presenting a unity of content through a variety of multiplicities. In suspending the content in its presentation, the teacher will present *a variety of ways of relating to and understanding it.* As a result of such a multidimensional reduction, the content is empirically reduced to a single form *because of the plurality of interpretations of it.* It is, in this sense, an individual content *because* it is multidimensional. Through such bracketing and requiring fulfillment, the educational content is a multilayered, multidimensional object which requires, for both its completion and its identity, the imaginative interpretations and acts of all of the students. The educational object, it follows, is a singular identity because it is comprised of the multiple interpretations of the students, the different ways of presenting it by the teacher, and the manner in which the teacher connects it to other subjects and the present reality of the group. It is a peculiar identity which continues to strengthen its identity through all of the imaginative interpretations of it. Through an imaginative reduction of the reality of the content, the knowledge of the particular object is achieved by the class both individually and collectively as a singular plurality of interpretations comprising its identity. The empirical essence of the educational object, in this case the knowledge of the given subject-matter, is attained through the dialogical imagination of the teacher and the students made possible by the imaginative epoché. The imaginative reduction has the task of both making possible the cultivation and use of the imagination, and therefore of uncovering the students in their essential character as imagining. Through this cultivation of the imagination, this appeal to the "free play" of the students, the teacher teaches them to imagine, and has the ultimate goal of making them conscious of the use of the imagination as the realization of their transcendental freedom. As such, the teacher is a transcendental condition for the presence, development, and future use of the imagination, and serves as an origin of the imagination in the group.

COMMITTED STUDENTS

The theme of the imaginative response to the content presented by the teacher leads to the question of the character of committed students as thirds in the educational group. The students, although in a manner different than the teacher, as well as other members of the group, are themselves group members with corresponding tasks, functions, and responsibilities. As such, they too manifest a particular form of the transcendence-immanence tension. They are, on the basis of their educational tasks and functions, immanent to the group as are all other group members. However, as in the process of being educated and in this sense personalized, they are also in the process of becoming full group members. This, of course, can vary with age, level of education, the subject being pursued, and so on, but regardless of the moment of the educational process, committed students are also defined by an additional tension within the group. They are, perhaps paradoxically, group members who are not yet full group members. They are, in this respect, also third parties who are not yet complete third parties, and whose totalizing act uniquely applies to their educational status and role in the group. Thus, as *being personalized*, as "assuming and negating" the content presented and the history of the group, they are both part of and not yet part of the group, future members with future tasks and functions which are rooted in their present educational tasks and functions (Sartre 1987, 7).

Regarding their status and contributions within the group, the task of the student *is to be a student, and only a student*, and this task is further defined and characterized by the particular level of education, relation to the teacher and fellow students, and so on. But what is essential and to be emphasized is that their future tasks and functions, in general their future life in the group, while founded on and involving the capacity to imagine learned through the process of personalization, are secondary, future tasks of which they are cognizant, but which do not bleed into, affect, and restrict the present task of the student to be a student. Their present educational status leads into their future roles in the group, and with varying degrees of proximity depending upon their age, desired future role, and so on. Thus, though there is not, or not necessarily, a one-to-correlation between the process of personalization and the individual future of group members, the arch-task of education provides the necessary resources for the desired future. Committed students are therefore immanent to the group in the process of transcending it through their personalization and as their tasks and functions become clearer and begin to take shape.

As a complement to the demands placed on the students by the teacher and the group as a whole, the students place demands on the teacher, the group, and themselves. The demand of the students is a present demand that bears both on their current educational status as well as their future in the group. At different phases, the students make demands which correspond to the level of education they have reached, and their orientation toward their individual and collective future. They demand from the group that the resources for education be available, and this can range from the physical space of education, to the opportunity for the proper education of the teacher, the necessary materials, and so on. Secondly, and following from this, the students demand from the teacher that they fulfill their task so that they can fulfill theirs. That is to say that they demand that the teacher provide the appropriate atmosphere, that they be prepared, and knowledgeable. And this, of course, can vary with the conditions and culture of each individual class. This demand is in truth a demand on the group that it provide the necessary personalization in order for the teacher to be capable of teaching the necessary content in the appropriate manner. Finally, part of the task and function of each student is to demand that all of the other students fulfill their tasks and functions, that is, that they are prepared, engage in the necessary, imaginative dialogue with the teacher and each other, and in general contribute to the educational atmosphere of the class. Thus, part of what it means to be a student in an organized group is to both fulfill the designated task and to demand that the other students fulfill theirs.

One particular point I would like to emphasize here is the relation between the age of the students, their level of education, and the demands they place on the group. For example, while the demands of a university student will differ from those of an elementary school student, they do so concerning a particular temporal orientation. The demand of the university student is *simultaneous* with the education being pursued. As the teacher places demands on the student to complete the various assignments, so does the student place demands on the teacher regarding their knowledge of the material and ability to teach effectively. This demand, however, can develop over the course of the educational career of the student, such that it may only be implicit early on in the educational process, continue to acquire determinacy, and ultimately become fully explicit as the student reaches a given level of education. As a result, for example, retroactively and depending on the education received, the student may realize that they did in fact have educational demands without fully being aware of them, and that those demands either were or were not met, which, in the former case, means that the system of education fulfilled its tasks and obligations, properly taught the material, and—now present—made possible the future of the student in accordance with the now explicit and present educational demands. It is, paradoxically, a *present demand* on a *past self* whose demand was not explicit. Therefore, the educational demands of the students evolve as their education continues, and as a result a student does, in fact, *implicitly* make such an educational demand insofar as they will make it *explicitly* in the future. In this regard, the process of education is itself a constant reflection, one in which the expectations and demands continue to develop with the progression of both the teacher and the students.

The students, as unique thirds to themselves and to the teacher, mediate the transmission of knowledge in the classroom and the general pedagogical experience. This totalizing mediation is the presence of the student to the classroom and serves as the correlate to the presence of the teacher discussed earlier. This presence, being part of the dialogue in the classroom, contributes to the knowledge and ignorance of the other students, placing their understanding, be it partial, insufficient, and so on, of the given material in relation to the other students as well as the class as a whole. As the teacher is able to establish relations of knowledge and ignorance between the students at a given moment, so are the students, in their dialogue with one another, their communal imaginative orientation toward the incomplete content presented, able to totalize as thirds the level of knowledge and ignorance present in the classroom as a whole. The students as thirds therefore help regulate the appearance of knowledge in education and the relations with the other students that make it possible. As a result, each student synthesizes the relations of the other students and the binary of the teacher and the other students, and in so doing helps found conscious, reciprocal, educational and epistemological relations within the group. The relations of truth, knowledge, and ignorance, though in certain respects originating with the totalizing act and look of the teacher, are completed by the students assuming these relations, building on them in their dialogue with one another, class discussion, their various assignments, and so on. Each student as a third helps found unique relations of knowledge and ignorance between the other students and the material taught, leading to a continuous, necessary, and constellational process of mediation within the classroom as a whole.

In their educational totalization, the students also totalize the teacher as a third in their singularity. From the point of view of the educational acts of the students, the teacher becomes a uniquely, collectively totalized third put in relation to each student and the students as a whole by virtue of the presence, attention, and demands of the students. As I discussed earlier, the teacher, as transcendent, creates the immanent space for education. In so creating this space, the teacher also continues to inhabit it. However, now, their "place" in the pedagogical space created is constituted from "the other side," through the students and their educational, constituting totalization. This "other side" is the complement to the imaginative epoché initiated by the teacher, the manner in which the students, once dwelling in it imaginatively after having been brought into it by the act of the teacher, continue it and further situate the teacher within it as knowledge is attained. Through dialogue and their imaginative responses to the content, the students transcend the teacher and bring them further into the immanence of the group as they continue to demand that they fulfill their pedagogical task. The relations of reciprocity between the teacher and students are of such a nature that, after the teacher creates the space for truth and knowledge, the students then incorporate them into it. The teacher does not remain "outside" this space, or passively occupy it by indifferently lecturing, but is constantly engaged such that—in a positive sense—there is a constant heightening of the transcendence-immanence tension. There is, therefore, a play of transcendences and immanences, an overlapping, a totalizing reciprocity wherein each constantly demands more from the other. The relations between the students and the teacher and the students themselves are mediated and mediating in the context of transcendences and immanences where all the members demand that each fulfill their task and contribute to the "directed creation" of truth (Sartre 1988, 53).

The reciprocity between the students as well as the students and the teacher possesses an additional character. Sartre writes: "It is the individual's *praxis*, as the realization of his project, which determines his bonds of reciprocity with everyone" (Sartre 2004a, 110). The educational *praxis* of each member of the group, in either presenting or responding to imaginative content and establishing relations of knowledge and ignorance, constitutes the constellational "bonds" necessary for the educational group to maintain itself and to continue to develop (Sartre 2004a, 110). The educational process, moreover, is constituted by the *praxis* of each individual as they work collectively to totalize and transcend the material presented in order to attain truth. And, as is clear in the term "process" itself, this collective, educational *praxis* and the reciprocity it gives rise to continue to develop for the academic period, be it a semester, an entire year, and so on. These "bonds," then, as foundational, make possible the continuous development of the students, the culture of the academic setting, as well as new relations of knowledge and ignorance which build on the relations previously established (Sartre 2004a, 119). On the one hand, the reciprocity remains fixed, a condition for the group and its future, while on the other hand the character of the reciprocity changes as knowledge is transmitted, the class advances in the subject, and the culture of the imagination continues to change and adapt to the changes in the educational relations.

On the basis of the continuously developing relations of reciprocity through the educational process, a further character of the educational group, one consistent with the ultimate definition of the Organization, presents itself. This organized educational group, as a process of resisting, imagining, and establishing relations of knowledge and ignorance, is a group that is *never fully constituted.*[20] The teacher and students create the space for such educational engagement, and through their continuous, imaginative dialogue, the group itself continues to inherit, inhabit, develop, and ultimately transcend its own "historical legacy" across the temporal distance of the educational period. It is a group which, regardless of the attention to the detail of the content taught and the emphasis on the agency of the students in their active engagement with the material, is always established in outline, as a sketch, and *continues to complete itself* throughout the educational process. The beginning of the process, then, in the early exchanges between the teacher and the students, in the setting of the terms of the class, the introduction to the subject matter, and so on, is an indication of what the group can and should be. As a continuous dialogue in images, the group is never a fully constituted group, it remains a particular "totalization without a totalizer," reflecting on and redefining itself as new knowledge is obtained (Sartre 2004a, 69). Though prepared for teaching and fashioned as group members through the educational process, the teacher and the students are dialectically interwoven such that their educational personalization is a continuous and necessarily incomplete process. Finally, as Sartre says that the Organization is "permanent reorganization," so is education permanent reeducation, and personalization permanent re-personalization (Sartre 2004a, 457). Education is therefore a process of perpetual reflection and development, the perpetual relearning of what was learned through constant reflection on it, deeper understanding, and future action. For both the teacher and the students, it is a continuous, incomplete process of personalization which is achieved through the transmission, acquisition, and development of knowledge and truth.

Although I have just discussed the educational group as a constant process, as correlative to an age, subject, and so on, it is necessarily temporally bounded, such that once the tasks of a particular class have been fulfilled, the students move on to the next stage or fully enter the group, and the teacher may continue to teach the next group of students. What happens, more specifically, however, to the teacher as an educational third once this process comes to an end? This leads to a further, unique quality of the teacher as an educational third. The teacher, in their capacity as an educational third, *teaches in order to be surpassed.* The task of the teacher is to make possible an understanding of the material, an orientation toward the group, and a future within the group, which transcend the previous knowledge and forms of the group. Their task is one which has the character of eventually no longer being the same task in the life of the students. As one incarnation of the collective memory of the past of the group, the teacher subsequently becomes part of this collective memory in belonging to the memory of the students. In fulfilling their pedagogical task in the particular historical moment, the teacher has transcended their present pedagogical task to fall back into a new educational immanence, which may be that of a new educational group or another aspect of the organized group. Regardless of the duration of the educational group, and even if they join new educational groups in accordance with the process of the group as a whole, the teacher is a temporary third. Teachers are, even if for a prolonged duration, linked to their task and function in such a way that once fulfilled, their constitution as a present third party comes to an end, and is either passed on to another educational third, or another part of the group.

The manner in which the students surpass the teacher as a third is also paradoxical. In the future of the students, the teacher is surpassed *insofar as* they are integrated into their action within the group. That is to say that insofar as the teacher has fulfilled their educational task, that is, taught the subject, cultivated the imagination, and made resistance possible, they will be surpassed by the students as they continue to remember in continuing to build on the knowledge obtained, by imagining, and by resisting. Initially an individual serving as an instance of collective memory, the teacher then becomes part of the collective imagination as the students continue to imagine. The teacher is therefore a vanishing third, a unity of the seemingly contradictory qualities of disappearing and perpetually remaining part of the group. Moreover, as helping fashion the character of the group, as a particular origin, their totalizing action is incorporated into the future of the group as surpassed, but also as remembered and immanent in the group's present and functioning. The totalization of this third, therefore, is immediate in its teaching, mediate in its future presence, and temporary because permanent. Furthermore, this permanent totalization occurs in the absence of the teacher as a totalizing third, but in their presence in the future group members as an origin of knowledge, imagination, and resistance. As the teacher emerged from the prior two group forms, they are then immersed in the progressive history of the Organization. In continuing to totalize the past students, as well as the future of the group, the teacher, as a third to the students and the group as a whole, blindly totalizes them as they continue to develop the group through their education. The teacher, as a transcendent-immanent third, is transcended by the students they have educated, returns to a new immanence as temporary and permanent, a past to be present in the future of the group through the imagination and resistance.

NOTES

1. Sartre's original French text is not divided into chapters. For the complete discussion of the Organization in the original French, see Sartre (1960a, 459–506).
2. In what follows, I will translate "le groupe en fusion" as "the group in fusion," as opposed to "the fused group," which is the official English translation by Alan Sheridan-Smith in his translation of the *Critique*. For the original French, see Sartre (1960a, 452–511). For the English translation, see Sartre (2004a, 345–404).
3. As noted in the introduction, the divisions of *The Family Idiot* in the English translation do not fully correspond to the original French text. For the accounts of personalization in both versions, see "School Years" in Sartre (1989, 3–352) and "Le Collége" in Sartre (1971b, 1107–464).
4. Henry Giroux also calls attention to this concept and its importance for critical pedagogy. See Giroux (2011, 41).
5. Although there are overtones of Kant's schematism in the *Critique of Pure Reason*, the manner in which I am using the term "schema," though sharing certain affinities with Kant's account, should not be confused with it. The notion of the imagination I am developing here is also related to, but different from, the transcendental imagination as discussed in the first *Critique*. Moreover, as the schema in Kant is "a third thing, which must stand in homogeneity with the category on the one hand and the appearance on the other, and makes possible the application of the former to the latter," as I am using it here, it is the manner in which, through education, the organized group mediates its self-understanding, resists ossification and external groups, and ultimately lays a basis for future action (Kant 1998, 272).
6. Sartre uses the term "football" instead of "soccer." However, since soccer is the term used for the sport in the United States, I have decided to alter the translation for the sake of clarity and familiarity.
7. For Sartre's concept of the second pledge, see Sartre (2004a, 485).
8. These concepts serve as the Sartrean, educational correlate to the various essential forms discussed by Husserl in *Ideas I.* See Husserl (1998, 11).

9. The importance of the imagination in education has been acknowledged by several education theorists and Sartre scholars. I have noted the scholars whose work is particularly relevant to the analyses here. For general accounts of the importance of educating the imagination and the particular role Sartre's theory of the imagination plays in such education, see Warnock (1976, 196–209) and Warnock (1977, 44–60). For the relation between existentialism, education, and aesthetics, see Kaelin (1966, 170–77) and Degenhardt (1975, 87–91). Maxine Greene has devoted several texts to the importance of the imagination and aesthetics in education, and their relation to the freedom of subjectivity. See in particular Greene (1988, 1–23, 117–35), Greene (1995, 17–31, 32–43, 122–33), and the lectures in parts 1 and 2 of Greene (2001, 5–130).

10. The theme of the imagination in Sartre has given rise to a wealth of literature. I will here cite the interpretations that I found most helpful in my research on this topic and which are most relevant to my task in this book. For two accounts of Sartre's early work on the imagination, see Casey (1981, 139–66) and Ricoeur (1981, 167–78). For an analysis of the distinction between the real and the unreal as it is operative in *The Family Idiot*, see Flynn, (1980, 105–23). For the relation between the imagination and aesthetics in Sartre, see Flynn (1975, 431–42). For a comprehensive account of the theme of the imagination in Sartre's philosophy, see Flynn (2014, 76–94, 104–36, 95–408). For an additional account of Sartre's thought as a whole, which discusses the nature and role of the imagination in the different phases of Sartre's thought, see Howells (1988, 9–14, 116–44). For Sartre's role in the development of the theme of the imagination in phenomenology, as well as in an attempt to develop a comprehensive phenomenology of the imagination, see Casey (2000, 1–20).

11. For an example of an orientation toward tradition that leads to the kind of ossification education is in part meant to prevent, see Marrou (1956, 305).

12. Both the teacher and the students are a form of what Flynn termed "the mediating third" in Flynn (1973, 11). For the complete discussion, see Flynn (1973, 10–31). See also Flynn (1984, 116–19)

13. This would involve a situation comparable to that of the waiter in *Being and Nothingness.* In this case, both the teacher and the group would be in bad faith if they expected the teacher to be a teacher *who is only a teacher.* The teacher, then, would attempt to repress their subjectivity to fully coincide with their role as a teacher, *to be a teacher*, and thus to be nothing more than a personalized group member.

14. For a relevant discussion of the relations between knowledge and ignorance, see Sartre (1992, 28).

15. For the complete discussion, see Contat and Rybalka (1977, 113–20). For a contrasting, critical view of the role of empathy in education, see Gordon (1985, 48–49). For discussions of existential psychology as "an attitude," and the related concept of presence, which is also at work in my account, see May (1969, 15), Bugental (1978, 36–38), and Bugental (1987, 49–66).

16. For an account of Sartre's concept of the look and its relation to dialogue, see Martinot (2005, 43–61).

17. For discussions of eidetic variation, see Husserl (1973, 352–54) and Husserl (1970, 69–72). For the phenomenological epoché and reduction, see Husserl (1998,

57–83). For a related discussion of bracketing in the act of teaching, see Greene (2001, 112). Flynn also discusses an "'aesthetic' suspension" in Flynn (2014, 388). For a discussion of Sartre's use of the reduction in his early philosophy, see Busch (1980,17–29).

18. For a further discussion of the importance of incompleteness in teaching, see Keefe and Keefe (2001, 68).

19. This empirical, phenomenological reduction also has interesting relations to the different ways into phenomenology. According to Iso Kern, there are three ways into phenomenology, namely, "The Cartesian Way," "The Way Through Intentional Psychology," and "The Way Through Ontology" (Kern 1977, 126, 134, 137). Education, however, on the basis of its empirical, imaginative epoché and reduction, can serve to motivate the change in attitude required for the turn to phenomenology. For example, on the basis of the cultivation of the imagination, it may pose the following question, "What must consciousness be, in order for it to freely imagine?" As a result, it is a peculiar, mediate way into phenomenology insofar as the suspension proper to education can serve as a fourth way into the question of the nature of transcendental subjectivity.

20. For an account of the importance for educational groups to continue to reflect on and develop themselves, but with an emphasis on the group-in-fusion, see Blenkinsop (2012, 183–95).

Chapter 2

The Temporality of Committed Education

In the previous chapter, I analyzed the nature of the Organization and the unique task that education plays in the organized group. Moreover, I demonstrated the role and function of both the teacher and the students, as well as the concept of the imagination in committed education. In particular, I emphasized the importance of the Organization as a form of reflection on itself, and the manner in which education was both an additional form of reflection and contributed to the general reflection of the group as a whole. There is, however, a theme that is intrinsically linked to reflection in Sartre's thought, and essential for a Sartrean phenomenology of education, namely, time.[1] And situated within an analysis of the logic and development of groups, a phenomenological analysis of education naturally assumes a relation to such development in its temporal character. Moreover, on the basis of the brief discussions of time in chapter 1, which concerned the multigenerational quality of the teacher, certain aspects of the past and future of the students, and the particular educational significance of memory, it is necessary and appropriate to inquire into the unique temporality of committed education in more detail. The present chapter will provide the necessary, fully developed temporal counterpart to the analyses of chapter 1 and, in so doing, will move from static to genetic phenomenology.

The problem of time was discussed by Sartre in several places, and a sufficient account of it requires an analysis of several texts. It is analyzed phenomenologically in *Being and Nothingness*, and, while preserving much from his early thought in the *Critique* and *The Family Idiot*, Sartre subsequently expands his analyses to include an explicitly diachronic dimension.[2] In addition to the discussions in *Being and Nothingness*, therefore, I will account for the temporality of the group as a whole and its history by making use of these later texts.[3] In the *Critique*, there is, on the one hand, synchronic temporalization, which Sartre defined as "a work of unification of simultaneous multiplicities in light of a common objective" (Sartre 2004a, 666). On the other hand, the diachronically totalizing dimension, "the result of the retro-anterogressive unification of temporalizations" (Sartre 2004a, 666). And, in discussing the relation between them, he writes: "In this sense, diachronic evolution is present (as past—and, as we shall see later, as future) in synchronic totalization" (Sartre 2004a, 54). In order to adequately address the temporality of committed education, both "levels" are necessary, and need to be understood both individually and in relation to one another. Regarding the synchrony of the group, I will provide a phenomenological analysis of lived-time, such that the problem of time in education is understood as *the problem of the lived-experience of time in education.* And as its complement, its diachronic fulfillment, I will discuss the role of generations, their succession, interrelations, and conflict in the education of the group.

As part of these analyses, I will also explain the temporality of resistance, that is, the various ways in which it is temporally operative within the present of the group understood synchronically and in accordance with its diachronic development. In this regard, I will emphasize resistance to the ossification of the group across generations, to its past and traditions, and to various threats from within the group itself. Education as a form of resistance, as I will show, temporally appears in the group on the basis of a particular diachronic development and the culture established by the teacher and the educational apparatuses in the group. Finally, as I am further defining the term in this chapter, resistance is not a purely "negative" concept, but rather both an appropriate way of integrating the past into the present and the temporally lived component of the imagination as it was discussed in chapter 1. Temporality itself, in its committed, educational dimension, and as rooted in the conditions of need, scarcity, and the practico-inert, must unfold *as a form of resistance to such conditions* in order to ultimately respond to and overcome them.

THE DIACHRONIC TEMPORALIZATION OF COMMITTED EDUCATION

The theme of the diachronic temporality of education introduces the problem of the relations between generations within the group as well as that of the identity of the group across time. Moreover, and concerning its past, it raises the question of the status of the practico-inert of education and the manner in which the present group relates to, and lives through, its practico-inert history. Building on what I discussed in chapter 1, and as was analyzed specifically concerning the teacher, the practico-inert history of the organized group involves its development from the group-in-fusion and the statutory group. However, concerning the educational history within the Organization itself, there is a particular form that the practico-inert takes, and which is simply the history of the established, institutionalized educational forms.[4] There is, therefore, a dual status within the practico-inert, involving the prior group forms that solidify in the present, which, regarding the theme of education, serves as their culmination, as well as the unique history of education within the group itself.

As a result of this twofold character of the practico-inert, the question of generations, of their succession and interrelations, and of their significance within the present of the group presents itself in a few different ways. First, as the Organization emerges out of the two prior group forms, it is comprised of generations and group members which do not belong to the Organization. As comprising the previous groups, and as each is a progressive articulation and development of what came earlier, the preceding generations of non-group members serve as a condition of possibility for the current form of the group. However, their status as historical, constitutive group members, as precursors of the present group form, gives them an *indirect*, or *a more distantly mediated* relation to the group. The prior generations and their corresponding forms of education in the Organization itself, however, have a *direct* and *more immediate* bearing on its present form. The diachronic temporalization of education, it follows, temporalizes the present generation in relation to previous generations within the group, but also in relation to non-group members who served as a condition of its possibility. As I will show, the nature of such educational temporality involves the interrelations and the conflict between different kinds of generations within a single group. As a result, extending Sartre's claim from *Being and Nothingness*, it is not only the case that "the *Mitsein* is conflict," but rather, when understood diachronically, "the *Mitsein* is generational conflict" (Sartre 1984, 555).

This character of the generational temporality of education takes on further complexity when the different descriptions of the practico-inert, across both the *Critique* and *The Family Idiot*, are taken into account. The practico-inert is often discussed in volume 1 of the *Critique* in negative terms that involve the passivity, inertia, and oppressive weight of prior, solidified, human *praxis*. For example, Sartre writes: "At this level we will discover an equivalence between alienated *praxis* and worked inertia, and we shall call the domain of this equivalence the *practico-inert*" (Sartre 2004a, 57). And later: "The moment of the practico-inert field is in fact that of the anti-dialectic. . . . In this field, everyone's action disappears, and is replaced by monstrous forces which, in the inertia of the inorganic and of exteriority, retain some power of action and unification combined with a false interiority" (Sartre 2004a, 320). As such, the practico-inert conceived as the accumulation of individual and group *praxes* has the effect of altering *praxis*, alienating it, turning it against itself, and of unexpectedly modifying an earlier *praxis* such that a new *praxis* corresponding to the new state of affairs becomes necessary.[5] Within the context of the *Critique,* it would appear that no positive role can be ascribed to the practico-inert, that previous *praxis* is necessarily a burden, distorting, and oppressive, and that once *praxis* becomes fixed in the past, in the in-itself, it a priori weighs *negatively* on the individual and the group.

There is, however, a different way of interpreting the practico-inert, one which I would argue is implicit in the *Critique*, and which, on Sartre's own terms, lends it a *positive aspect* and is also a further development of his account of the Organization.[6] The particularly significant positive descriptions of the practico-inert are found in the discussions of the Objective Spirit in volume 5 of *The Family Idiot.*[7] To begin, Sartre writes: "In fact, the Objective Spirit—in a defined society, in a given era—is nothing more than culture as practico-inert" (Sartre 1993, 35). Moreover, one central component of the Objective Spirit are the "demands and ubiquitous imperatives" that previous generations of writers, and as such, place on later generations (Sartre 1993, 46–47). Finally, and as Sartre himself notes, his accounts of the Objective Spirit "have no negative intent, no voluntary deprecation" (Sartre 1993, 38). From these statements, it is clear that there is a shift in the account of the practico-inert in Sartre's thought and that the earlier formulations, while preserved in various respects, are not exhaustive.[8] Moreover, as can be seen in the vocabulary of the later work, there is considerable overlap between the analysis of the relation between the Objective Spirit as embodied in the demands of literature, and that between the group and the individual in the Organization. Not only, then, is the practico-inert also a positive aspect of a given society or group, but part of what it means for the practico-inert to have positive value, to form a culture, and for it to make its own demands, to have its own requirements, and, in this case, to place a burden on the present generation to fulfill its tasks as it continues past traditions.

The introduction of this concept of culture into the positive account of the practico-inert extends the theme of demands as they were discussed in the Organization by *temporalizing them across generations*. In this later account, culture is the result of past *praxis* which solidifies and, if not reanimated through the present, will acquire the inertia and weight of the practico-inert as oppressive and begin to alienate the group. In a fashion analogous to the status of literature, there is both "une éducation-faite" and "une education-à-faire," and part of the development of the group, in its move from past to present, involves the manner in which the present generation assumes, responds to, and develops the educational demands placed on it by the past (Sartre 1972, 58). In this regard, present education has the task of *diachronically personalizing* the education of the past in order to make it valuable, significant, and meaningfully related to the present. In so doing, it extends the concept of demands discussed within the Organization proper, a concept which was largely fixed within a particular moment or generation of the group, and explicitly establishes the concept of *cultural demands* which are placed on the *present* by *past* group members. As such, it places an additional responsibility on the teacher, the students, and the group as a whole, namely, that of maintaining and developing the culture of the group.

These cultural demands, which are specific to a particular historical period, are also *educational demands*. In addition to providing the resources for education, the group has the accompanying responsibility of creating an educational culture. This involves producing and maintaining an imaginative culture of resistance through the use of the imagination, which will properly relate to the history of the group as well as the negative, and possibly threatening, manifestations of need, scarcity, and the practico-inert. In this sense, the culture of the Organization, in both its diachronic and synchronic dimensions, is ultimately the culture of the imagination. The system of education, as such a cultural product, requires a present, enlivening intention in order for it to maintain itself as a positive aspect of the current culture. In fact, Sartre writes that "the Objective Spirit can address itself to us only as an *imperative*," and it is by appropriately responding to this imperative that the necessary culture of education can be maintained on the basis of the past, but also further developed in accordance with the needs of the present (Sartre 1993, 45). There was, for example, a revolutionary culture in the group in fusion which lasted for the duration of the spontaneous, revolutionary action in the city of Paris. Subsequently, there was a sworn culture, one rooted in the need to maintain cohesion, to preserve the unity of the group in differentiation through the pledge and which lasted until additional structures and relations became necessary.[9] In the Organization, then, on the basis of these two groups, and with its own educational concerns, the temporal demand of previous generations, as well as the demand of the present group on itself, is to create a foundational, perennial, and historically situated educational culture.

The demand of the previous generations within the Organization, moreover, is placed *on the group as a whole*, but also on the appropriate educational apparatuses, to make possible an educational culture within the group such that the educational standards, institutions, and values will be maintained and will continue to develop with the history of the group. While not entirely determining the material taught, the methods of education, and so on, the past *praxis* of the group which has materialized as culture, as *a past, collective look on the present*, demands that the "same" environment, that is, one wherein the task of education is capable of being fulfilled, is provided and that ultimately resistance through the imagination is maintained.[10] In this sense, and perhaps paradoxically, past generations, in order to avoid the ossification, rather than the potential freedom, of the practico-inert, demand that the present educational system resist its past forms, its own traditions, and its own potential inertial form that will distort individual and group *praxis*. In truth, the constant reflection of the Organization on itself is both the constant potentiality, and at times the actuality, of resisting its past in order for it to have the appropriate role in the present. Moreover, in addition to being a reflection on itself in its synchronic form, the Organization is also a *generational reflection* which integrates and transcends its past educational forms.

In looking at the present, the previous generations—directly within the Organization, and indirectly in the previous groups—serve as additional third parties which, in their absence, totalize the educational relations between the teacher and the students, the other aspects of the educational institutions, the material taught, and so on. The past of the group as a third provides a basis and a corresponding expectation of the group in order for education to continue to be possible and to fulfill its task. It is because of this continuous totalization by the past as present that Sartre writes: "I find myself dialectically conditioned by the totalized and totalizing past of the process of human development" (Sartre 2004a, 54). And later: "This means that my life itself is centuries old" (Sartre 2004a, 54). Regarding its present form, the educational culture of the group is a demand that the group has made on itself, but also one that is continuously placed on it through prior generations as a collective third whose look totalizes the relations of knowledge. In addition to the generations that preceded this group form, there are also demands placed by the generations within the Organization, and with varying degrees of immediacy and mediation. There is, moreover, the ambiguously situated, peculiar demand of previous generations that are still group members, that continue to comprise and constitute the group, and which are present members who in certain respects are past and make past and present demands on education. They are the correlate of what Sartre referred to as "the older brothers," and in general the more immediately preceding generations of authors (Sartre 1993, 94).[11]

At this point, however, a question regarding the nature of the relation between the past and present of the group presents itself, namely: How is the educational demand of previous generations integrated into the group? Moreover, is it not possible that one can find here, rather than the smooth transitioning between generations, for example the extension and continuous development of literary forms, *conflict* between them? Is education not another form of generational conflict? Each of these questions involves several answers, and in truth, as much as there is continuity between the generations, it is also necessarily the case that there is discontinuity between them as well. As much as the past of the group demands resistance to itself for the sake of the present, the material taught, the form of teaching, and all the elements of the present form of education, do not necessarily coincide with one another across generations. Thus Sartre writes: "Each generation is a natural and social product of the previous generation; but each generation separates itself from the previous one and, as a *material condition of its praxis*, transcends the objectification of the previous *praxis*" (Sartre 2004a 666). As result, despite the possible educational continuity between generations in the Organization, there is also conflict regarding what ought to be taught, what education in the classroom should look like, what curricula should be developed, and so on.

In the historical sequences of generations in the organized group, there is a continuous development of educational tasks and functions, but one which is also comprised of discontinuous moments and interruptions in the previous forms of education. However, to the extent that the past needs to be modified it is also the case that the present, in recognizing the needs of the present historical moment, will alter the system of education in such a way that there is, or at least in principle can be, a conflict between the educational content, values, and aims of the different generations. As a result, while there are certain fixtures in the diachronic development of education in the group, such as the demand for an educational culture, the methods of teaching and use of the imagination will vary and possibly conflict. It is not simply the case that different subjects could be taught or emphasized, that new subjects which have emerged with technological advancements and newly discovered knowledge would be offered, and so on, but rather that both the meaning of what is taught, how it articulates the present and connects to the past, as well as the necessary language of images for the present generations, will shift, change, and potentially be at odds with one another. In this regard, while objectified by the look of the past, the present looks back, objectifies the system of education as a whole, and both resists and modifies it as needed. Therefore, while there is consistency in the demand for education across generations and the recognition of its necessity for the group, the nature of the demand and the form that the demand takes will vary, and in so doing will place the different generations in conflict with one another. Thus, although diachronic and synchronic temporalizations are interwoven, the nature of synchronic totalization, of the present education of the group, does not coincide with its history, that is, the prior development of a system of education across the previous generations. Diachronic temporalization therefore reaches its limit in the synchronic temporalization of the group, and while continuing to serve as a point of departure, it is just as much a point of conflict.

The temporal demand that the Objective Spirit places on the group serves to complement the unique task of education in a number of ways. The issue of educational demands situated within the organized group is further complicated when one remembers that its present form is comprised of a history that also includes non-group members. What, then, does it mean for a member of the group in fusion, or of the statutory group, to place a burden of responsibility on the present group member, such as a student, when the current student belongs to a group with a different character? The present form and needs of education, as specific to a particular location and moment in history, have the additional weight of inheriting traditions that made possible the present, but that in a fundamental sense are discontinuous with it. As education was a condition for the functioning of the group, it is now clear that such a system of education relies upon a particular history that both made it possible, but that also makes its own demands on the group as a whole. As a result, not only is education a present demand on the group that makes all other tasks and functions possible, but it is also a historical and present demand that requires a present, collective act on the part of the teacher and the students in order to be fulfilled. The tasks and functions of education, in other words, are not only static, but also genetic, in that they are inherited from previous group and non-group members and require their active assumption and negation to be perpetuated.

Moreover, the diachronic, temporal demands are placed on the present in various ways. The prior group forms that made the present group possible indirectly place demands on the present in order for the paradoxical, "pre-historical" origins of the history of the particular group to be maintained. Although not explicitly formulated by either the group in fusion or the statutory group, their legacy as necessary stages that led to the Organization places a demand on the present of the group to maintain their significance and necessity for the present moment, that is, *they demand to be remembered.* The Organization, then, in reflectively comprehending itself as comprised of generations unique to it as well as indirectly present within it, completes a demand that was implicitly made by prior group forms. One such demand from the statutory group, for example, would be to maintain the cohesion of the group and its internal differentiation through the development of education, by preserving its aims, achievements, and significance for the present. What Barnes referred to as "the cultural heritage" and "our interaction with this inheritance at any present moment," involves the explicit recognition and completion of educational imperatives implicit in the action of the non-group members who made the present group form possible (Barnes 1981, 248).

The question of the nature of the interrelations between the diachronic and synchronic elements within the group leads to that of the relations of the teacher and the students to these two elements. It is clear that the culture built on past *praxis* is handed down through generations, but how exactly is it inherited by the teacher and the students? How, in other words, does their synchronic temporalization as a moment of the group relate to the overarching diachronic temporalization of the group as a whole? The teacher, as discussed in chapter 1, is a member of a past generation that contributes to the articulation and development of the present generation. They are, as discussed, in several groups and generations at once, a member whose past is comprised by their present educational totalization, and whose present is informed by, and an extension of, the past that made possible their role as a teacher. There is, therefore, in this particular generational member, a further, temporal immanence-transcendence tension insofar as they are part of a prior generation, educated by a prior education, and a product and inheritor of traditions that are in need of being made present. This figure, then, has the educational demand of simultaneously preserving and modifying, making accessible and appropriate to the present, the past of the group crystallized in its education. They are, however, part of the present generation to the extent that they interact with it, help fashion it, set a model for it, while also remaining transcendent to it, incapable of being made fully immanent insofar as they are a condition for the present generation that did not emerge with it. As such, the entirety of the past of the Organization, beginning with the generation to which the teacher belongs, is embodied in the teacher. This means that "the life of the teacher itself is centuries old," a collective, historical sign of the collective past of the group that continues to totalize itself in and through the educational totalization of the teacher (Sartre 2004a, 54). The past of the group, moreover, continuously present in its diachrony, also reaches its limits with the manner in which the teacher assumes and negates this very diachronic process.

An additional complication arises when the teacher is understood as equivalent to the older brothers, to those immediately preceding, who, while belonging to their own, previous generation, are not necessarily *wholly* of the past and present generations. They maintain a particular distance from both the "older methods" of the system of education several generations prior, and yet are far enough removed from the present generation of students for there to be a qualitative distance between the two such that the kinds of images, technologies, and cultural understanding, present themselves as possible points of tension. They place the past generations in relation to the students, forming a link between them as both a member of the past and present, and educationally constituting their reciprocal relationship through their gaze. The temporal look of the teacher, therefore, is twofold insofar as it is a present look at a present generation, but one which establishes an educational relationship between the present and the past. It is not a "static look."[12] The look of the teacher is a historically constituting look that "objectifies" the students, that is, recognizes them as members of the Organization, but also *historicizes* them by temporally connecting them to previous generations and showing them that and ultimately why their lives take such a particular, present form.

The teacher, as a temporalizing educational third, mediates between the generations, totalizes the knowledge and ignorance of the students in relation to the material taught, and establishes their relation to the educational apparatus within the group. The temporal demand of the group on the teacher, as a demand that stretches across generations and across groups, alters with each subsequent generation, is modified in such alteration, but requires that the continuity and therefore the *identity* of the group in its *difference*, in its new generational form, be preserved in the necessary, new, and present form. Therefore, the demand on the teacher is a demand of past generations on a member of a past and present generation who has the unique present significance of maintaining the past life of the group but does so by *rejuvenating* such life in keeping it *present*, meaningful, valuable, and recognized as an integral component of the present of the students and their lives. The diachronic temporality of this demand culminates in a synchronic temporalization that rests on a previous development, is continuous with it, but necessarily discontinuous through the necessary educational modifications. The teacher, therefore, regarding the "objective," historical temporality of the group, is a synthesis of a multiplicity of generational temporalizations which are maintained in the present and, through the act of teaching, handed down to the students as *the inherited diachronic temporality and knowledge of the group.*

The students, as themselves members of the group who are not yet full group members, also inherit the educational imperatives of the past. Their situation, in a sense, is the opposite, on "the other side" of that of the teacher. Rather than belonging to group forms that preceded the Organization, or members who belong to an earlier generation, they are members of the present generation who have not yet realized the synchrony of their temporally extended and indeterminate generation. While the teacher inherited a tradition as a past member of the present group, the students are not-yet-present members of the group insofar as their educational personalization has not yet been formally completed. They therefore receive a demand from the past *to become educated*, to become group members, to, albeit at a particular distance, coincide with the group as group members whose lives are still centuries in the past. The students, in a paradoxical sense, are appealed to as temporally prior and subsequent to the group, as members of the group that will continue its identity in their difference, in new cultural forms, but which are also after the group, after its identity has been solidified in the past. They are seen by the past in such a way that their objectification is part of the process of making them full group members. In this regard, they are themselves historical thirds of the present, totalizing one another through their educational temporalization, but they are thirds that are not yet full, constituting thirds in the group. They are, as discussed earlier, totalized in their knowledge and ignorance by the absent gaze of the past in their relation to the teacher and the material taught. The diachronic look of the past makes possible their status as educational thirds insofar as it *historically* places them in relation to the various elements of the educational apparatus and the history of the group.

The students, in looking back, also mediate the relations between the teacher and the past of the group, totalizing the prior generations in their diachronic temporalization, and establishing present relations between the present and past. They are, though incomplete, still thirds to the prior generations and the teacher, and place them in relation in such a way that they have a meaningful presence in the synchronic process of education. In general, the inherited look of the past generations helps integrate the students into the group, into its past, its developing present, and ultimately its future. It provides a sketch for the group members to fulfill as they continue to articulate, differentiate, and develop the group through their education and eventual, full membership in the group. Through their own status as third parties, the students help keep past generations and the teacher as their historical sign in the present. The synchronic education of the students is therefore interwoven with the diachrony of the past, but in such a way that the prior generations are formative, more determinative, and serve as the basis on which the students temporally enter and begin to inscribe themselves in the life of the group.

THE SYNCHRONIC TEMPORALIZATION OF COMMITTED EDUCATION

The account of the diachronic temporalization of education across generations within the group has led to the question of the temporal character of the lived-experience of education. I showed the different ways in which the teacher and the students respond to the educational demand placed on them by various generations, and the manner in which they contribute to the temporalization of the "objective," historical time within the group. What, however, is the nature of the temporality of the experience of education? And building on the analyses of the imagination from chapter 1, what is the temporality of the lived-experience of the imagination in education? Finally, what is the nature of the lived-educational temporalization of the teacher, the students, and the intersubjective character of the educational experience? The response to these questions involves a phenomenological account of the temporality of education within the present, synchronic moment of the group which continues and responds to its diachronic development. In this section, I will provide an eidetic analysis of the lived temporalization of the teacher in their act of teaching.

As I discussed in the previous section, the teacher inherits an imperative to educate the present generation in accordance with the present circumstances of the group. The teacher, however, in belonging to multiple generations and groups, is also the symbol and embodiment of multiple temporalities. How, as a complement to the prior, diachronic account, does the inheritance of generational temporality and its corresponding demands bear upon the temporality of the teacher in their act of teaching? First, the teacher has the synchronic task of resisting the ossification of generations in the group through their act of teaching. The inherited demand is a burden placed on the teacher to resist the potential, negative weight of the practico-inert by discovering and putting into practice the educational form necessary for the present. As such, the teacher is caught "between" times, and they find themselves in a particular tension, insofar as the content of a particular subject has to be both preserved and transcended, appreciated in its historical significance while being appropriately expressed in a new, present form. The teacher, therefore, has the dual task of continuing an educational tradition, while also resisting it by finding the appropriate way in which it can be incorporated into the present reality of the group. The resistance to the potential internal ossification of the group, as well as the concomitant threat of using inappropriate, outdated methods and failing to incorporate new subjects and technology into the act of teaching, involves finding the right way to introduce the object of knowledge into the group in a new, modified, imaginary way, which continues to preserve its identity. As such, the teacher is simultaneously a form of resistance to previous educational systems, rhythms, and methods, as well as their necessary historical extension. They find themselves between several past, generational temporalizations and the future of the current generation of students. In beginning the immediate, lived-process of education, the teacher is in a temporal tension between generations, and in their immediate lived-relation to the past generations continues them by interrupting them in creating the new, necessary, and present pedagogical forms.

One element of particular significance that is inherited by the teacher is a cultural and temporal rhythm. Each previous generation, and each previous group, had a particular rhythm in its orientation to its immediate objectives, its ultimate aims, and so on.[13] In the group in fusion, for example, the group was spontaneously formed on the basis of an imminent threat and the realization of its ends was linked to an appreciation of the threat, and the manner in which it had to utilize time to accomplish its goals. In fact, as Sartre writes, "a group defines its own temporality, that is to say, its practical speed and the speed with which the future comes to it" (Sartre 2004a, 391). The revolutionary rhythm of this group, it follows, corresponded both to its ends, its reasons for founding, the urgency of the situation, and the manner in which the storming of the Bastille itself unfolded. Again, the sworn group, a settled revolutionary group, now defined by new concerns, above all that of its internal cohesion and perpetual unity, had a slower rhythm, one that was more considered, involving a necessary distance and perspective, and various practices, such as the swearing of an oath, that continued to make possible the very existence of the group. As part of the transition of these two particular group forms, there is a slowing of the rhythm, a redefined relation to the other group members, and a general reevaluation of the aims of the group and its future. One essential component of the rhythm of each group individually as well as the shift in rhythms in their chronological development, is the relationship that each has to *the manner in which time will unfold.* Again, in the group in fusion, as there was an immediate threat, that group had to move quickly, and decisions had to be made without the possibility of sustained reflection. Later, in the statutory group, it was possible for the group to slow the experience of time, the kind of future it would have as well as the way it would approach and appear in the group. The rhythm in each group is in part constituted by a particular orientation to time, which can itself be rooted in external threats or issues internal to the group.

In the case of the Organization, its temporal rhythm changes in light of the shift to reflection and its more general organizational character. This group, therefore, in reflecting on itself, further reflects on its *temporal functioning*, that is, its relation to its history, the present circumstances, and its short- and long-term goals. It reflectively determines the appropriate rhythm of the present moment and does so through a considered reflection on itself and the preceding group forms. For example, while recognizing the urgency of the group in fusion, the Organization both appreciates its accomplishments and foundational character, while also being careful not to allow such a rhythm, such an orientation toward and use of time, to seep into the temporal orientation of its present, which, as part of a process of reflection, is of a qualitatively different sort. Moreover, due to the circumstances of the previous two groups, the temporalization of individual and collective *praxis* largely maintained a single manner of unfolding. There is little room, for example, for the revolutionary action to "slow down," or for the statutory group to "speed up" without causing a particular temporal disequilibrium. One of the merits of the Organization, as an incorporation, development, and resistance of these two group forms, is that it can more deliberately regulate its temporalization. Its history, for example, can become a theme for it, and different distances both within and to the future can become objects of consideration. And if it is necessary to more quickly approach a certain objective, it will be possible for the group to do so, as it will also be possible for it to reflectively modify the rate of its functioning to find a more suitable approach to fulfill its aims. Finally, the synchronic temporalization of the Organization is further differentiated through its plurality of generations. As each prior group form had its own rhythm, so too does each generation, and thus each subsequent generation has to be mindful of this state of affairs, and, in resisting its own history, incorporate the prior temporal rhythms into its own by modifying them.

In the case of education, the teacher inherits a corresponding rhythm and understanding of the temporal process of education. However, part of the temporal component of their pedagogy, and as the complement to their use of the imagination, involves first discerning the temporality of the present generation of students, and subsequently finding the appropriate temporal manner of presenting imaginative content. In this sense, the teacher is a particular origin of time in the organized group as well as the proper relation to it. To prevent the present from being weighed down by the previous temporal rhythm *as practico-inert*, and more generally to prevent time itself from taking on the negative characteristics of the practico-inert, the teacher will therefore have to sufficiently understand the subject being taught, the present generation of students, and the relation between them. On this basis, they can then establish the appropriate temporal atmosphere in the classroom, properly temporalize their own imaginative act of teaching, that is, find the necessary rate for its presentation, and as a result initiate and continue the process of temporalizing the imagination of the students and their own imagination. This involves a further instance of finding the correct image for the material being taught, an image that articulates the subject-matter, the group, and will be accepted and actively engaged with by the students. The teacher, in their temporal-imaginative role, is a unique synthesis of temporal rhythms who embodies past educational rhythms, creates the necessary rhythm for the present, and *lives this temporal tension* between the generations.

There is an additional component to the temporalizing, educational act of the teacher in relation to the present generation of students. Part of what it means to be attuned to the temporality of the present, is also to understand how it needs to be modified for the sake of the education of the students and the future of the group. The teacher needs to begin to instill the *necessary temporal rhythm* for the life of the group. The teacher thus serves as a temporal condition of possibility for the students to fulfill their tasks as students as well as future group members. For example, in a technologically oriented society, one wherein the pace of the culture has increased in various ways and may possibly be "too fast" in the transmission of information, it will be necessary for the teacher to create the necessary temporal context to address this state of affairs. And such a context has a twofold significance. First it is the context proper for the particular subject, lesson, and in general for the educational object to temporalize itself on its own terms. Secondly, in creating such an atmosphere, the teacher has the additional responsibility of simultaneously *bracketing out* the general pace of the present generation, while also *responding to it* such that it can adjust as needed. To an extent, then, the teacher has to *bracket time itself* in order for it to appropriately appear in an educational setting and to ultimately have the necessary relation to the other aspects of life in the group. As a result of this latter role, there may be a peculiar diachronic conflict in the synchronic present of the group. There is, more generally, a conflict of rhythms, and the teacher has to resist the past rhythms in addressing that of the present generation of students, and must therefore integrate what is necessary from both past and present rhythms into the present.[14] As part of such a situated, temporal-imaginative pedagogy, it may be necessary to provide "slower" lessons, instill the proper way to read a text of a certain subject-matter to both introduce students to the content and to education as an issue of time.[15] For example, concerning a certain text, fewer pages or passages can be assigned, with general, interpretively open questions that require rereading, explicit interpretive acts, rather than more narrowly focused questions, whose "answers" can simply be found in the text, and so on. The point, in this case, is to "slow down" the act of reading, in more general terms the act of learning, in order to instill the necessary temporal orientation toward a text and the understanding of the importance of such an orientation.

The concern with finding the appropriate temporal rhythm for present education and the multigenerational situation of the teacher leads to a few further questions regarding the temporalization of the act of teaching. First, what is the essential nature of the temporality of the teacher in their act of teaching? Secondly, how exactly does the teacher temporalize their own imaginative pedagogy? And lastly, what is the relation between temporality and knowledge? As I demonstrated in the previous chapter, the knowledge of the teacher gives them a unique, educational transcendence-immanence tension. The nature of this transcendence-immanence tension, however, complicates when the knowledge of the teacher is connected to the temporal aspect of the act of teaching. The knowledge of the teacher places them at a *temporal distance* from education in the organized group and adds a temporal layer to their epistemological transcendence-immanence tension. The unique situation of the teacher ascribes them a unique temporality both regarding the fulfillment of their own task of teaching as well as the temporality of the students.

First, the temporality of the teacher is comprised of a dual past. On a diachronic level, which maintains a presence and continuity with the synchronic present, they inherit and presently incarnate the past of the group. Therefore, their immediate, subjective act of teaching, their imaginative, rhythmic presentation of content, is continuous with the objective, temporal succession of generations within the group. In this regard, each act of the teacher is a synchronic act which forms a chain with the diachronic past of education as such, which was itself comprised of the pedagogical acts of teachers, the students, the decisions of the specialized apparatuses, and so on. In the language of Husserl, the far retention of the teacher is connected to and encapsulates the past education of the group. Secondly, the immediate act of teaching has its own, synchronic past. The imaginative presentation of content, in this case, temporalizes itself in accordance with a few aspects of teaching in its lived-present. It is immediately continuous with the portion of the lesson that has been given, the questions and discussions of the students, and broadens out to include the previous class meetings, the earlier parts of the semester, and so on. The immediate, synchronic present of teaching is therefore a contextual whole comprised of the various degrees of mediation within immediacy that constitute the past of the teacher. This past is "subjective" insofar as it is the past of the teacher *with regard to their act of teaching*, and while also continuous with the diachronic temporalization of the past, is irreducible to it. Each individual pedagogical act, therefore, is a unity of diachronic and synchronic temporalizations which are continuous individually and with one another but are also distinct.

In addition, as a correlate to the dual past of the teacher, they also possess a dual future. However, there is an essential difference that needs to be taken into account concerning the future. While their past is their own as well as that of previous generations, so is their future their own as well as that of the students who will collectively attain knowledge. Both the past generations and the students have unique futures as well. The future of the past generations is the meaning and role they will have in the future of the group. It is not, that is, a direct result of their *praxes*. Similarly, the immediate future of the teacher is in part comprised of the manner in which the past content is incorporated into the future of the unit, class, the students' understanding, and so on. It is also comprised of the material to-be-taught, and the future, presently indeterminate elements of the experience of teaching. Their immediate future, in this sense, coincides with that of the students insofar as their future is that of the particular class for which they are responsible. However, as the students were not members of the generations comprising the diachronic past of the group, so those generations are not members of the present generation or the future. Understood in this way, the diachronic past is therefore comprised of the past generations, while both the synchronic present and future are comprised by the students. The teacher, and only to a certain extent, is the sole member who is present in both and makes possible the continuity and transition between all of the pasts and futures of the group. And as the students advance in the process of education, there is a continued distancing from the temporalizations of the earlier periods of education. In this regard, the temporalization of education is the process of moving from the students' dependency on an initial temporal orientation toward the independence of such an orientation insofar as it is instilled, developed, and lived individually and collectively by each student.

There is, however, one particular aspect of the temporalization of teaching that needs to be noted, and which is connected to the process of personalization discussed in chapter 1. One part of this latter process, which may appear to be an undue restriction, is the understanding that education needs to be prescribed appropriate temporal limits. Through the process of personalization, and their eventual teaching in the group, the temporalization of the teacher in their unique individuality is necessarily bounded in such a way that they are able to designate the appropriate time to a given lesson, unit, level of education, and so on. The communication of knowledge has to take place within the appropriate temporal boundaries of the temporal process of education. This is a form of "objective-subjective" time insofar as it is the immediately lived objective time of the process of education but is not at the level of the diachronic temporalization of generations within the group. Thus, the teacher, guided by the material taught, the necessary educational rhythms, and their process of personalization, is temporally limited in their teaching insofar as they are only able to devote a particular amount of time to the given subject-matter. This limitation, however, is not a restriction. It is simply a determination that the educational apparatuses within the group have reached based on an appreciation of the level of education, the circumstances of the system of education, as well as the needs of the group as a whole. The free temporalization of the teacher individually and collectively with the students requires that the process gradually complete itself within a given time frame.

Furthermore, the appreciation of the temporal limits of education demonstrates the manner in which the educational apparatuses, as well as the various systems of education, recognize the need for appropriate temporal rhythms. Such appreciation contributes to the teacher's task of creating such a rhythm in the individual class by outlining limits to the process within which the temporality of teaching can naturally unfold. These limits serve as a point of departure for the educational process, and do not confine it such that the teacher feels unable to adequately communicate a lesson, that it is necessary to rush through or to skip certain essential elements. In fact, these temporal boundaries both help and demand that the teacher fulfill their task and that the act of teaching cohere with the standards of the group, its other concerns, and the short- and long-term aims of education. In this regard, the synchronic temporality of teaching reaches a particular limit insofar as it is bounded by beginning- and end-"points" within which the lived-time of teaching can unfold. As a result, the educational apparatuses and the system of education, collectively with their various roles and responsibilities, serve as thirds that further totalize the relations between the teacher and the students, knowledge and ignorance, and the past of the group. These elements of committed education, in their dual capacity as presence-absence, of establishing a framework and remaining at a distance to appreciate and maintain the freedom of the teacher and the students, totalize all of the parts involved in creating a temporal framework within which the individual temporalizations and rhythms of the teacher and the students can unfold.

THE INTERSUBJECTIVE TEMPORALIZATION OF COMMITTED EDUCATION

The analysis of the temporality of the teacher, as well as the temporal context within which education takes place, leads to the following questions, namely: What is the nature of the lived-time of the students? How do the individual and collective temporalizations of the students contribute to the temporal process initiated by the teacher and whose aim is realizing the truth of the educational object? First, it is important to recognize the lived-temporal situation of the students within the group as well as within the temporal, educational framework of the classroom. As was the case with the teacher, the students possess their own transcendence-immanence tension. Unlike the teacher, however, as well as the other, educated group members, their tension takes the opposite form. In accordance with the present stage of their educational process, the students are still "before" the time of the group insofar as they have not yet been fully integrated into it. As such, they are peculiarly transcendent to the temporal functioning of the group. Regarding its diachronic temporalization, they are "after" it, the generation which will inherit it. However, insofar as they have not yet done so, they are in an indeterminate, ambiguous, *presently historicizing* location, and remain temporally transcendent to the group to which education has the aim of making them immanent. They are in the process of becoming continuous with the past insofar as they are obtaining the knowledge required for them to establish a meaningful relation to it. Their transcendence is in their immediate, temporal lived-experience of not yet fully belonging to the group or their own generation but being in the process of becoming so. They are, in this sense, *a-synchronous.* Through the dialogue of images between the teacher and the students, the inheritance of the past of the group, in accordance with the level of education and the subject-matter, is individualized in the life of each student and becomes part of both their individual and collective past. The imaginative-temporal process of education makes the past of the student continuous with the past of the group and allows the latter to serve as a basis for their present education and future life as full group members.

The temporal transcendence-immanence tension of the students is further complicated by the fact that they do not yet have their own educational rhythm. Moreover, as they do not a priori relate to their role as students and the process of education, their own educational temporalization is dependent on the teacher and the group. To start, it is important to note that, while the teacher begins the process and, in a sense, both begins and continues the process with each class meeting, the teacher does not impose a temporal rhythm on the students. Much as the group establishes a temporal context for education, the teacher begins a process of learning, comprised of a given subject, its manner of presentation, and dialogue, in which the necessary orientation toward the subject matter and knowledge can be developed. Such an orientation, moreover, is in part determined by the subject matter itself, that is, *by the intrinsic temporality of the given educational object.*[16] The teacher, then, orients the particular lesson on the basis of the prior recognition of the nature of the educational object, the stage of the lesson, the history of the class, and so on. Moreover, the imaginative content is presented in accordance with the imaginative dimension of the object, which itself outlines, demands, and makes possible the necessary temporal sequence for its imaginative fulfillment. As a result, the object of education is its own temporal object.[17] As such an intrinsically temporal and temporalizing object, it has the additional quality of not remaining identical in its content and the presentation it demands across all stages of education. For example, a particular text taught for the first time and at an earlier level of education may require a slower, more compartmentalized approach, such that the given sections, chapters, terms, and so on, are worked through in line with its character as a new educational object. However, the same text, read at a later stage, and on the basis of the subsequently obtained knowledge, may be able to be read faster, discussed more comprehensively in class, in relation to other intellectual traditions, other texts by the same author, and so on. In this sense, the object is both identical and different as the understanding of it deepens over the course of the educational process. And in this sense, *the object resists itself* insofar as it prevents an exhaustive understanding or presentation of it at a certain stage of the educational process.

The temporal character of the object of education guides the temporalization of the lesson and the general process of education. Moreover, it helps the teacher present the content in a manner consistent with its intrinsic temporal character and the stage of education. As there is mutual recognition between the teacher and the students in their temporal dialogue, so is there *mutual recognition of the intrinsic nature and temporality of the educational object which appears in such dialogue.* Moreover, phenomenologically understood, such "objective" time is not "vulgar," degraded, or even necessarily linear, but rather the intrinsic temporality of the object which requires the corresponding temporal orientation in order to be adequately imaginatively grasped and appreciated.[18] The object contains its own rhythmic orientation toward itself which also corresponds to the level of education. It is part of the task of the temporalization of education through both the teacher and the students to recognize such temporality to establish the appropriate relation between the object of education and the students. There is, therefore, a *temporal adequation* between the teacher and the students on the one hand, and the educational object on the other, the increased understanding of which is a result of the deepening of the educational process.[19] And insofar as committed education is concerned with cultivating the imagination, there is an imaginary dimension to such adequation. On the basis of the temporalization of the object, *there is a further adequation between the imagination and time.*

The manner in which the teacher chooses to imaginatively present the material, on the basis of the intrinsic temporality of the educational object, guides the manner in which the students imaginatively engage with it to collectively attain truth. There is, in the imaginative dialogical process, a correlation between the temporalization of the object, that is, the temporal stages which lead to its understanding, and the imaginative-temporal acts of the students in their study of it. Understood through the lens of time, it becomes evident that the teacher's presentation of content is not only not a temporally neutral, incomplete presentation of static content, but also *an incomplete temporal process*, one which, in its future-oriented character, leads the students to participate in the completion of this process through the use of the imagination. The temporalization of the act of teaching, as well as that of the object in its educational significance, in pointing the way to their own fulfillment, are future-oriented and guide the students to imaginatively temporalize the content presented in a future-directed manner.[20] The lived-time of the education of students, in its dual imaginative and temporal dimensions, is intrinsically directed toward the future as it continues to approach the object in its truth. In beginning with the teacher, the images produced indicate their own fulfillment, and in being properly fulfilled by the students, have the temporal process up until then completed. The truth obtained then becomes its own imaginative-temporal sign, a sketch, a temporal indication of the work for the students to do to obtain further knowledge.

As a result of the individual, temporal engagement with the objects of knowledge, there is an a priori indeterminacy, an inherent uncertainty, in the temporal unfolding of the individual temporalizations and the manner in which they both relate to one another and contribute to the establishment of an overarching, single, intersubjective temporalization. Moreover, part of what this orientation accomplishes within the classroom is to create an intersubjective, reciprocally constituted, and dependent temporality. Each student, as a third to all of the others and the teacher, in their unique temporal relation to their education and in dialogue with the other students, temporalizes the other students and the teacher. As a result, each temporalization in the classroom is intrinsically connected to all of the others, and constitutes a collective, temporal process toward knowledge which has been initiated by the teacher. In following the temporal order of the object, the play of individual temporalizations forms the necessary, intersubjective temporal rhythm. The lived temporalizations of the students in the classroom individually connect with the material as part of a collective, dialogical, imaginary process that allows knowledge to be gained by a *temporal-imaginative creation.*

Within such temporalization in the classroom setting, there is a plurality of each temporal dimension, and each dimension overlaps with others, partially coinciding with them, while remaining distinct. For example, the past of each student is unique to the manner in which it is *lived* by the student. However, as oriented toward the same object, the "pasts" of the students coincide, and ultimately establish a collective past of education. The same can be said of the present, insofar as each student is presently oriented toward the object, and the "present" of the class is that of the flowing simultaneity of imaginative acts. And the future, insofar as it is partially sketched through the object and the teacher, is *the same future* for all of the students. From the side of the object, the future of the class is the truth to be obtained, and in this regard, however indeterminate a place it may occupy, the truth of the object bounds the process of obtaining it. From "the other side," as each student relates to the object individually and imaginatively, they all intentionally relate to the same educational future. Their futures all overlap and ultimately coincide with the attainment of truth. However, there are obvious descriptive differences insofar as each student relates to the content uniquely, on the basis of their own temporalization, and grasps the truth on their own terms and integrates it into their lives in their own way. There are, therefore, different rates at which the future as truth is obtained by the students, but insofar as all the students are imaginatively oriented toward the same object and have the same educational aim, they comprise a single, collective future, which appears more quickly or slowly on the basis of the student's relation to it. The students are accordingly transcendent to one another in their individual temporalizations while establishing the immanence of an intersubjective temporal process. The pluralities of the past, present, and future create a temporalization wherein each dimension, as unique to each student, coincides with, and remains distinct from, all of the others, and contributes to an overarching, unstable temporalization which is continuously refashioned and reexperienced through the educational process.

As can be seen from the discussion above, the potentiality for conflict inheres within the educational process because of its fundamental uncertainty. There is, at least potentially, a tension between the teacher and the students, the students among themselves, as well as between the teacher, the students, the educational object, and ultimately the group as a whole. And, though there is conflict in such relations, this does not involve the degradation to an alienated group form but merely shows that conflict, tension, asymmetry are possible, if not also in certain respects, necessary parts of the relations built upon the foundational relations of reciprocity. Again, as discussed earlier, the group attempts to create a temporal framework within which the necessary educational process can fulfill itself. However, the objective temporality of the group may very well conflict in various respects with the teacher and the students. The educational process, therefore, cannot be understood as a preestablished harmony. The time allotted to a given subject, stage of education, and class, while necessarily an estimate, may very well be limiting, and this can only be determined after the process of education has begun. The teacher may realize that there is not enough time, that there is not an appropriate correlation between the time allotted and the educational requirements, and so on. Moreover, the students themselves, in their experience in the classroom, as they temporalize the material taught, may not feel that sufficient time was provided, that the temporal rhythm of the class as a whole did not allow for the necessary connection with the material for knowledge to be sufficiently obtained. The students, as dependent thirds, temporally establish the relations of ignorance and knowledge in the educational process, but it is not a priori certain that the plurality of temporalizations will cohere or coincide with one another in the process of obtaining truth. Nor is it guaranteed that sufficient time has been allotted for the students to meaningfully relate to the material as such, and therefore, though the dialogical, imaginative, and future-oriented totalization may have in part fulfilled its task, the conflict which emerged between time and knowledge did not allow for the appropriate personalization of the material. Thus, though the process of education is guided by the temporal-imaginative acts of the teacher, the intrinsic temporality of the object, and the temporal-imaginative responses of the students, conflict in education is a perennial danger which the different members of the process need to constantly keep in mind and address as needed.

NOTES

1. For Sartre's discussion of reflection in the chapter on "Temporality" in *Being and Nothingness,* see Sartre (1984, 211–37). On this point, see Barnes (1973, 20–30, 66–74). For a recent account of reflection in Sartre, see Williford (2020, 89–103). For an analysis of the theme of temporality, with an emphasis on the early, phenomenological theory of time, see Somerlatte (2020, 198–211). For a text with a similar emphasis on the phenomenological character of Sartre's early work on time, see McInerney (1991, 149–74). For an article that historically situates Sartre's analyses of time, particularly in his early period, see Cormann (2020, 76–86). For a discussion of time in the *Critique*, see Flynn (1997, 129–32).

2. For relevant analyses in the *Critique*, see Sartre (2004a, 53–56, 666). From *The Family Idiot*, see Sartre (1993, 3–56) and from the original French (Sartre 1972, 9–66). For the accounts of synchrony and diachrony in *The Family Idiot*, see Barnes (1981, 278–309). Annabelle Dufourcq draws attention to the manner in which Flaubert uniquely experienced the future on the basis of the situation of his family and the relation to it during infancy. See Dufourcq (2014, 59).

3. For the analyses of static and dynamic temporality, see Sartre (1984, 187–211).

4. The term institution as used in this chapter should not be confused with its use in the second half of this book, wherein institutionalized education, as a degraded form of committed education, is discussed.

5. In the *Critique*, for example, this is discussed with regard to the Spanish economy and deforestation in China. See Sartre (2004a, 161–84, 225).

6. Gyllenhammer has argued for a positive reading of the practico-inert as well. See Gyllenhammer (2015, 3–12).

7. For the complete chapter on the Objective Spirit in the English translation see Sartre (1993, 33–56). For the original French, see Sartre (1972, 41–66).

8. For Sartre's understanding of the practico-inert in the *Critique*, see Barnes (1981, 249).

9. I will take up the theme of the culture of the group in fusion and the sworn group again in the next section concerning the lived-time of the cultural rhythms of education in the organized group.

10. This further involves an extension of the concept of the look as inherently dialogical insofar as in this case different generations are in dialogue with one another. In this regard, see Martinot (2005, 53–58).

11. On this point, see Barnes (1981, 262).

12. Sartre's examples of the man bent over the keyhole and the man in the park in *Being and Nothingness*, for example, can be considered instances of a "static look." See Sartre (1984, 341–54).

13. My analysis here has an interesting relation to the two notions of rhythm discussed by Jaeger in volume 1 of *Paideia.* See Jaeger (1945, 125–26). He writes: "We must not be misled by his words into thinking that Archilochus' rhythm is a *flux*, although the modern idea of rhythm is something which flows, and some derive the word itself from ῥέω, 'to flow.' Obviously when the Greeks speak of the rhythm of a building or a statue, it is not a metaphor transferred from musical language; and the original conception which lies beneath the Greek discovery of rhythm in music and dancing is not *flow* but *pause*, the steady limitation of movement" (Jaeger 1945, 126). Jaeger also notes that Democritus referred to "the rhythm of the atoms" as their "pattern," and that Aristotle translated the term for rhythm as "schema" (Jaeger 1945, 126). I am using the term in both of these senses. Educational rhythms "hold" and "pattern" generations (Jaeger 1945, 126). I am adding a particular emphasis to the element of time to develop the concept of a temporal rhythm which is the result of a particular form of education.

14. It is important to note that, while Sartre discusses this group in the absence of alienation, that does not rule out the possibility of conflict in the group, especially if it is necessary for its development and to avoid alienation. See Sartre (2004a, 455).

This is a form of lived-conflict, operative on a different level than that of the conflict between generations discussed in the previous section.

15. In a similar, albeit more critical vein, Nietzsche in *Daybreak* writes: "A book like this, a problem like this, is in no hurry; we both, I just as much as my book, are friends of *lento*" (Nietzsche 1997, 5).

16. Again a quote from Nietzsche in *Daybreak* is relevant to my analysis here. The following lines serve as an example of the manner in which a particular subject-matter and educational object have an inherent temporality, and are situated within the temporal, cultural rhythms of the present: "For philology is that venerable art which demands of its votaries one thing above all: to go aside, to take time, to become still, to become slow—this art does not so easily get anything done, it teaches to read *well*, that is to say, to read slowly, deeply, looking cautiously before and aft, with reservations, with doors left open, with delicate eyes and fingers" (Nietzsche 1997, 5).

17. I am using the term "temporal object" in the way in which Husserl has defined it in his 1905 lectures on internal time-consciousness. He there defines it in the following way: "By *temporal objects in the specific sense* we understand objects that are not only unities in time but that also contain temporal extension in themselves. When a tone sounds, my objectivating apprehension can make the tone itself, which endures and fades away, into an object and yet not make the duration of the tone or the tone in its duration into an object. The latter—the tone in its duration—is a temporal object. The same is true of a melody, of any change whatsoever, but also of any persistence without change, considered as such" (Husserl 1991, 24).

18. The "objective time" of the object is therefore a second instance of objective-subjective time in the group, insofar as it corresponds to a form of objectivity, which helps determine the temporalization of education by the teacher and the students. However, it is different from the "objective" level of diachronic temporality. Moreover, and as the vocabulary indicates, this demonstrates that "authentic" time in education is intersubjective, or, perhaps better, comprised of the temporality of the individual, the group, and the object of education. This stands in contrast to Heidegger's view as discussed in *Being and Time.* See, for example, Heidegger (1962, 311). Education, in this respect, while itself rooted in the orientation toward need, scarcity, and the practico-inert, is also rooted in an orientation toward time. Similarly, as Heidegger argued in *The Metaphysical Foundations of Logic*, logic is in fact grounded in metaphysics and the temporality of *Dasein.* See Heidegger (1984, 103, 154, 196–219). Nevertheless, though he does address the relation between being-with and authenticity, he did not emphasize the intersubjective character of temporality to the extent to which I am emphasizing it here. In this respect, see Heidegger (1984, 139).

19. The notion of the temporal adequation between the subject and object has a significant relation to the theory of adequation as it was developed in the Middle Ages and the etymology of the term. See Carruthers (2008, 28–29 and footnote 34 on p. 376). Most important for my purposes here is the following: "*Adequatio* is a word of relationship, 'adjustment,' 'fitting' a word to what one wants to say. The prefix is crucial to its meaning, not a dead metaphor. *Adaequatio*, being a matter of

relationship and not identity, admits of many grades and degrees of approximation" (Carruthers 2008, 28).

20. For an account of Sartre's views of the future, see Hollier (1986, 20–21, 199–200).

Chapter 3

Literature and the Culture of the Imaginary

The previous two chapters were devoted to the analysis of the unique task of education in the organized group in both its static and genetic dimensions. The first chapter demonstrated the role that education plays in the group, its nature and methods, and the necessary form of the imagination for committed education. Chapter 2 deepened these analyses by reinterpreting them through the lens of time, providing both a historical, diachronic, as well as a phenomenological, synchronic account of the temporality of education. There are, however, a few questions that emerge on the basis of the previous two chapters concerning the theme of the imagination, and which extend it to the life of the group as a whole, namely: How does education in images translate into future, collective imagining? How does education further make possible the reading in images necessary for committed literature? And how, finally, does it produce a particular culture, what I am terming a culture of the imaginary, which is also a form of resistance?

In order to respond to these questions, and to demonstrate the *effects* of committed education for the group as a whole, its significance, and its nature as a perennial task and condition for the future, a few steps are necessary. First, I will show the kinds of group members produced by committed education, and how it serves as a point of departure for their temporal and imaginative orientation toward their lives in the group. This will involve a renewed consideration of the relation between perception and the imagination, and the manner in which perception continues to serve as a necessary basis for the derealizing acts of the imagination. I will, however, emphasize that the two are not as separate or disconnected as Sartre had initially interpreted them in *The Imaginary* and his other early work.[1] As part of the account of the individual group member's use of the imagination, I will develop the corresponding concept of an *individual image*, which is an image produced by a single group member that bears directly upon their role in the group and is not explicitly addressed to the group as a whole.

The theme of the individual orientation in the group leads to a second, more comprehensive theme, namely, that of the precise manner in which the group continues to educate itself after the period of formal education has come to an end. This section will be guided by the following question: How can education be understood as a perennial task in the organized group, and how does it contribute to the fulfillment of individual tasks and functions? In order to demonstrate the cultural context of such a form of education, I will draw, in a positive sense, a parallel with Sartre's concept of "the objective neurosis" from *The Family Idiot.* Moreover, from the same work, I will expand on his concepts of "the social imaginary" and "the social image" (Sartre 1987, 130; 1993, 510).[2] This description of what I will also refer to as the public imaginary will involve an account of the imagination after the period of education and the manner in which such a cultivated imagination is operative in the Organization.

Finally, after these first two steps have been completed, I will turn to the theme of committed literature. This section will be guided by the following question: How does committed literature educate the group as a whole and meaningfully affect the tasks and functions of the group members? The analysis of literature within an educated group itself involves the reconceptualization of a number of Sartrean themes and the relations between certain of his texts. In particular, the relation between volume 1 of the *Critique* and *What is Literature?* needs to be reinterpreted such that the latter work, though chronologically prior, is a fulfillment of the later text insofar as it allows for the appropriate integration of literature and education in the theory of groups. This section will further address the nature and role of the educated, *literary imagination* in the Organization, and how it contributes to the group's continued reflection on itself. Lastly, as a complement to the concept of individual images, I will develop the concept of *collective images*, which are the images produced by literature, and extend to the group in all of its dimensions as it continues to direct itself toward a necessary future.[3]

THE PUBLIC IMAGINARY AND THE TRUTH OF THE ORACLE

After having established the essential character of committed education and its temporal character, the question as to the nature of such education for the organized group and collective action presents itself. In order to address the effects of education in the group, this section will be guided by four central questions. First, how does the previous form of education translate into a particular culture and form of life in the group? Secondly, and more generally, what is the nature of the cultural context the previous students enter and within which a life of the imaginary is further made possible and actualized? Thirdly, how does the relation between teacher and student, and the constellation of relations among the students, develop into the constellational relations of the individual group members attained through the fulfillment of their tasks? And lastly, how do the imagination and perception operate in such an educated group?

To begin, the group establishes the necessary public, imaginary culture for it to continue to educate itself and within which the individual acts of imagining can take place.[4] As such, it has created and continues to create the context within which the life of the group understood, both collectively and individually, that it can be determined and guided by the imaginary. It maintains the emphasis on the imagination developed throughout the formal process of education, and the appreciation of the appropriate relations between the imagination and perception. Despite a certain priority of the real and its status as "a permanent center of derealization," the imaginary is the primary term, and is the essential component of a public, collective life in the group (Sartre 1987, 130). There is, in the culture of the group, a fundamental continuity between the educational experience, demands, and expectations of the period of formal education and its present reality. In a positive sense, the public imaginary is the equivalent of the concept of "the objective neurosis,"[5] which, in being such, is an open imaginary, inherits past images, and modifies them as needed as part of the future-directed process of the group.

Moreover, such a public imaginary is concerned with raising the consciousness of the group members, dialogue within the group through literature, and therewith intersubjective, imaginative creation for the sake of the freedom of the group. In this regard, following *What Is Literature?*, what is of such significance is that the reader demands a particular literary work, and the author produces such a necessary, imaginary text, because of the historical circumstances the public finds itself in. The culture of the educated, organized group produces the culture it needs, a space for imagining, and a context within which *public life can be imaginary.* The culture of the organized group is, as an alternative to an objective neurosis, an objective, free imaginary which is comprised by the demands of the author and the public, generosity, and the appropriate, balanced relation between the imagination and perception. Thus, as educated, the Organization is ultimately a context within which the group members imagine with the aim of further integrating themselves into the group, and which continues to be present to reflectively articulate itself through the appropriate production of images.

There is a particular manner in which Sartre's discussions of the oracular character of Flaubert are operative in this context as well (Sartre 1993, 452).[6] The students enter a context that was already prophesied through their education, but they do so in such a way that they now have the obligation to freely continue and develop in accordance with the present demands of the group. As a result, though there is continuity in the succession of generations and the stages of life in the group, there is, as discussed concerning diachronic temporality, a necessary form of conflict and tension between the generations. Thus, in entering the group, the students find themselves in a culture of the imaginary wherein they are further situated concerning past generations, and in which the prophecy of past generations, the educational demands continuously placed on the subsequent group members, are in the process of being freely and spontaneously fulfilled. Moreover, in a paradoxical sense, from the side of the students, the oracle of education is both true and false. It is true insofar as the temporal-imaginative process of education serves as a point of departure and model for their imaginative lives in the group. In this regard, their education, as preparation for life in the group, is also a precursor of such a life and provides them with the resources necessary to live a free, spontaneous, collective life. In another sense, the students' personalization, the manner in which each student individually, and each class and generation of students collectively, integrates the inheritance and educational content of the group, instills an orientation to their future lives. And this life is itself continuously personalized in order for the organized group to maintain its essential character, achieve new ends, and resist its own ossification. Their process of personalization, in this regard, primarily provides *the form of life* in the group, insofar as it establishes the necessary imaginative and perceptual abilities for a future, free and collective life.

The oracle, however, is also false in its predictions concerning the future lives of the students. In addition, within the organized group, this falsity belongs a priori to the oracle of committed education. The oracle is such precisely because it is incomplete, at best a mere sketch, a prediction whose fulfillment is dependent upon the future, unknown circumstances of the group, the ability to imagine on the part of the students, as well as the manner in which the former students and the other group members choose to interpret and respond to the circumstances. As a correlate, *the content of life* in the group is largely uncertain, yet not without a meaningful relation to the nature of this group form insofar as, at the very least, its skeletal structure and other essential features will be acknowledged as helping comprise the content of future life in the group. In a sense, then, precisely what makes the oracle true is also necessarily what makes it false, insofar as the preparation for life in the group provides students with resources which will transcend the present moment and discernable future through their own individual, unique uses of them. The students, ultimately, are oracles to themselves as they fulfill the process of personalization, but in such a way that their future lives in the group are only *partially schematized* by education. Each student, then, as uniquely situated in the group, has a particular *imaginative style* which traces back to the manner in which they engaged with the imaginative dimension of their education.

The process of education can also be understood as oracular from the side of the teacher. Through the content taught, the various lessons, and their individual use of the imagination in their pedagogy, the teacher helps indicate the kind of group members the students will become. Through the various creative methods in the classroom and their ability to serve as a model of imaginative engagement with the subject-matter, the teacher serves as a model of the kind of imaginative orientation appropriate to, and required for, future life in the group as full group members. Moreover, as demonstrating the appropriate relation between the imagination and perception in the presentation of content, that is, as showing the latter to be a basis for its own transcendence through an imaginative act, the teacher prophecies the future orientation of the lives of the students as they continue to reflect on and develop the relation between perception and the imagination. Although they reach a particular level through education, perception and the imagination are not *exhausted* with the process, and the students, in part, will continue to imaginatively transcend the reality given in perception on the basis of the model the teacher provided in presenting imaginative content to be completed by the students. The teacher is therefore prophetic insofar as they establish the foundational understanding of the proper use and relation of perception and the imagination but leave the manner in which they will interact largely undetermined.

In addition to the students and the teacher prophesying the future of the group through the process of education, the past generations themselves have a peculiar, ambiguous status as oracular manifestations in the life of the group. The past generations of the Organization, in the demands that they placed on the students and continue to place on the group as a whole, predicted the form of life the students would lead insofar as it preserved the order of the group. However, in placing such demands, they also recognize their intrinsic limitation in appreciating the unpredictable and unforeseeable character of future life in the group. The past demands that the present maintain a public imaginary culture, but the form such an imaginary takes and the content of the images with which it is fulfilled are necessarily open and unrestrained by their past correlates. As a result, though the past maintains a presence in the group, it does not weigh on the group, but is in truth a particular lightness, an openness to the new dimensions of the group, and an awareness of its own limitations that recognizes the need for later generations to alter the group as necessary. On the basis of the system of education and the culture established, with varying degrees of accuracy depending upon their distance from the present, previous generations prophesy future life in the group, but also, as a complementary element, only to a certain extent, such that the future group members are recognized as free to develop the group as they see fit. The new group members, then, enter the culture of the group as both an extension of the period of education and as a point of departure, and experience themselves as the present form of a succession of generations which continues to place demands on the present but recognizes that they will be fulfilled freely and uniquely.

The originally pedagogical imaginary, through its cultivation of the imagination of the students individually and collectively, both serves as the necessary basis for such an imaginary life and is continuous with it as continuing to serve as its condition of possibility. In a sense, the act of imagining is limited by the educational process insofar as it is oriented and developed in a particular manner. However, the concept of the initially pedagogical, and subsequently public, imaginary, is open, and the manner in which it is operative in the group, its ability to fashion particular images, is *not unduly restricted.* The history of the group and the process of education, then, are transcendental conditions for the present acts of imagining, and fashion the group in a way that makes the corresponding and necessary form of imaginary life in the group possible. As a result, though freely determined by the group members, on the basis of their historical situation and the process of personalization, *the imagination of the group members itself is schematized.* The schematism of the imagination in the organized group is a result of the educational, historical, and now uniquely public context the group members find themselves in. It is a comprehensive historical, educational process that serves as a transcendental ground for the possibility of the appropriate use of the imagination, but does so by simply making it possible, and, in this sense, subsequently stepping back in order for it to take on its own character and life. Ultimately, then, the preceding stages of the group are a process of providing open limits to the imagination, and by further establishing such a use of the imagination within the overarching, continuously schematizing context of the public imaginary.

One of the essential elements of such an educational schematism is its incomplete, constantly developing, and spontaneous character. The use of the imagination in the public life of the group is a result of the prior process of education but is not reducible to it. The presentation of incomplete content with the concomitant expectation of its fulfillment has produced an imagination that is able to transcend the present reality of the group in order to complete it as necessary for the future life of the group. The public imaginary, as necessarily a historical and continuously imaginative context, bounds the imagination of the group members by allowing them to transcend and modify it. It is itself incomplete, comprised both by the content of the images produced and the totality of imaginative acts of the group members, but does not demand that the use of the imagination remain consistent with it. To the contrary, in addition to maintaining the traces of past generations, it itself recognizes that the imaginative framework will need to be refashioned, and that the previous standards of public imaginary life in the group may no longer be appropriate, or need to be modified in various ways. Therefore in serving as *an objective transcendental condition for the imagination,* it holds itself back in order to make possible the necessary present acts of imagining. At the same time, however, it must be understood that any break in the tradition of imagining, any rupture by the present moment, maintains the past of the imaginary insofar as it does not interrupt it simply to diverge from it, but rather, disrupts it in order to remain continuous with it. The novelty or the difference introduced into the public imaginary through the imagination is a necessary condition for the temporal and imaginative identity of the group.

There is, however, a paradox in this emphasis on such an imaginative culture. Although the imagination has a priority in the group regarding its freedom and transcendence, the imagination maintains an intrinsic, necessary connection to perception. The group members imagine altering the reality of the group as needed but do so with an interest in precisely that reality in a future form. Thus, while the imaginary is always both founded on and a transcendence of a prior reality, it has a twofold aim in its *Leistung*.[7] On the one hand, it produces imaginary content which is the necessary fulfillment of the presently lacking state of affairs in the group, and in this sense finds one of its ends in the image produced. On the other hand, however, it is producing images *for the sake of the real.* The imaginary culture, it follows, enshrouds perception, and creates an atmosphere within which the imagination can freely produce the necessary images, but always does so in accordance with an interest in, and concern for, the reality of the group in its present and future. Therefore, the act of imagining and the context within which it occurs are always of a twofold sort and continue to develop as the dialectic between realization and derealization unfolds. In this sense, the images produced are ultimately *bounded images* insofar as they intrinsically relate to the future realization of the image as a necessary, constituent part of the reality of the group. The aims of the group, as situated within a culture of the imaginary, are continuously achieved and transcended through the dialectical process of perceiving and imagining. As a result, the process of imagining in the group is defined by the repetition, *always in a new form,* of the process of individually and collectively derealizing the real and subsequently returning to a new reality.

In addition to the dialectical interrelations between perception and the imagination, there is a necessary tension between the public context of the imaginary and the individual acts of the imagination. The social imaginary of the group is a point of departure for the imagining acts of the individual group members. It serves as a guide for the imaginary life in the group, for how the images should be produced and their content, but all it does is guide the group members. There is, in principle and as needed, conflict between the individual acts of the imagination and the context within which such imagining takes place. In this instance, there is a necessary conflict between the individual image produced by the individual group member and the collective image of the group which the past and, with varying indeterminacy, present group members have produced of the group. There is a fundamental coincidence and non-coincidence of the acts of the imagination insofar as they are situated within a context they transcend and, by so doing, *resituate themselves and the public imaginary in accordance with a newly fashioned image.* Moreover, this involves the further extension of the claim from *The Family Idiot* that "Irreality is not the absence of all reality, but its *contestation*" (Sartre 1971a, 595).[8] In this case, the imaginary itself serves as a contestation to the imaginary, a challenge that the present, and still derealized image makes to the previously established image that has come to take on a reality in the group. Different forms of the imaginary, both present and past, individual and collective, on the basis of a given reality, contest themselves and are in a constant state of tension in order to make possible the continued development of the appropriate images for the group.

The public imaginary, it follows, is not a static concept, but itself continues to develop in accordance with the present individual, modifying acts of the group and its own character as a *constant demand* to be so modified. The social imaginary therefore precedes and makes possible the imaginative acts which will alter it as needed, and this process of preceding and modifying continues throughout the life of the group. In this regard, there is a particular practico-inert of the imaginary, and it is a positive, light, liberating element of the group through which the past of the group continues to accumulate in order for the group to remain new. It is an instance of what Sartre refers to as "the practico-inert of the imaginary" (Sartre 1987, 131).[9] Therefore, the past acts of the imaginary, their various images, and the collective image of the group understood as its constantly changing self-understanding, congeal into a *real image* whose task as inert is to serve as a constant basis for unique acts of the imagination (Sartre 2004a, 416). The practico-inert of the imaginary is a perennial, positive demand on the group members to imagine, and provides, in broad strokes, a constant origin for imaginative acts by present group members.

There is a further manner in which the acts of both perception and the imagination are continuous with the history of the group. Upon entering the group, the group members find themselves caught in a tension between perception and the imagination. As stated, the imagination is the context for perceiving. However, there is an additional aspect built into the thetic character of perception which makes it more than simply positing its object as "existing" (Sartre 2004b, 12).[10] Reality is also perceived as *to-be-imaginatively modified.* The act of perception therefore gives the reality of the object, the task, and the group *in propria persona*, but it does so in such a way that the reality is perceived as open, situated within the imaginative context of the group, and to-be-modified. Perception, it must be noted, is not instrumentalized for the imagination, but rather serves a transcendental function in its additional, open thetic character insofar as the imagination could not derealize the real if the latter were not previously perceived as such and as capable of being modified through the imagination and *praxis.* Perception is therefore an opening onto the group and a particular manner of dwelling within it. It is, however, a perception which is always more than itself both in perceiving an identical object in its manifolds and presence and absence, but also in implying its own imaginative modification which serves as a basis for the future reality of the group. Enshrouded by the imaginary, perception is still *a center* of the group, and the imagination that derealizes it is capable of doing so precisely because of its intrinsically open and future-directed character. The act of perception, in this case, is temporally directed insofar as it involves a particular instability of the present reality perceived. As the complement to the imagination, perception preserves its own integrity as a fundamental manner of being open to the present and future of the group, and as such it helps orient the imagination without imposing on it.

Through the interrelations of the acts of perception, the imagination, and their contents, the group dialectically temporalizes itself into its future. Perception is an origin of the imagination, and the imagination is an origin of perception. As a result, there is a constant, dialectical tension between them, such that the openness of perception is derealized, modified, and fulfilled through the appropriate imaginative act. Moreover, through such transcendence of the real, the imagination produces content which, with various degrees of identity, is realized as the future of the group. Therefore, the future-directed, dialectical development of the group is not the *Aufhebung* of its past, a preservation and destruction, or a sublimation of content *on the same level.* Rather, the imagination, as a response to perception, personalizes it and integrates the imagined content into the group in such a way that it becomes intrinsically related to, even if only a basis for, the future, necessary reality of the group. The *Aufhebung* of the group is therefore comprised of two unique elements and the overcoming of the one by the other which results in a new form which preserves each, but as two prior and present forms, namely, those of the real and the imaginary. The dialectical development of the group, it follows, is not only not a purely linear progress insofar as group forms can progress or regress, move in different directions, and change suddenly or gradually, but also because the dialectic is comprised of *a plurality of continua of qualitatively different elements* whose unity as a constant process of overcoming is a preservation and supersession of two distinct "realities" in the group. The context of the group, therefore, is a multidimensional, unresolved because constant and incomplete, dialectical interplay between the two terms of perception and the imagination, whose conjoined products simultaneously preserve different realities while continuously demanding their imaginative modification. This *single* dialectic is a multidimensional dialectic of qualitatively different intentional acts and their correlates.

This multidimensional dialectic takes on a further structural feature when understood concerning the diachronic temporality of the group and the corresponding coincidence and non-coincidence of images in the group. As I said earlier, the group maintains itself as *the same group* as it develops itself imaginatively. What, one may now ask, is the relation between such a notion of identity and repetition? What, concerning the group as a whole, is the relation between the dialectic of perception and the imagination and repetition? The images, as being rooted in the past of the group and corresponding to the essential form of the organized group, contribute to its continuous repetition as a particular group form. As intrinsically linked in various ways to prior images, the images of the present repeat or, said somewhat differently, themselves serve as various forms of repetition of the past images. However, as in part comprised of new, present content within a new, present public imaginary, the images of the present do not wholly repeat or reproduce the identical images of the past, but either, in their novel character challenge it as they interrupt it or modify it and therefore rejuvenate it. Regardless of the particular, present relation to the images of the past, the present of the group is both a repetition and a new origin of the group. The group is structurally of such a sort that it repeats itself in its essential form and order, alters in its imaginative self-understanding, and continues to transcend and remain immanent to itself as it repeats in its rejuvenating temporalization. At most, one can say that the present and future forms of the group, with their appropriate culture and public imaginary, are implicit and seen with various degrees of accuracy which correspond to the immediacy and mediation of the past generations. However, such implicit images do not need to have the character of an actualization of potential which was perfectly consistent with the previous actuality, but rather may very well be slightly visible forms which may, only upon their imaginative realization, be seen and understood as fundamentally at odds with the group, as the fulfillment of the identity of the group in its past as its difference in the present. The group, therefore, is a blend of repetition and rejuvenation, identity and difference, and the dialectic of the imagination and perception that constitutes it is comprised of old and new images and content.

THE TEMPORAL DIALECTIC OF PERCEPTION AND THE IMAGINATION

The previous section provided an account of the public imaginary the students enter after the completion of their formal education and the manner in which the context of the imaginary, particularly concerning its historical, diachronic dimension, serves as a point of departure for their future imagining and lives. In order to develop the concept of the imagination appropriate to the educated, organized group, I also described the character and role of perception in a group with a primary orientation toward the imaginary. As a result, I was also able to show how the imagination and perception relate to and build off of one another, and the intrinsic, incomplete, and continuous process of derealizing and realizing reality in the group. However, a few questions pertaining more specifically to this life present themselves. How, given the essential character of the Organization, do group members orient themselves perceptively and imaginatively as they fulfill their tasks and functions? In addition, and as also follows from the diachronic component mentioned above, how are the group members temporally oriented toward their roles in the group? In what follows, I will show that there is a further dialectic of temporality and the imagination wherein each complements and extends the other to allow for the necessary, future-directed orientation to the particular task. The relation between these two themes will allow the task to be completed both through the appropriate imaginative modification as well as in accordance with its own unique temporality. The temporal opening to the future is accomplished on the basis of the imaginative transcendence of the present reality, and such transcendence is itself possible on the basis of an intrinsically future-directed process of temporalization. This imaginative transcendence is part of what I am terming the aesthetic attitude, which serves as a correlate to the natural attitude and inheres in the present reality of the group.[11]

As part of their imaginary lives, the group members further understand the fluid character of their tasks and functions. As part of the imaginative a priori of this setting, the group members recognize their roles and designated tasks as a blend of fluidity and fixity, spontaneity and inertia, and requiring constant imaginary modification. The group members accordingly understand their tasks as *empirical, fluid essences* and perennial points of departure for imaginative acts. Both the subject- and object-poles of life in the group are open, partially unstable, and mutually affect one another through their continuous dialogue. And as the relation between the individual and their task develops, so too does the relation between them and the other group members and tasks. The structural relations of the distribution of particular tasks are preserved, and the fact that this group form is defined as such a distribution continues, *but the nature of the constellational relations to all of the other group members and tasks in the group will alter.* Therefore, in imaginatively modifying a particular task as needed, the group member also modifies the relation between that function and all of the others, and, reciprocally understood, is itself modified by the other imaginative modifications carried out by the other group members. In a similar way, in modifying their relation to the task, in revising their own role in the group, the group member will relate differently to their assigned task but will also alter the relation between their role and all of the others, and is again reciprocally modified by the other group members changing their own understanding of their particular roles. In this regard, both the role of the group members and their tasks are further understood as being what they are and what they are not, designated roles in the group which are irreducible to their present incarnation. Both individually and collectively, the tasks prescribe a necessarily open, incomplete, and imaginatively modifiable course of action which guides the group members. In this regard, the tasks as the object-pole of life in the group serve as the focal point around which, and in relation to which, the individual roles are carried out and developed.

In this respect, the concept of tasks and functions demonstrates a character that was only implicit in Sartre's analyses, namely, of being *intrinsically educational.* In addition, they maintain various relations to the temporality of the education of the group in both its diachronic and synchronic dimensions. Conceived in this way, tasks and functions are *educational objects*, and they continue to educate the group through the manner in which they prescribe their own fulfillment. In this sense, the "distribution of tasks," which defined the Organization, not only has to be further defined as an "educational distribution of tasks," but one wherein the tasks themselves have an educational function (Sartre 2004a, 446). Moreover, due to the orientation they demand from the group member, they both maintain continuity with the previous process of education and extend it by continuing to educate the group member. The task, though also capable of being modified by the group member, itself continues to reinforce the previous education by prescribing, in the form of a sketch, its own fulfillment and, depending on the circumstances, requiring the group member to alter it to meet the needs of the group. The object makes possible the future education of the group member by leaving open new possibilities of relating to it, learning from it, and requiring the appropriate modification of it. The tasks, in this regard, are not *static*, but constantly demand new orientations toward them. As such, the task in its educational dimension continues to make the necessary, imaginative life in the group possible.

As a correlate to this demand and continued education through the object, the individual group members continue to educate themselves through their constant reflection on their role in the group. Moreover, they understand their own tasks and the constellation of relations they form with the other tasks in the group as flexible and in a perpetual state of readjustment. The group member therefore relates to their own role as something that requires constant education and reeducation, and through their constantly developing imaginative orientation modifies it and its corresponding object. In this regard, one could say, *one is never in the same group twice*, insofar as the individual place in it, as well as the object worked on, are constantly developing as the group fulfills its short- and long-term aims. The group members relate to themselves as more than their functions in transcending their roles as free *praxes* in order to properly fulfill them. However, through such constant reorientation, it should not be thought that the group members impose on the object, or that the object imposes on the group member. Rather, through an imaginative, dialogical relation between the two, each demands from the other what the other demands of it, and this reciprocal demand, being educational, requires the proper understanding and approach in which both appreciates the nature of the task and object, but also recognizes the need for an appropriate development and modification of them. The group members therefore continue to educate themselves, perhaps paradoxically, by continuing to reinforce the education they received and recognizing that life in the group requires constant reeducation.

This foundational reciprocity between the group member and their task leads to a particular, necessary tension in this relation and the general functioning in the group. This also requires an extension of the concept of reciprocity as the necessary basis for human relations. Sartre writes: "Reciprocal ternary relations are the basis of *all* relations between men, whatever form they may subsequently take" (Sartre 2004a, 111). First, as a necessary supplement to such relations, it is necessary to add the reciprocal relations between group members and their tasks. Secondly, the relations between individuals are further mediated by their relations to objects and the manner in which the objects relate to one another as relative to the particular group members. The foundational relations of this group form therefore involve reciprocal relations between the group members themselves and the group members and their corresponding tasks. And again, the relations between the group member and their object, and the other group members and other tasks, involve a particular tension. Each object, as I've shown, prescribes in an open, sketched manner, its necessary fulfillment. There is a constant correlation between them, but as both subject and object educate the other, they also advance at different rates, such that, in one instance, the object may be "ahead" of the subject and demand that they adjust their orientation toward it. In another instance, however, through their own reflection, the group member may transcend the object and therefore need to work to modify it to bring it into the present of the group in the appropriate way. The reciprocal demands of each therefore place a burden on the other to "keep up" with it, and to necessarily adjust itself on the basis of changes in the other.

In this regard, through a continuous process of reciprocity, the present demands serve as new, discontinuous, interruptive moments that allow the dialogue between subject and object to continue, but precisely *because of the interruption of novelty into their reciprocal relations.* Again on the model of the author and the reader from *What Is Literature?*, the object becomes an author, teacher, or guide of experience, and in its relations to the other tasks, requires the group member to adapt to it. The group member too, serves as an author, teacher, and guide, both concerning the task before them and their own role in fulfilling it. And what is to be emphasized is that both task and group member are *fully able to be what they are by always being more than what they are at present in their reciprocal, educating relationship.* Each, in other words, is what it is precisely because it is not what it is, irreducible to its present, and a future-oriented, educational-temporal sign of continuous education and fulfillment. They mutually conform to one another within the general context of the life of the group. In so doing, they mutually overcome one another and return to one another in a sublated form, and constantly do so because of the necessary tension between them.

Moreover, this tension between the subject and the object complicates when considered in relation to the theme of the imagination. The tension in the perceptual relation to the object is also a basis for the same tension in imaginative form. How, then, does the subject imaginatively reorient through reeducation to the object, and how does the object, as its own imaginary, and as an imaginative complement to the reflection of the subject, respond to the subject and make its own corresponding demands? First, to continue to fulfill their role in the group, the subject alters the images created in relation to the object. Such images, as stated above, are individual images, which uniquely relate to the particular task and are rooted in the public imaginary and its history. However, with each change in the group, the subject, or the object, the group member newly derealizes the task and makes imaginative contact with it in order for it to be subsequently modified as a moment of its own fulfillment. *The image is therefore a primary mode of access to the perceived object in its present.* Of course, and as discussed earlier, by the very nature of its character as a derealization of a prior reality, it is founded on what it transcends. However, in transcending the particular object through the imaginary variation of it in order for it to continue to be the particular object that it is, the truth of the object as it is perceived, with determinate relations to other objects, and situated within the present reality of the group, necessarily lies in its imaginative modification. In this sense, there are two moments of the temporalization of truth. The truth of the object is attained in its imaginative modification by the group member, but this derealization, as leading to a future reality, is "complete" once the realization of such derealization is attained. Therefore, the image created corresponds to the object derealized, and as the latter will be modified through its fulfillment, so too will the subsequent, individual images of the "same" task change as well.

The object itself, as the objective correlate of the subjective, imaginary orientation toward it, has its own imaginary dimension. Although it is a point of departure for its own derealization, in order for the individual imaginary act of the group member to be meaningful, in order, that is, for it to be realized as the derealization of *this object* in accordance with what is necessary for the group *at this moment*, the object itself demands its own corresponding modification. The subject, as so educated, and dwelling in this group with its public imaginary, is capable of recognizing the imaginary dimension of this particular object and, on the basis of its history, fulfilling its own imaginary demand. The object, as possessing such a dimension, *is an analogon of itself*, an imaginary sketch of itself which is recognized by the group member and with which they carry out their act of imagining. Such objects are therefore future-directed, imaginary objects which are ultimately *temporal analoga* which serve to orient the group member individually and the constellation of group members collectively. And yet, as the correlate of the subject, the analogical indication of the object appreciates the subject, corresponds to it, and is symmetrical with the present act of imagining within the overarching present of the group. As a result, the derealization of the subject is the derealization *of this object*, and the act, though free and spontaneous, is appropriately limited by confining itself to this particular object, in truth this particular aspect of it which is in need of imaginative modification, and which will lead to its corresponding, indicated, future reality.

In addition to being future-directed imaginative analoga, tasks and functions also contain an intrinsic temporal rhythm which changes with the circumstances and needs of the group. Moreover, in containing such a rhythm, they help contribute to the general temporal rhythm of the functioning of the group as a whole. Again, the temporalizations of the group member and the object are reciprocally interrelated and build off of one another. They form and maintain their own temporal adequation throughout the process of continuous education in the group. However, due to its intrinsic temporal character, and its connection to the other tasks and the present state of the group, the task requires not just an appropriate imaginative orientation toward it as imaginatively relating to *this task*, but also, and as part of such an orientation, requires the particular, corresponding temporal rate of the imagination to engage with it appropriately. The object, in temporally and imaginatively analogizing itself, establishes a rhythmic relation to it in accordance with which the group member must harmonize to fulfill the needs of the task at hand. There is, it follows, a temporal correlation between subject- and object-poles, such that the temporalizations of the group member and the task correspond to and fulfill one another. There is, therefore, a temporal form appropriate to the fulfillment of the task, which respects the temporality of the task itself, is guided by it and, in so doing, does not impose a temporal order on the process "from outside."

There is a further temporal rhythm in the task when it is conceived as a whole comprised of various sub-tasks, which must be carried out in a particular sequential order for the task to be completed as a whole (Sartre 2004a, 391). The object itself is unity of a multiplicity of temporalizations, a constellation of mutually related temporalizations, each of which has its own temporal rhythm, demands, and rate. Within the identical task there is a manifold of temporality insofar as its completion is dependent on the necessary completion of its temporal parts in accordance with their prescribed temporality. Therefore, there is harmony internal to each task, which requires the necessary understanding of the play of the different temporalities within the task itself. Moreover, when the task is understood "intersubjectively," concerning the other tasks in the group, there is an intersubjective temporalization in which the different temporalizations of the parts of all of the tasks, and ultimately the temporalizations of the tasks themselves, complement and complete one another. As there is a constellation among the parts of the object, so is there a constellation among the objects in the group, and *the manner of the temporalization of the group* is in part a result of the fulfillment of the temporalizations of the various tasks and sub-tasks.

From the complementary side of the subject, the orientation toward the task, in appreciating its temporal, educational demands, harmonizes with it in its essential nature. The subject, in this case, allows the demands of the object under the present circumstances to serve as a temporal sign of its own process of completion. Reciprocally, however, the group member can also alter the temporal course of the object through the recognition that their own role in the group is in need of being temporally *re-situated.* Through reflection on their own temporalization of their particular role, they may come to see the need for a new orientation, and in so doing, take a different approach to the object in both its imaginative and temporal dimensions. Therefore, in appreciating the intrinsic temporality of the object and its various stages, and simultaneously recognizing their own situation in the group, the group member, on the basis of their own self-reflection, may realize that a different pace for the fulfillment of the task is necessary. As a result, their imaginatively and temporally reconsidered relation to the object will result in the particular task being fulfilled at a new pace, *in accordance with a new time.*

In such temporal reorientation, it must be further understood that the subject is not imposing its own time or a preestablished time on the object. Rather, they are simply recognizing the state of the dialogical relation between the two and the manner in which it is presently situated and adapting their relation to the object and their own role as needed. In this instance, allowing one side of the relation to dictate the temporality of the process, with the concomitant exclusion of the general functioning of the group, would not be allowing that single temporality to flow smoothly, but would rather, surreptitiously, introduce a one-sided domination of the process by one of the terms. In order, therefore, for the temporal process to be respected, at times the subject will need to adjust to the object, and at times the object will need to adjust itself to the subject, allowing for the free, open, and spontaneous temporalization of the fulfillment of the task at hand. The group members and their corresponding tasks accordingly personalize themselves *dialogically* throughout the temporal process of their fulfillment. And in this sense, *temporalization is personalization* insofar as the task, both on the basis of the education received as well as the history of the task, is "assumed and negated," and therefore *temporalized* in and through its fulfillment (Sartre 1987, 7).

COMMITTED LITERATURE AS COLLECTIVE PERSONALIZATION AND PRAXIS

The discussions of the previous sections described the cultural context the students enter after the period of formal education and the manner in which they are temporally and imaginatively oriented toward their lives in the group. In order to complete these two prior stages, I developed the concept of the public imaginary and the generational and cultural conditions of possibility for the production of images in the organized group. In so doing, however, I confined my analysis to the individual images the group members produce in their relations to their tasks. Moreover, I demonstrated how such an imaginative approach contributes to the dialectical development of the group, as well as how the temporalizations of the individual imagining acts comprise an intersubjective temporalization.

In addition to such individual images and their temporalization, the group also produces *collective images*, that is, images that extend to all tasks and functions, to all group members with varying degrees of immediacy and mediation, and which articulate the group to itself *as a whole.* And these images are produced through the various media of committed literature. Such images serve both as an additional form of reflection of the group, a form of continued education, and personalize the group as a whole. Furthermore, they are intersubjectively constituted through the reciprocal relations between author and reader in the dialogue in images in which the author produces an imaginative, literary work that is fulfilled by the reader in their engagement with it. Several questions present themselves on the basis of this understanding of literature and its role in such an educated group. First, what is the character of a collective image in the organized group? Secondly, how does it serve a unique educational and personalizing function?[12] Thirdly, what does it mean to read in this particular group form? And lastly, how exactly does literature, in both its imaginative and temporal dimensions, contribute to the dialectical development of the group? In order to respond to these questions, I will divide this section into two parts. In the first part, I will analyze the form of reading and imaginative engagement with literature proper to the organized group. And in the second, I will describe the temporalization of the imagination in its engagement with literature and how such temporalization contributes to the orientation and direction of the dialectic of the group.

Literature and the Collective Imagination

As I have explained, the students enter a context of the imaginary after the completion of the formal period of education. Within this context, they continue to form images on the basis of the present culture, their previous education, and the diachronic images of previous generations. In being immanent to the public imaginary, the individual group members transcend it through the free, spontaneous use of the imagination and are irreducible to it.[13] The collective images within the group, which literature has the task to produce, are also immanently situated within the public imaginary as they transcend it. In so doing, they will extend to all of the tasks and functions in the group, the various group members, and the previous generations insofar as the present articulation of the group reorients the relation to, and understanding of, the past. Such collective images continue to *rejuvenate* the group, to ensure that it always remains young, and that the present is always new. The author, to use Sartre's term, "renews" the group (Sartre 1988, 63). Literature as a whole, then, and its incarnation in the act of reading, has the role of simultaneously keeping the past of the group in the present while allowing the present to be its *own present.* And as a necessary, positive, future-directed element, there is a tension within the very concept of the collective images of committed literature insofar as they develop out of a previously established imaginative context, on the basis of the prior generational images, but vary them, modify them, and even challenge them as needed in order to produce the appropriate images for the present. There is, then, a temporal dialectic internal to the image that involves the conflict and overcoming of individual and collective images in both their synchronic and diachronic dimensions. In fact, the continued freedom of the group is intrinsically linked to this dialectical tension of the imaginary.

Before carrying out the analysis of the author, the reader, and their dialogical relation in the act of reading, it is necessary to provide a brief account of the form of consciousness that further situates the different group members in the group. First, the author, in the role of producing images, has additional structures of consciousness that extend and complicate the intentional character of consciousness as it is described in the introduction to *Being and Nothingness.* Sartre there states that all consciousness is positional consciousness of an object, and non-positional consciousness of itself. It is, therefore, conscious both of itself and the intentional object, but the form of consciousness it has of itself does not posit itself as an object.[14] The author, in addition to these fundamental structures of consciousness, has the further qualities of being conscious of himself as an author and of the group. The *conscience (de) soi* of the author is therefore also a *conscience (de) group*, and the ultimate, intentional correlate of the act of writing, the images produced, also have the character of being images-for-the-group and must be so understood by the other group members. The author, then, in order to properly understand his role in the group, as well as the importance of the images produced, requires this additional, twofold conscious structure.

The reader, as the complement of the author, contains the same, additional twofold intentional structure, but rather than initially producing the images, completes them in the intersubjective act of reading. In so doing, the readers comprehend their literary engagement in the group as itself structurally composed of their consciousness (of) themselves as a reader as a consciousness (of) the group. The author, in his work, produces images that are necessary for the group, and the readers, as the necessary complement to such work, engage with the images *in the form needed by the group at present.* Thus, on the basis of their reciprocally structured self-consciousnesses, author and reader engage in the dialogue in images necessary for the group to continue to develop. They are, in this regard, collectively and individually oriented toward the same intentional, collective object, the collective image of literature, on the basis of the particular work produced, which can be a novel, a play, sculpture, and so on. From different "sides," then, the author and reader produce the necessary images of the present through a dialogue made possible in part through the structure of consciousness in the organized group.

The two-sided intentional relation to the object further develops the concept of the noematic correlate of a noetic act of consciousness. The object of the literary image, as well as its presentation in and through the literary image itself, is necessarily incomplete. The author has not exhausted the work in the presentation of it, with its particular form, style, and so on, nor has the individual reader, or the community of readers, exhausted the meaning of the text and its value for the present. There is a peculiar sense here in which the work of literature, in appealing to the freedom of the reader, gives rise to an individual-collective fashioning of images which are meant to articulate and guide the group, but necessarily do so by holding back, by requiring interpretation and subsequent action on their basis, but without the text imposing itself on the group and fully prescribing the necessary course to take. Of course, it addresses the present needs of the group, but it creates an identical object with outlines of the future, which is necessarily understood and lived differently by the different group members *as part of the same present of the group.* It is, in this sense, uniquely situated within time, within the present of the group, and yet *inter-temporal*, existing across the different temporalizations of the author and the readers, yet without existing entirely independently of the temporal setting of the group.

This leads to the concept of *the temporal a priori of literature*, which shares paradoxically in both the objective time of the group, while being instantiated in all of the individual acts that engage with a literary text and help produce it. Such an object, therefore, is outside of time insofar as it transcends the individual temporalizations of the group members, and yet within time insofar as it is situated within the objective, historical moment of the group and its public imaginary. Such images, therefore, are not *wholly* "outside time."[15] As such, they preserve the unique temporality of the imaginary object, but given their role in the group, they also participate in the temporalization of the group.[16] While it is true, then, that they have "their own time," as a necessary complement for images in the organized group, they are irreducible to such time, and contribute to the temporalization of the reality of the group. Furthermore, these images are irreducible to any single imagining consciousness or interpretation of the work. They are, therefore, *open, indeterminate, intersubjective images.*

And here, the question of the truth of literature in and for the group presents itself. As noted, committed literature is concerned with the present circumstances of the group, and provides the necessary moment of reflection for the group to *know itself* and subsequently carry out the necessary collective action. On the one hand, there is the truth of the work that the author presents through various media, and which can be understood as a particular, first-order truth. This form of truth is meant to be grasped by the reader as "the meaning" of the work. On the other hand, however, the work is incomplete, the images in need of fulfillment, and therefore the act of "writing" is not complete until the act of "reading" has been carried out. This second, more comprehensive, intersubjective truth requires the active engagement of the different group members. These are, it follows, two interrelated and independent concepts of truth. In a given work, there is a plurality of surfaces, in which the primary truth provided by the author is a point of departure for the secondary truth of the community of readers, and this latter truth involves a deeper and collective imaginative engagement for its fulfillment. In this sense, there is a coincidence in the noetic, imaginative acts of reading directed at the "same" collective object, and in such a way that the noematic correlates and the object established on the basis of the plurality of intentional acts of reading are inexhaustible. The truth of reading in the organized group is on various levels in the work itself, as well as in the present and future of the group insofar as literature is an articulation of the present which is also an indication of a necessary future. The aim of the collective acts of reading is accordingly twofold insofar as it is directed toward the preservation of the group, but *in a new form*. In reading, therefore, the reader is directed to different levels of truth, with their own different emphases on the present and future temporal dimensions, guided toward a future which requires the individual and collective imaginative acts of reading and eventual action on their basis.

These discussions of the truth of the literary object point to the pedagogical role of literature in the educated, organized group. Such further education itself reflects the process of formal education. The group members, in this respect, are educated by the author who, comparable to the teacher, "teaches" through their particular representations and interpretations of the present. In a sense, the author has also lived the life of these group members before them. They have, in this regard, comprehended the present, and are now attempting to make it *known* to the group members.[17] The group members have themselves comprehended the present, but it is made explicit in certain knowledge in the literary work. As such, the author has lived the life of the present in a way that coincides with the other group members, yet is also fundamentally distinct, insofar as they are tasked with articulating it as a unique moment of reflection. Moreover, they have not yet fully lived the future of the group but have begun this process by indicating the necessary direction for the group. The author, as having lived the life of the group in revealing it, has also not lived it, and paradoxically has not lived their own life, as the completion of the images requires the intersubjective fulfillment of the other group members and the realization of a still uncertain future.

In the committed act of reading, there is an extension of the character of reality as it is perceived within the culture of the public imaginary. As I showed in the first section, reality is perceived as to-be-modified and as capable of being altered through the imagination. In the act of reading, the same reality is perceived through the literary text and with the same characteristic fluidity, but the literary text is also approached in the same way. In the act of perceiving the text, and as using it as a basis for imagining, it is always perceived as a basis for imaginative modification and in that regard a new form of the group. In the act of reading, the work is perceived as *in order to be imaginatively modified.* However, as situated in the group, the individual act of the imagination transcends itself in recognizing its intrinsic connection to the other imaginative acts in the group. Thus, there is, in the phenomenon of reading in images, an initial perception which is an opening to the imaginary of the text, of the group, and therewith of the other group members. Perception, as the necessary ground for the derealizing acts of the imagination in the engagement with literature, is a further point of departure for a literary text which is to be *collectively derealized* for the sake of future *praxis*. In this regard, the processes of perception and the imagination have to be understood in both their individual and collective dimensions. In the act of reading of the individual group member, there is a necessary, positive, future-directed tension between perception and the imagination, between reality as it is presently grasped, and the imaginary challenge issued to it through literature.[18]

As a structural component of a community of such readers, and as necessarily the case in order for reading to be more than just an individual, serialized, alienated and alienating experience, the perceptions of the different group members agree to an extent, though they do not fully coincide.[19] And as a result of this, the derealization of a prior reality is the derealization of an interpreted reality which can serve as a further basis for individual, unique acts of the imaginary which are not necessarily fully consistent. Through the images of literature, and a continued dialectic of perception and the imaginary, the group members issue challenges to the imaginative acts of the other group members in order for the act of reading to serve as a collective challenge to the reality of the group. In this respect, there is a tense dialectic within the imaginary itself in committed reading, which also involves a challenge to the other group members both to adequately fulfill the text presented but also to envision the necessary, future reality of the group. The act of reading, therefore, in extending the characters of perception and the imagination that permeate the culture of the group, leads to a collective process of imaginative literary engagement wherein each reader challenges all of the others and themselves, and in appealing to the freedom of the other readers, demands that they fulfill the requirements of the imaginary in the group. As a result, the acts of perception and the imagination do not fully harmonize in either the individual group member or the community of literary group members.

However, on the basis of the perceptual-imaginative relation to the text, and the transcendence accomplished through the imagination, one can further ask exactly what form the appeal of the author to the imagination takes. Is it perfectly harmonious, or are the author and the public at odds? Should they be? In a sense, the manner in which the author incites the imagination is diametrically opposed to what is found in Kant's aesthetics in the *Third Critique*.

Rather than having the imagination "quickened" in its coherence with the understanding in the harmony of the experience of beauty, the imagination is challenged (Kant 1987, 63). Through such a challenge, it follows, there is a particular tension between the author and the public. The author is charged with revealing the reality of the group, and that in part includes revealing discord in the group, issuing a challenge to the reader to interpret the text in the appropriate way, and to subsequently act on its basis. In fact, in issuing such a challenge, the author and the book serve as a discordant tone introduced to alert the reader to the lived-reality and dissonance in the group. The "faculties" of the group, that is, the different tasks, the members, their skills, and so on, come into conflict in the work of literary art in order to illuminate the present and to move toward the future. The literary text, in its appropriateness for the circumstances, incites the imagination through revealing dissonance and thus does not harmonize the faculties of the reader or of the group, but challenges all of them through the particular tension between what is the case and a sketch of what ought to be the case. The text, in appealing to the imagination, does not provide a complete form to be experienced in the harmonizing of the faculties, but rather an incomplete, future-oriented work that will disturb the faculties for the sake of future action. In other words, rather than having all the work of constitution already done, the reader, the public, the author, have all the work of the imagination, thought, and action still to do.

There is a further imaginative dimension to the dialogue between author and reader. The work of the author, on the basis of the challenge posed to the reader, makes possible the free play of the imagination, the possibility of the variation of forms of the future of the group that will lead it to correcting itself and continuing to develop. The unique form of the image leads to the possibility of varying the group in its present reality for the sake of future *praxis*. On the basis of this understanding of the imaginary it becomes possible to extend Husserl's concept of eidetic variation to develop a collective, educational eidetic variation and *Wesenschau.* The work of literature has its end in the audience imagining the necessary form of the future and carrying out the required action. However, the eidetic resolution of the present circumstances, while "permanent," in the sense that it resolves them, is also "temporary," insofar as the group will need to correct itself again in the future. Thus, the act of free phantasy brought about through the literary work is situated within the present of the group, ultimately a collective response to the present situation, and as such it is necessarily dated. It does not involve the variation of forms to reach a fixed essence, for example, "*of any* spatial shape whatever, *any* melody *whatever*, *any* social practice *whatever*, and so on, or the essence of a shape, a melody, and so on, of the particular *type* exemplified" (Husserl 1998, 11).[20] In this case, the eidetic variation is meant to discover the essential future, and a priori dated, form of the group.

There is an additional aspect to the act of reading which bears upon the individual group member and their relation to the rest of the reading public. The individual group member, as part of the organized group, and educated in the necessary manner, reads *individually*, but not in *isolation*. Their reading may occur in a variety of settings, either alone or with others, but the acts of reading of the different group members are not *disconnected*, but rather *continuous* with one another insofar as they individually contribute to and comprise the collective engagement with literature of the group as a whole. Each reader, as discussed above, connects with the material on their own terms, places demands on the other readers, and challenges them, the author, and the imaginative culture of the group. Therefore, though an individual activity, reading is necessarily and intrinsically a collective act insofar as it is layered with the demands and appeals of the other group members and situated within the reciprocal relations of the various group members. The group, in other words, does not fragment in the acts of reading, but maintains itself in the individual-collective character of reading and the orientation toward the group through literature. The experience of reading, therefore, is not only intersubjective insofar as it involves a particular relation between author and reader, but also insofar as all of the readers are implicated in the reading of the single individual.

The individual character of reading, moreover, is an additional reflective moment within the group, one wherein the group members reflect on what has been presented to them by the author as itself a form of reflection, and in so doing helps establish, through the collective reading in images, the concomitant collective reflection which is necessary for the group to continue to reorganize itself. As a result, through literature, and the collective recognition of the present of the group, its lack, and the sketched future, the organized group becomes a *communis imaginans* in which the group, through both individual acts of imagining, and individual and collective images, takes itself as an *imaginary object to be varied and modified as needed under the present circumstances*. The process that this *communis imaginans* must go through is that of varying the forms of the group to reach a situated eidetic truth. The dual play of immanence and transcendence in the act of reading, through the context of immanence and its continued transcendence, leads to a literary community which primarily relates to and understands itself through the imaginary and continues to act on this basis. And in so doing, the group members continue to re-situate themselves in the group and, possibly paradoxically, de-situate themselves through their free and spontaneous acts in order to do so. Literature as continued reflection is also a moment of de-situating the group members in order for them to ultimately re-situate themselves within the group that is continuously, imaginatively, reorganizing itself.

The Temporality of Literature

There is an additional element in the act of reading in the organized group, and which has been implicit in my analyses thus far, namely, the temporalization of the imagination and its bearing on the character of the development of the group. The author appeals to the imagination of the reader through the literary work, and the latter responds to the demands of the former in completing the image and truth presented. In so doing, the author and the reader, as the two terms of a dialogical process, temporalize the group and give a particular direction to the temporalization of the group. As I showed, concerning the tasks and functions, the imagination is temporalized and fashions its images in accordance with a particular temporal direction. The rate and temporal rhythms of the group are determined by its culture and present needs, and the dialogical act of reading which gives rise to action contributes to *the manner in which* the temporalization of the group unfolds.[21] In producing collective images that bear upon the lives of all of the group members, literature situates time within the group, and, in addition to providing it with a future-oriented direction, lays a particular emphasis on each of its dimensions. The temporality of reading, which is a multidimensional intersubjective temporality, ascribes the necessary importance to the past and present while giving a particular priority to the future. Within the educated, organized group, time is necessarily a future-directed process whose rate is continuously determined by the dialogues of literature and subsequent *praxis*.

In light of its importance for the group, the future must be properly understood in accordance with the two concepts in which Sartre develops in *The Imaginary*. He there writes: "There are in fact two sorts of future: one is but the temporal ground on which my present perception develops, the other is posited for itself but as *that which is not yet*" (Sartre 2004b, 182). In a sense, then, the group temporalizes itself toward a double future, or toward a future understood as itself comprised of two dimensions. In addition to being perceived as to-be-modified-through-the-imagination, such an act-character has the necessary quality of being directed-toward-the-future. Thus, the future as the general background serves as a further horizon of the imaginary within which the individual acts of the group members will unfold in both their individual and collective dimensions. The open future, in this general sense, is a further component part of the orientation toward the future insofar as it infuses the imagination itself with an open character. The imagination remains bounded through the education, culture, and needs of the group, but such a general future, which serves as a correlate to the general past of the group in its history, traditions, and images of past generations, allows for a contextual specification which serves as the determinate future of this individual act of the imagination and of this plurality of imagining acts.

Literature, in its production of images, contributes to the opening of a general future as a *fore-ground* on which individual modifications of the group can take place. However, in making such a contribution, and as itself situated, it speaks to a present that requires *this particular future*, and as a result, further opens the future, but in this case as a determinate, necessary state of affairs. The collective images of literature possess a twofold directedness insofar as they continuously open *a future as such* in the group, but are primarily directed toward *this particular future* of the group as the future necessary for *this present.* The images of the author, it follows, and their completion by the community of readers, dialogically constitute a dual future which prioritizes a particular future but appreciates the importance of a general future as the "back"-drop against which particular futures can determine themselves. The group, on the basis of its reading in images, temporalizes itself toward two distinct yet interwoven futures which are both opened by the imagination and continue to make the opening of the imagination itself possible. Thus, the group temporalizes itself in accordance with a multidimensional imaginary act which derealizes the past, present, and future of the group, holds the future in a particular suspense, and does so in order to produce the necessary images to modify the group and for the group to temporalize itself in the appropriate way.

As a result of this particular process of temporalization, there is a harmonizing of the temporal dimensions, the ability for past, present, and future to play off of and complement one another, but always with the recognition that the act of reading is primarily future-directed. As such, the concept of demands takes on an additional temporal character. The demand that the author places on the reader, and that the reader subsequently places on the author, determine the demand as a demand for a particular future, which, depending on the circumstances, will be more or less continuous or discontinuous with the past and present of the group. The demand of literature is ultimately an *imaginative-temporal demand* for the production of images across a process of temporalization which makes possible the necessary dialectical temporalization of the group. Reading in images, it follows, is necessarily future-directed and appreciates the importance of the past and present for the life of the group. A synchronic demand, then, is overladen with a diachronic dimension insofar as it requires the present of the group to act for the sake of *its future*, but to do so in such a way that the past and present to be surpassed maintain their significance as the past and present of *this group* whose form is preserved as it imaginatively modifies itself. In this regard, all of the temporal dimensions of the synchrony and diachrony of the group are implicated in the temporal demand to imaginatively refashion the group in its past and present for the sake of the future. Through the collective images produced, the various generations in the group and the images historically passed down are modified as the group determines how best to integrate them into its new and necessary future.

There is, as a correlate to the two forms of the future just discussed, a reciprocal, twofold form of the past. First, there is the general past of the group as a whole, its diachronic past, and the generations which comprise it. And this past, as the general background of the group, with the various images it has handed down and the culture it has established, serves as the context within which, and the point of departure for, future imagining acts. Moreover, in this capacity, the general past is a general form of memory, which preserves the past in the present as such a point of departure for the imagination. In this general sense, the diachronic past of the group, as the foundational memory for the act of the imagination, is a further, transcendental condition for the ability to imagine in the organized group. As a result, and speaking concerning this general past, it becomes clear that *memory is a present and continuous transcendental condition of the imagination.*

The second form of the past, which is the correlate to the determinate future, is a determinate past which, with varying degrees of immediacy and mediation due to its distance from, and significance for, the present, is integrated into the various images of literature. Thus, in producing the necessary images, an author may in fact incorporate an element of the more distant past, return to certain elements of more distant generations, and, given the needs of the present circumstances, place less of an emphasis on certain aspects of the present or the immediately preceding generations. The immediate past, then, understood as both the immediately preceding generations but also the significance of past generations, serves as the necessary, specified ground for the determinate future. In this regard, *a determinate memory is the transcendental condition of a determinate imagining act.* The determinate past is accordingly integrated and derealized in a present imagining act directed toward the future in both its synchronic and diachronic dimensions. Moreover, in order for this to occur, the imagining acts themselves have to be of a new character, that is, in addition to being consistent with the past in being future-directed, the manner in which they orient themselves to the future and temporalize themselves is necessarily different. Such unique, present imagining acts continue the tradition of imagining, but do so by creating new literary images whose temporalization corresponds to the present of the group. The dialectic internal to the image, as well as that between perception and the imagination, as integral components of the act of reading, temporalize the group into the future on the basis of a three-dimensional temporal derealization which makes a new future possible.

As a result of the unique temporalization of the imagination through literature, the life of the group becomes a dialectical play of memories and images, of pasts, presents, and futures, of derealizing and realizing acts which produce a new future which is continuous and discontinuous with the history of the group. The temporalization of the imagination, achieved through the intersubjective imaginary of literature, is an open, free, indeterminate process which is itself constantly rejuvenated through speaking and reading in images. And such a temporalization itself unfolds at different rates depending on the present circumstances of the group and the character of the present generation. Time itself, then, in such a group, is a constituted and reconstituted process, comprised of the temporalizing imagining acts of the group members, and constantly reorganizing itself as needed. In harmonizing, all three temporal dimensions indicate and complement one another, leading to a collective future comprised of individual, future-oriented temporalizations that allow the group to preserve its structure in surpassing the present. Literature, therefore, as continuously educating the group and personalizing it, allows the three temporal dimensions to be what they are, to lead to and intertwine with one another, without unduly emphasizing or repressing one or more of them. *Literature and the act of reading, it follows, allow temporality to be its own temporal process.*

Committed literature in the organized group is therefore a dialectic of time, the imagination, and perception, with each element indicating its own supersession in the perpetual personalization of the group through literature. And yet, as being oriented by literature, the temporalization of the group is itself more than itself insofar as it cannot be reduced to a single rhythm, a single manner of unfolding, or a single dimension in the group. In this sense, it *over-flows* the group as allowing the group to itself be more than it is in its opening to the future and a genuine past and present through a threefold derealizing act that serves as a transcendental condition for a determinate future. As a result, and regarding the question of truth, in its incarnation in literature, reading and the imagination, it is a constantly temporalizing aspect of the group. It is, in this regard, the group's "comprehension of its own time in *the imagination.*"[22] It is itself a constant process of temporalization, imagined and reimagined on the basis of new and reinterpreted memories that stand at the foundation of the group. The act of reading, then, as a collective, epistemological act *par excellence*, is therefore an a priori indeterminate and uncertain process of learning whose truth in images is a continuous dialogical process.

NOTES

1. For Sartre's own views on the development of his thought and the limitations of his early theory of the imagination and its relation to perception, see Rybalka, Pucciani, Gruenheck (1981, 47). For a detailed account of the imagination in the Flaubert project and Sartre's later philosophy, see Aronson (1980, 325–54).

2. The first concept is discussed in the sections on personalization. See Sartre (1987, 130) and Sartre (1972, 786). The latter is in book 2 of volume 5 of the English translation, and book 2 of volume 3 of the original French. See Sartre (1993, 510) and Sartre (1972, 548), respectively.

3. These issues led to debates within *Les Temps Modernes*. See, for example, Beauvoir (2004, 269–77) and Merleau-Ponty's response in Merleau-Ponty (1964, 26–40). For a further account of Sartre's aesthetic, one which focuses on theater, politics, and the imagination, see Dort (1981, 32–43).

4. The analyses I am carrying out in this chapter have parallels with Sartre's discussions of "the social image" and "the social imaginary." For a discussion of both terms, see Sartre (1993, 510). The elements of these definitions that serve to deepen the analyses here involve an understanding of the relation between an individually created image and its location within an overarching, social imaginary which contextualizes and makes it possible. I am not, however, concerned with the particular content of the images or the nature of their relation in a particular historical period, but the manner in which an individual and their context, or the part and the whole, are operative in a culture that values the positive use of the imagination.

5. See Barnes's section "The Public Neurosis" in Barnes (1981, 278–86). Also see Flynn (2014, 399–401) and Flynn (1997, 190–95).

6. On this point, see Catalano (2010, 199) and Barnes (1981, 290).

7. I am here using the German term to demonstrate the character of an act of imagining as both a performance and an accomplishment.

8. The original French reads as follows: "Mais, nous le verrons, l'irréalité, pour Flaubert, n'est pas l'absence de toute réalité, c'en est la contestation" (Sartre 1971a, 595). The English translation reads: "But as we shall see, unreality for Flaubert is not the absence of all reality, it is the challenge to it" (Sartre 1981, 575). Throughout this chapter, I have largely translated the French "contestation" into English as "contestation" and its cognates, but will also use the term "challenge" when it is more appropriate in the given context. Moreover, I have translated "l'irréalité" and its cognates as "irreality," "the irreal," etc.

9. For the complete quote see Sartre (1987, 131).

10. For the positing character of perception, see Sartre (2004b, 12).

11. For a discussion of Sartre's aesthetics and the role of the imagination which is particularly relevant here, see Howells (1988, 116–44). Also see Howells (1979, 3–23, 143–69). For Husserl's concept of the natural attitude, see Husserl (1998, 51–62).

12. As an example of this, in *What is Literature?* Sartre writes: "Thus, whether he is an essayist, a pamphleteer, a satirist, or a novelist, whether he speaks only of individual passions or whether he attacks the social order, the writer, a free man addressing free men, has only one subject—freedom" (Sartre 1988, 6).

13. Pucciani has also drawn attention to the importance of the imagination for groups. See Pucciani (1981, 520).

14. Sartre writes: "The necessity of syntax has compelled us hitherto to speak of the 'non-positional consciousness of self.' But we can no longer use this expression in which the *'of self'* still evokes the idea of knowledge. (Henceforth we shall put the

'of' inside parentheses to show that it merely satisfies a grammatical requirement)" (Sartre 1984, 14). And in the accompanying footnote, Barnes writes: "Tr. Since English syntax does not require the 'of,' I shall henceforth freely translate *conscience (de) soi* as self-consciousness" (Sartre 1984, 14).

15. For further analyses of this point in *The Imaginary*, see Sartre (2004b, 193).

16. For relevant analyses of the temporality of the imaginary, see Sartre (2004b, 192–93).

17. On this topic, see Flynn (2014, 339).

18. In his text on Sartre, Flynn cites the following relevant lines from Scrivener: "'the value of literature, like education, is in its ability to disturb the consciousness of the contemporary reader'" (Flynn 2014, 388).

19. This is one of the views discussed in Sartre (1993, 42–45).

20. For the complete quote see Husserl (1998, 11).

21. Guerlac has also analyzed the temporality of reading in Sartre, and has connected it to his discussions of the group in fusion. See Guerlac (1997, 83, 235).

22. This is a modification of Hegel's claim from the preface to the *Philosophy of Right.* The original quote reads as follows: "Philosophy too is the apprehension of its own time in thoughts" (Hegel 1942, 11).

PART II

Institutionalized Education

Chapter 4

Education as Assimilation

The first part of this work was devoted to developing a genuine, Sartrean phenomenological analysis of education. In chapter 1, I provided an account of the task of education in the Organization, the nature of the teacher, the students, and their relationship, as well as the role of the imagination. The second chapter deepened the previous analyses by integrating the theme of time into education. I provided an account of the temporality of education, with an emphasis on both its synchronic, phenomenological, lived dimension, as well as its diachronic, "objective," generational component. Finally, in chapter 3, I developed the consequences of the previous analyses of education for the group as a whole. I explained the imaginatively oriented relation to tasks and functions, the role of literature as a task for the group as a whole, and the manner in which the group temporalizes itself through literature and the culture of the imaginary.

As discussed in the introduction, there are two phenomenological orientations toward education implicit in Sartre's work, the first being spontaneous, free, and imaginative, the second degraded, ossified, and oppressive. In the present part, I will develop the educational counterpart to committed education, what I have termed "Institutionalized Education," which both inverts the previous discussions of education and introduces new elements into the nature and results of education. In this sense, to use a phrase from Husserl, it is "umgestülpte Bildung," or "education turned on its head" (Husserl 2001a, 17). As also discussed in the introduction, the Institution is a degraded Organization and therefore lends itself to a corresponding analysis through the lens of education. In the chapter on the Institution, Sartre writes: "Thus it is characterized by the same features that enabled us to define organized practice: but, *insofar as it is an institution*, its real being and its strength come to it from emptiness, from separation, from inertia and from serial alterity" (Sartre 2004a, 603). I will accordingly focus on the aspects of the Institution that are essential to providing an account of an oppressive theory of education which alienates the group members and the functioning of the group as a whole.

Before beginning the analyses proper of part 2, I would like to make a few general remarks about this form of education in order to further contrast it with committed education, to clarify its essential character, and to situate it within Sartre's project in the *Critique.* As he stated in *Search for a Method,* one of the essential aims of his later thought is to integrate existentialism and Marxism.[1] And within part 1, I attempted to show the manner in which education contributes to this unification. Education, I showed, plays a unique role in providing the resources for the individual to become a member of a group while maintaining their individuality. If, however, this is one of the accomplishments of liberating education, the question of the relation between existentialism and Marxism has to be posed again concerning an oppressive group and its corresponding oppressive form of education. In this case, the question concerns the nature of such a group member, the group itself, and the relation between them when the group has the task of structurally and systematically oppressing group members in their individuality in order for them to become members of the group. In an institutionalized educational system, rather than genuinely unifying the individual and the group, education attempts to keep them distinct, isolating the individual as a necessary condition of belonging to the group. Institutionalized education, in other words, maintains the individual, *as an individual,* in their seriality, as well as the group *as a group*, as an ontological unity.[2] The Institution, in its essential aims, unifies individuals to fracture them, and fractures them to unify them, and therefore both terms are preserved while also attempting to be unified in a false synthesis.

There is an additional point I would like to make at the outset to further characterize the concept of institutionalized education. The understanding and approach to education in the Institution parallels the attitude toward the paintings of the aristocracy of Bouville described in *Nausea.* There, Sartre writes: "Their souls at peace that day as on other days, with God and the world, these men had slipped quietly into death, to claim their share of eternal life to which they had a right. For they had a right to everything: to life, to work, to wealth, to command, to respect, and, finally, to immortality" (Sartre 1964, 83).[3] Institutionalized education, as it is being developed here, believes that it has a right to exist in its present form, that its historical forms and the actions of previous generations are justified, and therefore that its system of education and its history are justified and necessary.[4] The orientation toward the education of the group as such is thought to be necessary, intrinsically legitimate, and justified in its hierarchy, culture, and oppression. The existence of this educational form is beyond question, and the kind of group it produces, its culture, and the role and concept of literature within it, are viewed as part of the order of things. This educational form is therefore imbued with the spirit of seriousness, propagated by serious individuals, and producing serious group members.[5]

Concerning the relation between parts 1 and 2 and their corresponding forms of education, part 2 is an inverted image of part 1, its identical opposite, yet a reversal which also introduces its own, peculiar elements. It is also, more generally, a shift from dialogue to monologue, and represents the danger present in all groups of either declining from a free, spontaneous, and imaginative form to an ossified, degraded, and oppressive form, or, if already oppressive, toward increased alienation. As a general guide, then, each aspect in part 1 and the order of the chapters themselves will be taken up again and modified in accordance with the character of the Institution. In this chapter, I will begin with an account of the task of education in the institutionalized group. I will then turn to the institutionalized teacher and describe both how their personalization is a form of depersonalization and their orientation and pedagogy in the classroom. Finally, I will discuss institutionalized students, their status and experience of education in the Institution, and how in their case too personalization is ultimately a form of depersonalization.

THE INSTITUTIONALIZED TASK OF EDUCATION

After having introduced the concept of institutionalized education and its place within Sartre's thought, the following question presents itself, namely, what is the task of education in the institutionalized group? In order to articulate this task as foundational and a condition of possibility of the group, I will focus on a few central aspects of this group form that bear directly on my task here, namely, reflection, seriality, and sovereignty. As a degraded Organization, the Institution maintains a number of the characteristics which defined the Organization. It reflectively articulates itself, distributes roles and responsibilities, and produces the group members it needs to sustain itself. Sartre writes: "Similarly, as a detailed practice, it can and must realize itself through individuals who have been selected or produced by the group; it therefore presupposes powers, tasks, a system of rights and duties, a material localization and an instrumentality" (Sartre, 2004a, 603). However, these very features not only lose their original meaning, but change their sign such that they serve as a condition of possibility for the opposite educational form.

As a mechanism of reflection, education serves as an extension of the reflection of the part of the group that reflects on and guides the group as a whole. As a result of this totalizing reflection, the Institution produces group members who define themselves solely through the Institution. The reflective articulation of the Institution, the manner in which it is present to itself, is such that the sovereign element of the group reflects on the group as a whole *for the other group members*. It is not, therefore, a reflection which integrates all of the group members as free *praxes*, but a totalizing reflection of an individual or sub-group which governs the other group members. The form of reflection specific to the Institution, then, is a form of impure reflection.[6] As such an impure, distorted form of reflection, the tasks it assigns, the functions of the group members, and the relations within the group are alienated, oppressive, and hierarchical.

On the basis of the reflective determination of the group, what does it mean to say that the group members are "inessential" in the Institution? There are in fact two responses to this question. The first involves the nature of functions in the group, and the second is a result of the system of education which is designed with the explicit aim of producing inessentiality. To begin his analysis of the Institution, Sartre develops a contrast with the group in fusion. This contrast, in fact, highlights the inversion of freedom, individuality, and collective action which characterized earlier group forms. He writes: "In the living moment of the group (of fusion in the first stages of organization), the common individual is not inessential because he is the same in all. Everyone comes to everyone, through the community, as a bearer *of the same essentiality*" (Sartre 2004a, 599). This, as just mentioned, alters in the case of the Institution. Rather than the essentiality of all group members in the fulfillment of their tasks, a "balance" between the individual as a group member and as a free, unique, *praxis*, in an institutionalized group the individual loses their essentiality in relation to their function. The function maintains its importance for the group, but the individual responsible for its fulfillment becomes insignificant, replaceable or interchangeable, and subordinate to it insofar as the function fulfills itself through them.[7] Thus, Sartre writes, "freedom, conceived as a common transcendent subject, denies individual freedom and expels the individual from function; function, positing itself for itself, and producing individuals who will perpetuate it, becomes an *institution*" (Sartre 2004a, 600). In its domination over the individual who performs it and the culture that "sustains" it, the function inverts the essentiality characteristic of the earlier group forms.

At this point, the question concerning the status of sovereignty in the institutionalized group presents itself. I have referred to the sovereign part of the group responsible for determining the direction of the group, but what exactly is sovereignty in such a group form, and how does it relate to the theme of education? Sovereignty, though not confined to the Institution, possesses a unique significance in the Institution and for the theme of education. Early in the chapter on the Institution, sovereignty is defined in the following way: "By sovereignty, in effect, I mean the absolute practical power of the dialectical organism, that is to say, purely and simply its *praxis* as a developing synthesis of any given multiplicity in its practical field, whether inanimate objects, living things or men" (Sartre 2004a, 578). Moreover, in illustrating this concept, Sartre returns to the example of the soccer club from the chapter on the Organization. As a free, spontaneous, and positive instance of sovereignty, the action of each player involves an arrangement or rearrangement of the other players, their possibilities and responsibilities, and the field in general. As such a regulatory third party, each group member totalizes all of the others, and integrates them into the play. This account of sovereignty takes on a different character in the Institution. Sartre writes: "But if the exercise of sovereignty were complete, the sovereign would have to be external to the group and to totalize it as totality-object in his practical field" (Sartre 2004a, 579).[8] Sovereignty, then, from an immanent and reciprocal totalization becomes a transcendent and one-sided totalizing act of an individuated sovereign. In relation to education, the sovereign institutes a process of education to make the group members inessential. The system of education, with all that it entails, from the preparation of the teacher to the development of curricula, is the *essential* means to produce inessential group members.

As discussed in chapter 1, education in the Organization is a point of departure, a beginning for the group members, and a second pledge through which the students as future group members enter the group. However, in the Institution, these aspects of education change their character. It is true that in the Institution education is also a point of entry into the group. It is a second pledge that serves as a point of departure, but in such a way that the group members, both during the period of formal education and as full group members, remain locked within the immanence of the group. As a point of departure, education is used to produce a type of group member who will not transcend the group or even be able to do so. They will remain perfectly consistent with it, assimilating the content taught and the expectations of the group. Education is therefore both a beginning and an end, a point of entry into the group from which the group member cannot escape because the possibility of transcending the group is denied. The individual is produced in order for the fulfillment of their possibility in the group to be the elimination of their possibility as a subject. They are produced within immanence with the concomitant negation of transcendence, whether concerning the particular task and function or the group as a whole. Rather than allowing for the transcendence by the group member of the immanence of the group in order for the group to transcend itself while maintaining its immanent form, there is a tightened immanence which does not provide the necessary space for transcendence. In truth, there is continued action within the immanence of the group with the result of the perpetual replication of confined immanence.

In order to achieve such identity with the group, the concept of education and its imposition take an appropriate form. First, the responsibility of education is distributed differently. Whereas there was symmetry in the Organization, there is a marked asymmetry in the Institution. The sovereign has the responsibility of determining and providing the necessary education for the group members. And this sovereign responsibility takes a few forms and manifests itself in various ways in the group. As a form of determining reflection, the sovereign individual or sub-group is responsible for creating a system of education, decides what will be taught, how it will be taught, and so on. Moreover, as a correlate to the formal establishment of a system of education and a constitutive element of it, the sovereign also creates a culture wherein the necessary orientation in the group is developed, the necessary values are instilled, and the material taught is reinforced. The students, on the contrary, have the responsibility to obey and assimilate the education provided in order to acclimate to life in the group.[9] This responsibility, on the one hand, is reciprocal insofar as both sides make demands on one another. However, on the other hand, the responsibility of the sovereign to the students is to provide the education which will allow the students to enter the group, but ultimately to serve the sovereign and the group. It is, therefore, not a genuine responsibility toward the students, nor one that will be genuinely fulfilled, insofar as the educational personalization of the students leads to their depersonalization as group members. The students, moreover, have the responsibility to be educated, *but to exhaust their education in what is provided*, and ultimately to maintain such a responsibility as their future responsibility to the sovereign.

There is an additional element to the character of demands in the institutionalized group. The organized group members placed demands on themselves in order to fulfill their aims and potential both individually and collectively. Here, the sovereign also makes demands on the students. However, such educational demands requires them to fully cohere with the will of the sovereign. The students, too, as did the members of the soccer club, place demands on one another, but only to ensure that the will of the sovereign is carried out. Their demands on one another are not meant to allow each group member to fulfill their life in the group both individually and collectively, but rather to do so as an individual whose individuality is repressed for the sake of the sovereign. The constant tension, then, in the organized group members which led to the fulfillment of the potential of the group, is here replaced with a passive acceptance and submissive harmonizing of group members. There is, in the relation between the students and the group, a passive acceptance of the demand of the sovereign and the passive placing of demands of the students on one another in simply extending the initial demand of the sovereign. Tension, then, if it exists at all, is a result of group members acting contrary to the educational demands and culture of the group. The harmonizing of the group members, in this form of education, is a passive assimilation of the educational content presented and the expectations of the group.

There is a final point to be emphasized in this introductory account of institutionalized education, which will also further contrast it with committed education, namely, literature. Institutionalized education also makes possible the engagement with the necessary literature of the group in the future. And again, literature is understood in a comprehensive sense involving the production and use of images, whether through novels, plays, artworks, and so on. Such literary engagement will perpetuate the education of the group members, and continue to make them into the passive and inessential group members necessary for the group. The period of formal education prepares the students to be passive group members when they fully enter the group. The author and the reader in this case are not engaged in a genuine dialogue in images. Each does not demand and promote the freedom of the other. Rather, the author, as an educational extension of the sovereign, directs the creation of the engagement with images, that is, imposes content which is passively received and absorbed by the reader. As was the case in the process of education in the relation between the teacher and the students, the demand of the author is for the passive acceptance on the part of the reader. One central aspect of the task of such education, then, is to produce passive students who will maintain their passivity in the life of the group, and in particular in their engagement with literature and the necessary action it demands. During the period of formal education and through literature the group infuses the group members with an orientation which will either allow them to passively accept and fulfill what is asked of them in the group, or, if necessary, to find ways to develop and modify the assigned tasks and functions to better serve the sovereign.

THE DEPERSONALIZATION OF THE TEACHER

After having provided an account of the nature and aims of education in the institutionalized group, it is necessary to explain the manner in which this group form, through the action of the sovereign, produces the teacher it needs to serve its particular ends.[10] In the Institution, the personalization of the teacher is a process of depersonalization. Rather than personalizing the teachers in their freedom to creatively fulfill their individual task, the depersonalization of the teachers involves having them exhaustively personalized such that their own freedom, spontaneity, and creativity, in truth their subjectivity, are eliminated from the task of teaching as much as possible. This requires a reconsideration of the definition of personalization as "assumption and inner negation" insofar as the teachers "assumes" their necessary role as a teacher and does so by "internally negating" their subjectivity to identify themselves as an institutionalized teacher (Sartre 1987, 7). Moreover, there is a corresponding inversion of the principles of Sartre's existential psychoanalysis, affecting the orientation of the teacher toward education and the object of knowledge, the students, and the nature and possibility of their life-choice in the group. The account provided here will be both descriptive and prescriptive, demonstrating not only the character of this form of personalization, but also the process by which it is imposed on the individual group member.

The context within which institutionalized education takes place involves a necessary role of need, scarcity, the practico-inert, and the structures that have been built on them. These very conditions contribute to the character of institutionalized education. This form of education, as ultimately designed to serve the sovereign, harmonizes with them and continues to integrate them into its functioning. Rather than resisting the weight of the practico-inert, institutionalized education makes use of it to preserve the order of the group. In this regard, it continues to add to the weight of the practico-inert, with the aim of making it as difficult as possible to resist or modify it. Thus, while it is true that different conditions for history would help give rise to a different form of education, it is also the case that the same conditions, given the orientation toward them, can contribute to the founding of a system of education which is consistent with them. In an educational form that harmonizes with such conditions, the group produces a teacher who themselves harmonizes with and helps maintain both these conditions and their manifestations in education and the group in general. Institutionalized education therefore serves as an alternative to committed education as well as the possibility—present or future—of any form of education with a different relation to such conditions.

The Institution will produce teachers who passively accept and reinforce the past and present of the group as well as its own ossification and degradation. The sovereign must ensure that the teacher produced relinquishes their subjectivity in order to, as much as possible, identify with the group. The teacher too, if they are to cohere with the will of the sovereign, is forced to personalize themselves by depersonalizing themselves in order for their task, as an extension of the will of the sovereign, to be fulfilled. The group demands that the teacher depersonalize themselves as an individual in order to personalize themselves as a teacher. One of the main aspects of personalization in the institutionalized group is the production of the kind of teacher the group needs without recognizing and appreciating their subjectivity. The recognition, in this case, is one-sided. The future teacher is not recognized as an individual with various possibilities, a particular approach to education, and so on, but rather solely as a group member whose ultimate aim, and in general, whose ultimate task, is to serve the sovereign through teaching.

As such, the group is not empathetically oriented toward them, but relates to them coldly, from a distance, and mechanically in its imposition of educational standards regardless of their individual history, circumstances, or world-view.

As an additional element of the lack of recognition, the teacher is further depersonalized through the knowledge instilled. This knowledge is deemed necessary for the continuation of the group and requires a particular manner of presentation. Moreover, the knowledge is itself transmitted to the future teacher as a passive group member who will subsequently transmit the material in the same way to a group of passive students. It is therefore necessary for the group to promote passivity, acceptance, and a form of indifference in the depersonalization of the teacher. First, concerning the history of the group and its response to the conditions of its history, the various sovereign, educational apparatuses personalize the teacher by providing the context within which institutional education takes place and will do so in the future. In the recognition of the need for a teacher, there is also the recognition of the need for the teacher to maintain the continuity of the conditions of the history of the group, as well as the interpretation and response to those conditions on the part of the group. The depersonalization of the teacher assumes and requires the identity of the group across its history and that the present personalization of the teacher will be necessary and sufficient for their role in the group in the future. To personalize the teacher is therefore to depersonalize them as an identical group member across the past, present, and future of the group. As such, this process will also involve the teaching of the history of the group, the methods and curricula established, and the manner in which the subjects taught and the way they are taught contribute to maintaining the form, culture, and aims of the group. And what is of decisive significance in this case is that the history of the group, which involves a unique concern for its educational history, is sanctioned by the sovereign.

In contrast to committed education, in which the teacher in the process of personalization is a part of the process, a further reflective moment within it, in this case the established methods and content are presented as complete and in the absence of reflection and meaningful engagement. The personalization as depersonalization of the teacher is linked to their paradoxical status as a reflective moment of the group whose individual reflective act is repressed to allow for the emergence of the reflection of the sovereign through them. There is, paradoxically, a lack of historical context insofar as the only history provided for the teacher is that which has been formally approved by the sovereign. The restriction of historical understanding through reducing it to a single interpretation has the effect of historically de-situating the teacher such that the history internalized and taught is seen as necessary, justified, and *a-historical* insofar as it has eliminated any possibility of contextualizing the understanding of history itself. The question, therefore, of the truth of that history, of the interpretation provided and, in a more general sense, the historical understanding of the group itself, is not raised by the teacher, and not allowed to be raised at all. At most, differentiations within the group, and certain changes to the form and content of teaching, are presented as necessary to maintain the ideal form of institutionalized education or to stay as close to it as possible. The interpretation and response to the historical conditions of possibility of the group are presented as intrinsically necessary and universal. The teacher, then, becomes one more historical necessity as the group continues to act in accordance with such conditions.

As such a historical moment in the group, the institutionalized group has already lived the life of the teacher in advance and epistemologically hands it down to the teacher for the sake of a necessary future. Depending upon the particular subject the teachers will teach, the age of the students, and so on, the group provides the teachers with the life of the group in its past, present, and future, as they have not yet lived it but will do so through their education in order to educate the students. And again, this comes with various restrictions, as the past of the group was not lived-through, the future has not yet been lived-through and, as concerns the future of the students, will not be so. However, the group will depersonalize the teachers in such a way that they are confined to the knowledge obtained, and in this regard qualified to teach the required content. In addition, in instilling such knowledge and limiting their teaching abilities, the group produces a teacher which, again as an ideal and as much as possible, will already have lived the future life of the group regarding their education. In this regard, they are meant to repeat and reproduce the standards of the group in their teaching. Of course, they have not lived the future of the group, but in condensing the life of the group into the standards of the sovereign, and therewith reducing the present and the future to the past, the group has produced a teacher who has lived their own educational future and that of the students insofar as there will be a coincidence in the knowledge of the group and its past, present, and future forms.

In depersonalizing the teacher, the group does so across all of the temporal dimensions and attempts to have the group continue to culminate in the present in order to maintain the past and prevent a new future. The group therefore has the dual temporal and epistemological status of having already lived the life of the teacher in the past and future and of necessarily having done so in order to make their present role possible. The past, in this respect, is "open" insofar as it continues to be the point of entry into the group, while the future is necessarily "closed" insofar as it is limited to coincide with the past, and in principle represents a threat to the identity of the group. As a result, the group *temporally and epistemologically depersonalizes the teacher* in order for them to be capable of fulfilling their task in the group. Thus, the group both precedes and is subsequent to its own development insofar as it attempts to maintain the life of the group already lived in order to preserve its hierarchical order. And lastly, as I will show later in this chapter, this process of depersonalizing the teacher is intrinsically linked to, and finds its fulfillment in, the depersonalization of the students. Such a process of depersonalization, then, ultimately completes itself as an *intersubjective process of depersonalization.*

The lack of recognition of the subjectivity of the teacher is complemented by the imposition of the necessary historical and pedagogical content sanctioned by the sovereign. The historical understanding instilled in the teacher is complemented by the limitations and restrictions placed on the act of teaching. Along with the elimination of the subjectivity of the teacher, the group imposes clearly and rigidly delineated methods of teaching, assignments, curricula, and so on. There is a single method and standard of teaching. Of course, there will be differences as the necessary method of teaching will vary from one subject and level of education to another. However, across such differences in the process of education, the standard will remain identical insofar as it continues to maintain the hierarchy of the group. As a result, the process of personalization is complete, rigidly demarcated, and consistent and predictable. The style of teaching, which will largely assume the form of a lecture with a strict presentation of what needs to be taught, the various media and images that can be used, and so on, is determined and imposed in advance. There is, therefore, little, if any attention to the possible creativity of the teacher, but rather a process meant to standardize their approach to teaching and the relation to both the content and the students. On the one hand, such personalization is a point of departure insofar as it makes institutionalized teaching possible. On the other hand, in closing off the possibility of a free, spontaneous, and creative method and orientation toward teaching, it is ultimately a form of depersonalization.

As a further consequence of such depersonalization, the teacher is also made inessential. The teacher becomes another inessential group member who is made inessential in accordance with their unique, foundational, and unifying role in the group. The required skills are internalized, but are not made the teacher's own. In truth, it is the group internalizing itself through the teachers, forcing them to internalize the pedagogical standards of the group at the cost of their own subjectivity. The teacher is made into an instrument with which the sovereign is able to accomplish his ends. There is a single approach that the teacher is personalized to carry out, or, perhaps better, through their depersonalization, is carried out through them. In this respect, the personalization of the teacher contrasts with the training of the players of the soccer club in the Organization. There, each player was assigned a task and function, and the club as a whole developed the unique potential of each player. As a result of such training, each player developed their own style. Whether as a forward, midfielder, and so on, the players internalized what they were taught, made it their own, and uniquely fulfilled their task in the group. In the Institution, with minor differences, all of the teachers are the "same," that is, they have been identically personalized, and identically present the material to the students. Naturally, there are differences depending on the subject, level of education, and so on, but there is a single teaching style. Through a single, comprehensive process of personalization, all of the teachers in the group are depersonalized by being given a single style to be realized in the task of teaching.

As the process of personalization was complete, so will the teaching itself be complete. The exhaustive character of such personalization depersonalizes the teacher and prepares them to realize the will of the sovereign as not only another group member, but one with a unique, foundational role. There is, it follows, no "positive creative imperative" instilled in the teacher (Sartre 2004a, 450). The imperative given by the group to the teacher, what in general can be understood as the imperative of education, is a passive, *imitative imperative*, what I have chosen to term the "mimetic imperative." Again, such an imperative is an inversion of that found in the Organization. Sartre writes: "Function is both negative and positive: in the practical movement, *a prohibition* (do not do *anything else*) is perceived as a positive determination, as a *creative imperative:* do *precisely that"* (Sartre 2004a, 450). It is in fact the case that the institutionalized teacher is prohibited from doing "anything else," that is, teaching in their own style, modifying the content or curriculum, and so on (Sartre 2004a, 450). It is also the case that the teacher is required to "do precisely that," that is, to teach exactly how and what they were instructed to teach (Sartre 2004a, 450). The "creative imperative" in the process of personalization in committed education is degraded to a mimetic imperative in institutionalized education (Sartre 2004a, 450). In fact, in this case, the prohibition and creation coincide, such that the teacher, by not teaching in their own manner, is obeying the imperative of the sovereign, and in so doing is repressing their freedom. Through simply imitating what has been passed down and reproducing it in their teaching, the personalization of the teacher introduces a form of repetition into the group. The teacher repeats the methods and content of education in order to repeat the process of education for the students. The imitative imperative thus depersonalizes the teacher through its restrictions in order for the teacher to subsequently depersonalize the students through their teaching.

In order to accomplish this last goal, and to complete the process of depersonalization, the group will appeal to and cultivate the perception of the teacher and instrumentalize their imagination. The group will ensure that the material is understood as it is presented, that the methods and educational history of the group have been internalized, and that the teacher is prepared to externalize the information taught in accordance with its established character. Unlike the personalization of the committed teacher, there is no appeal to and a cultivation of their imagination to allow them to creatively present the material as needed, but rather an instrumentalization of it that will allow the use of images to the extent to which they are necessary to the group.[11] The group develops the imagination of the teacher to the extent that it will serve perception and the present reality of the group. The process of depersonalization is careful not to fully eradicate the imagination, but will condition it, in truth manipulate it, such that the images that it produces are used to reinforce the perception and acceptance of the group *in its reality*. In this case, the act of imagining is not the realization of transcendental freedom, but rather the assimilation to the needs of perception. In a manner that expands on Sartre's claims in *What is Literature?*, the teacher learns to speak in images, *but in images which serve the real.* The images presented are complete, and as such do not require any interpretive, creative, or imaginative engagement on the part of the students. They are accepted simply as they are, in a manner identical to the perception of material objects.[12] As such, the reality of the group will be seen and reinforced even in the variations of the images used to articulate it. And of course, the teacher must be able to produce such images, but, through the process of depersonalization, the images produced will be sanctioned by the group. They will cohere with the accepted, perceived reality of the group, and therefore the ability to speak in images is ultimately the ability to speak in *images of reality*.

THE INSTITUTIONALIZED TEACHER

The discussion of the personalization of the institutionalized teacher as a form of depersonalization leads to a number of questions concerning the act of teaching in the Institution. In general, one can now ask: How does the institutionalized teacher fulfill their designated task? How do they reinterpret the themes of perception and the imagination and incorporate them in their pedagogy? And how exactly does the act of teaching relate to sovereignty? The first topic to be discussed in response to these questions is that of reflection. As a degraded Organization, the reflection of the Institution is also degraded, which in this case means that a part of the group reflectively determines the group as a whole. This unique, individual-collective reflection has several consequences for the status of the teacher. First, the teacher is a moment of reflection in the group, but as an extension of the reflection of the sovereign. As such, the reflection of the teacher has the additional, peculiar, if not contradictory, quality of being unreflective. The teacher reinforces the reflection of the sovereign through their teaching, and in so doing does not freely contribute to the articulation and self-understanding of the group.

In a certain sense the institutionalized teacher is both a reflection of the sovereign as well as an extension of their reflection. This introduces a peculiar paradox into reflection. The sovereign is a transcendent group member which in their transcendent reflection determines the immanence of the life of the group. The sovereign as transcendent, as outside the group, still serves as one manner in which the group reflects on itself. As immanent to the group, however, as the necessary, educational sovereign incarnation that the group needs, they are also a group member and therefore included in the group as reflected on. The sovereign, as a more comprehensive form of reflection, is also a unity of identity and difference. As identical, they determine and comprise the essence of the group, the manner of its unification, and serve as the transcendental condition of its possibility, actuality, and continued existence. As so reflecting, however, they are also a moment of difference, distinct from all the other group members in being transcendent to the group and guiding it. As such, they are at a distance from the group, in this regard a peculiar essence which is removed and different from that which it defines, and their reflection on the group cannot fully coincide with it.

The status of the sovereign and their reflection affects the nature, role, and ability of the teacher to fulfill their task in the group. The teacher is an extension of the sovereign but is caught between the transcendence of the sovereign and the immanence of the other group members. In reflectively articulating the group through the act of teaching, the teacher serves as an immanent component of the transcendent act of reflection which is itself transcendent to the immanence of the other group members. The teacher is both a necessary component part of a more comprehensive act of reflection while also remaining their own individual, peculiar blend of reflection and the lack of reflection. They are a derivative reflection who carries out their task by cohering with the transcendent reflection of the sovereign in their pedagogical immanence. There are, therefore, orders of reflection in the Institution in general, and institutionalized education in particular. The higher-order reflection of the sovereign determines the ends of both the sovereign and the group. As a result, the teacher takes on a unique role in this situation as a further moment of the reflection through which the ends of the sovereign are realized and is able to fulfill this task by making the ends of the sovereign the ends of the students. The educational aims of the students, the knowledge obtained, the manner in which it is communicated, and so on, are ultimately part of the preestablished ends of the sovereign.

An additional question presents itself on the basis of the reflective situation of the teacher in the group, namely: How does the form of reflection proper to the institutionalized group, with the different levels within it, serve to mediate the group's relation to itself? Education in general and the role of the teacher in particular serve as the third thing necessary for the group to properly relate to and understand itself, and for the hierarchical order in the group to be preserved.[13] Is there, then, an identity in the act of reflection across the different group members, or given that some members of the group reflect on it in order to understand and guide it, while others reflect on it in accordance with the standards of the group, is there not a difference, or a discontinuity, in the reflection proper to the institutionalized group taken as a whole? As I have discussed thus far, and will continue to address, there is a difference both in the nature of the reflection, as well as in the possibility of reflection depending upon one's role, task, and function in the group. In a sense, the sovereign is the only individual to freely and genuinely reflect. The teacher, in extending this reflection, is a peculiar blend of it and their own, unreflective reflection. The students and the other group members, however, reflect in accordance with their education and the standards of the group. The imposed reflection on the group members therefore distorts and prevents their own ability to reflect, to genuinely grasp themselves in their subjectivity and the group in its transparent, collective functioning.

The nature of reflection and its various levels in an academic setting leads to the question of the third in such a group form. What happens to the educational third in such a reflective situation? And what kind of an educational third is the teacher? As I discussed in chapter 1, the committed teacher as a third was in part determined by, and emerged from, the reciprocity of all the group members in the Organization.[14] As an origin of the Institution, the reciprocity of "ternary relations" is also a basis for the relations in the Institution insofar as teachers comprise one of the possible manifestations of such relations. The teacher as a third therefore both constitutes alienated, educational relations, but is also constituted by them, a product of them, a continuity, in this sense, between what the group needed and continues to need concerning its education. Moreover, in addition to being constituted as a third by the other group members, including the students, it is important to emphasize that the teacher is also constituted as a third by the sovereign. Teachers are, therefore, a third comprised of qualitatively different forms of the Other insofar as their very role places them between the sovereign, the students, and the other group members.

The teacher as a third is also a unique condition of both the possibility and impossibility of the functioning of the group as a whole. Teachers are a derivative, transcendental condition of the possibility and actuality of the unity of the group because they are a transcendental condition of the impossibility of life in the group. And, further extending the status of the committed teacher, they are a mediated transcendental ground referencing both the previous groups and the sovereign. The transcendental character of the teacher is therefore a mediated and conditioned one, itself a product of the impossibility of a genuine life in the group because of its decline and the role of the sovereign. However, the institutionalized teacher continues to mediate between the past and present of the group, but now with the additional task of mediating between the past, present, and the sovereign of the group. The teacher's transcendental functioning is complicated accordingly because it is always conditioned by, and saturated with, the presence of the sovereign. As a result, the teacher does not relate directly to the past, with various degrees of proximity, immediacy, and mediation, but always with the a priori of the sovereign and the meaning that the past and present have for one another through the sovereign's presence.

This transcendental mediation, this depersonalized orientation, further develops and complicates the relation between the themes of transcendence and immanence. The situation of the institutionalized teacher as a degraded third has its own "transcendence-immanence tension" (Sartre 2004a, 374). I have already shown one form this tension can take in describing the form of reflection proper to the sovereign and the teacher. In this case, there is an additional form of this tension concerning the teacher's orientation to the students and the content taught. And here, it is possible to see a further break in the continuity of the previous group forms with the formation of the Institution. Concerning the development of the *Critique*, rather than remaining a moment of continuity in the immanence of a single history, the institutionalized teacher is a moment of discontinuity, a rupture in the freedom of the development of the previous group forms. On the one hand, as part of the logic of the development of groups, and as a necessary consequence of the alienation and ossification of groups, the Institution can be understood as part of a single logic unfolding in various ways. On the other hand, as distinctly new because of its alienated and oppressive form, and because of its constraints on the freedom of the group, it is necessarily at odds with, and therefore discontinuous with, the previous group forms. Teachers, as inheriting the continuity and discontinuity of the Institution, are therefore a tension between groups insofar as they are properly in one group while, and to a certain extent because, they are at odds with the previous group forms. Moreover, because of the presence of the sovereign, the transcendence of the teacher is reduced to a transcendence within their immanence in the group insofar as it is determined by the transcendence of the sovereign. They are, it follows, a transcendence-immanence tension concerning past groups, but also within the institutionalized group itself insofar as their transcendence cannot itself transcend the imposed immanence established by the sovereign. And yet, they are in part transcendent to the immanence of the students, such that they are comprised of a twofold transcendence and a twofold immanence in relation to both the sovereign and the students.

As a result of the tension in the role of the teacher, the "ideal distance" of the teacher from the group, which is in part due to their reflective character, is further modified as well (Sartre 1984, 123). Teachers are at a distance from the group because of their own reflective status, but also confined within it as subject to the sovereign. They are at a distance from the group in their reflection while also remaining proximate to it because of the unreflective character of their reflection and its determination by the sovereign. As a result, the institutionalized teacher is the group's "presence to itself," a moment of its educational articulation through the establishment of a system of education, but also "absent from" it insofar as their articulation of the past and present of the group, their transcendental function in the present, makes the group "present to" itself in separating it from itself in passively assimilating the group members to the life of the group (Sartre 1984, 124). Teachers are one way in which the group remains at a distance from itself and cannot be not fully integrated with itself because it is dominated by the sovereign. They are ultimately within the present of the Institution as an immanent group member, but their role as teacher, as an incarnation of its past and its condition of possibility, places them in the past of the group with a unique relation to the past groups that made the present group possible. They therefore inhabit several groups by remaining partially integrated, and partially cut off from them, a singular, derivative transcendence-immanence reduced to the transcendence-immanence of the sovereign.

On the basis of the transcendence-immanence tension proper to the teacher, one can now ask: How exactly is the setting for institutionalized education established? How does the teacher create the necessary atmosphere for such education to take place? To properly respond to these questions, it is necessary to invoke the look as it was discussed in *Being and Nothingness.* Through the look of the teacher at the students, which is in truth the twofold look of the individual teacher and the sovereign, the teacher objectifies them as an "us-object," but one comprised of their atomization and seriality (Sartre 1984, 537). The teacher's pedagogical gaze has the result of creating the necessary space for both knowledge and ignorance in the classroom setting. Moreover, this particular look introduces a relation between the content taught and the students. As such, the teacher, as a third who looks at the students, creates the space in order for the method of teaching appropriately to the institutionalized group be possible. The teacher objectifies the students in looking at them and fixes them both as group members and concerning their possibilities for knowledge. They are seen reduced to inert forms of the group, and as such bounded in their subjectivity and possibilities.

In addition, the look of the teacher homogenizes the students, it reduces them to a particular identity insofar as they are all required to learn the content sanctioned by the sovereign. The single look of the teacher collectively identifies the students as a singular whole, whose assimilation to the group will be accomplished through absorption of the necessary knowledge. The looks of the students, however, are secondary, and in looking at the teacher, do not have the force to reduce them to an object, but merely coincide with the manner in which the teacher looks at them. And again, it is important to remember that the teacher is under the gaze of the sovereign. Teachers too are fixed in place by the sovereign, ascribed an essence, and their subjectivity and potentiality have been reduced to their role in the group through the process of depersonalization. Furthermore, due to the immediacy of the look of the teacher at the students, and the mediacy of the look of the sovereign through the teacher, the students do not truly look at, see, or objectify the sovereign. As subordinate to the teacher, they do not truly objectify the teacher either but only, in a sense, part of the teacher's role in the group, as the individual responsible for teaching the material, but not as an object of the group produced by the sovereign. The students cannot equally objectify the teacher in their look because of their standing in the group, and are virtually incapable of objectifying the sovereign, whose look is not itself immediately or genuinely seen by the students.

After having discussed the necessary pedagogical space established through the look, one may ask: How does institutionalized teaching unfold? What is the nature, understood both philosophically and psychologically, of the relation between the teacher and the students? The response to these questions involves a renewed engagement with Sartre's concept of existential psychoanalysis. The concept of the teacher in this form of education is a distortion of the concept of the committed teacher and their essential qualities. As a distorted form of existential psychoanalysis, it is itself "an attitude" (May 1969, 15). As an attitude, however, it has a fundamentally different character. And what is to be stressed here is that this attitude is rigid, "inflexible," determined in advance and consistent with the needs of the group, not those of the students (Sartre 1984, 732). There is a single attitude, and a single orientation to both the students and the content taught. Moreover, such inflexibility is complemented by the appropriate form of absence, the diametrical opposite of presence defined by Bugental.[15] This absence, in truth, is also an indifference, the absence of concern for both the individuality of the student, but also for the atmosphere, setting, and meaningful engagement in the process of education with the students (Sartre 1984, 124). The teacher maintains a degraded form of presence, a blend of absence and indifference, so that the material can be properly presented and absorbed.

There is, as rigid, indifferent, and distant, a general lack of empathy in the teacher. Teachers are not empathetically oriented toward the situation of the students, the culture of the particular class, or the general, overarching historical context, but are rather concerned with establishing an atmosphere which both coheres with and continues to produce the hierarchical order of the group. The primary concern is the assimilation of content, to the neglect or exclusion of the students and their circumstances. If, however, there is to be empathy at all, it will only be present or invoked as needed to ensure that the pedagogy of the teacher, and the corresponding educational tasks and functions of the students, will be fulfilled. This form of empathy is paradoxically indifferent or, at the very least, instrumentalized such that any concern with the students is integrated into the educational process and the necessary functioning of the group. The orientation of the institutionalized teacher, it follows, creates the space for an educational monologue, the transmission of knowledge, and its passive acceptance.[16] Teachers continue their depersonalization through the strict application of the pedagogical rules acquired during the period of personalization. It is, in addition, standardized across the process of education in the group, and, while it will correspond in certain respects to the level of education, there is a single, monological pedagogy and distance that defines the process of education as a whole.

As was the case in committed education, the existential attitude leads to the question of how the teacher implements an appeal to both the perception and imagination of the students. And secondly, it leads to the question of the response of the students to this form of teaching. The teachers' absence in the classroom has a further bearing on the pedagogical space they are tasked with creating. Above all, the space of institutionalized education is *perceptual space.* There is an imaginative element to it, and a particular role of the imagination within it, but the imaginary space created is reduced to the space of perception, such that whatever appeal is made to the imagination, and whatever space is correspondingly created, will serve the perception and knowledge of the group *in its reality.* As a present-absent third, and through both the content presented and the manner of its presentation, the teacher serves to found *a collective perceiving.* They establish an attitude wherein what is given in the presentation of the material is accepted by the students as it is given and is accompanied by the thetic positing of its reality. *The space of perception is therefore the space of acceptance.*

Insofar as the imagination has a role in the classroom, the teacher will provide images, again of whatever sort necessary, in order to reinforce the perceptual content. In order to do so, the images will have two effects. First, they will complement the complete, perceptual content, continuing to show the validity of what is taught. Secondly, they will serve to instrumentalize the imagination for the students to learn to form images which are consistent with the perceptual content, and ultimately cohere with the needs of the group by cohering with the particular needs of the lesson, the level of education, the subject, and so on. The imagination is only appealed to in order to continue perception in education, and, as much as possible, to reduce the image to the given. In so doing, the space to imagine becomes bounded by the space to perceive. As a result, the teacher serves as a transcendental ground for the establishment, cultivation, and future use of perception in the group. *The teacher is, therefore, an origin of perception in the group.* And as instrumentalizing the imagination, *the teacher is an origin of the imagination.* However, instead of serving as an origin of the freedom of the imagination, the teacher restricts it by cultivating it to produce images which harmonize with the world of perception.

In order to achieve the reduction of the imagination to perception, the teacher effects the institutional correlate to the educational suspension discussed in chapter 1. However, in this form the epoché and reduction are inherently oppressive. The teachers initiate the process, remain transcendent to it, and can only be considered an immanent component of it insofar as they transmit the sanctioned knowledge in the appropriate manner. They are outside the process insofar as they are engaged in a monologue and do not empathetically interact with the students in the process of learning.[17] They will, therefore, in the act of teaching, effect their own empirical, imaginative reduction, *but will do so in order to reduce the imaginary to perception and the irreal to the real.* Paradoxically, through such an educational epoché, the teacher *posits the reality of the content taught* and excludes both themselves in their subjectivity and other potential ways of interpreting the content. Such an act of placing in brackets necessarily also brackets out any content that is inconsistent with the values and needs of the group, not in order to present or describe the material for it to be brought to intuition, but rather so that the reduced content is perceived as the only content and necessarily *being precisely as it appears and because of how it appears*.[18] This particular educational reduction does not involve a neutrality modification, but rather a necessary positing of reality.[19] Paradoxically, an oppressive, empirical, imaginative reduction posits the images used as either real or in the service of the real, and suspends the reality of educational content in order to impose it.[20] Moreover, as seen in its reality, the content is also viewed as complete. Thus, rather than an open, "infinite" task, the institutionalized reduction is "finite," closed, defined by an a priori limit on what is allowed to appear as well as the manner in which it does so.

Through the teacher's pedagogical suspension, the students are brought into the collective reduction, remain inside and outside of it, but passive, submissive, and accepting what is given through perception and on the basis of the minimal use of the imagination. The students, in so doing, become primarily *les hommes perceptuelles*, and secondarily *les hommes imaginaires*, with the latter serving their standing as perceptual in the former. It is therefore through an epoché with an emphasis on perception that the student is able to fully enter the perceptual space of learning, remain isolated, accept the content presented, and use the imagination to the extent necessary *in order to see the content taught.* The knowledge presented draws the students into the space of the reduction and allows them to internalize it as depersonalized, that is, as the knowledge proper to the subject-matter and group, possessing a "pure objectivity" which does not involve their engagement in the process of its attainment. The students, once the knowledge is obtained, once the lesson is complete, "leave" the reduction, and subsequently reenter it with the beginning of the next unit, lesson, and so on. The lack of knowledge, as the point of departure for the students, places them outside the reduction. They then enter it, attain knowledge through perception and the instrumentalized imagination, and then leave it with the obtainment of knowledge. In the space of the educational epoché, the students are largely static, simply absorbing what is presented, rather than imaginatively and creatively engaging with it. Although they enter such space with the effecting of the reduction, they maintain a particular exterior insofar as the content presented remains independent of them and the teacher does not actively integrate them into the process of learning.

Moreover, and as I explained in chapter 1, this educational reduction is necessarily an *empirical reduction.* However, whereas it was defined by a flexibility and an adaptability in the case of committed education, here it has a static, fixed form, and if it changes at all, it does so only to reinforce the knowledge and values that have been imposed on the students. As such, there is a minimal variation with the age of the students, the nature of the subject-matter, and so on, and, most importantly, it is designed so that the material cannot be grasped on its own terms, but rather on those of the sovereign. As a unique form of bracketing, institutionalized education also has a peculiar relation to the status of assumptions and views of the content. As empirical, such a reduction continues to stand on the ground of the world. However, rather than suspending assumptions about the content, it begins with the assumption that the material is as it appears to be, that its manner of presentation corresponds to it, and that it can be *passively comprehended.* It has, therefore, its own, limited, and restrictive a priori, insofar as it is constituted by aspects of the natural attitude which it also brackets to fashion and communicate the necessary content. It is, moreover, a process with fixed stages. It does not, in other words, develop with the culture of the class, the nature of the experience in the classroom, or the knowledge obtained. The suspension, in this case, does not help find the appropriate presentation of content for the appropriate, corresponding acts of the students to connect with it, but rather restrains both and continues to ensure the single, sanctioned approach to education. There is no variation of imaginative content on the basis of the history of the class, but a single, unwavering presentation that continues and, in its form, repeats itself throughout the process of learning. There is, of course, one exception insofar as what was initially taught is further integrated into the subsequent lessons and a part of the knowledge of the subject-matter. However, as it was originally presented as real, and was subsequently accepted as such, there is not a change from imagination to reality, but rather a continuous assumption of the reality and truth of the content.

There is, moreover, a paradox here. There is no space for ignorance in the group, but only the imposed and established space for knowledge. *As a result, the students are kept in ignorance precisely because there is only space for knowledge.* The students, by passively receiving certain content, and being forced to accept it as truth to the exclusion of other truths and interpretations which are inconsistent with it, are kept ignorant because they are restricted to particular knowledge. The space for knowledge, moreover, is itself limited insofar as it is constituted by what the sovereign has approved of and will ultimately serve him. In this case, ignorance is imposed through knowledge. The teacher constitutes relations of knowledge among the students that are ultimately meant to be relations of ignorance. And the knowledge presented, again paradoxically, is its own ignorance insofar as what is presented is presented as what must be the case. It is because knowledge is presented as complete that the act of learning is inherently also an act of ignorance, an act of oppression, which prevents the space of the absence of knowledge necessary for the obtainment of knowledge. The classroom setting is comprised of individualized, atomized, perceptual space, wherein the presentation of the content as complete, and its passive, perceptual acceptance is necessary and sufficient for the standards and needs of the group. The students, therefore, are kept ignorant in order to never be ignorant, that is, so as to know only what is taught to them.

INSTITUTIONALIZED STUDENTS

The account of the institutionalized teacher and their orientation in the classroom leads to the question of the role of institutionalized students in this form of education. I have already begun to indicate this role in explaining the fact that they passively accept what the teacher presents to them. However, on the basis of such passivity, how is the material internalized by each student individually and in relation to the other students? Moreover, in what sense are institutional students educational third parties? To begin with the second of these questions, as third parties they are thirds in the group like anyone else with designated tasks and functions. They are also, as regulatory third parties, constitutive of the transcendence-immanence tension of the group. In this case, this tension takes on an appropriate institutionalized form. First, like committed students, they are in the process of becoming full group members. However, unlike them, their regulatory act as third parties is accordingly restricted. They regulate or totalize one another as thirds and the teacher as a kind of third, but they are not able to regulate the sovereign as a third. The sovereign, of course, regulates and totalizes them, but they cannot totalize the sovereign in turn. Or, at best, their totalization of the sovereign, their relation to them and the hierarchical culture of the group, is an act of acceptance or obedience. They can carry out their educational tasks in the group as thirds, but the overarching context of education and the nature of the educational process involve a third they cannot reciprocally totalize or regulate. Thus, as I will continue to show in this section, their personalization through education is a form of depersonalization insofar as they will never develop as individuals but only as group members.

As such thirds, what is the task of the institutionalized student? Again, the task of a student is only to be a student, to be concerned solely with education, and the manner in which this task is carried out will vary with age, subject, the culture of the particular class, and so on. The concern with the future, which is implicit throughout the process of education with varying degrees of immediacy and mediation, is secondary to the immediate educational concerns at hand. However, as preparing the group members to enter the group in the future, the group personalizes them by depersonalizing them insofar as their future life is sanctioned by the sovereign and consistent with the ultimate aims of the group. The students therefore accept the education they are presented with, the history and present order of the group, and as part of this assumption, repress their own possibilities as free, unique individuals. The extent to which they make something of what has been made of them is therefore reduced as much as possible, with the ideal of them wholly being what has been made out of them, such that what they make of themselves coincides with what the group has made and continues to make of them. There is an approximation of transcendence to immanence, and of immanence to transcendence, with the result that any potential transcendence of the situation is restricted and turned back on itself in order for it to fall back into the previous immanence. These students are thus immanent to the functioning of the group, and continue to remain so insofar as they never transcend their education or the group but remain locked within both and reducible to them.

The limited nature of the regulatory action of the students as thirds also affects the status of demands within their education. As discussed earlier in this chapter and part 1, the different group members place demands on one another to complete their tasks and functions. However, the institutionalized group members are not seen or treated as genuine, free subjects, and thus the question of the possibility and nature of a demand assumes a corresponding character. The sovereign and the teacher place various demands on the students. But the students, as inessential, do not have the freedom or standing within the group to make genuine demands on either the teacher or the sovereign. There is a lack of reciprocity in such demands. As students and minimal group members, they place demands on the group to be educated as needed. The issue, however, is that their life in the group is determined in advance by the group. The demand to be educated is therefore a demand to be educated in accordance with the needs, standards, and culture of the group, and not as an essential part of the cultivation of their subjectivity. They demand, like committed students, that the group make education possible, that the teacher be properly personalized, and therefore that they receive the appropriate education. But in the Institution that means that they demand to be assimilated. In recognizing that their personalization is dependent on the role of the teacher, there is a specific demand that the teacher fulfill their task and function in the present in order for them to be able to fulfill theirs in the present and future. It is an incomplete demand insofar as it will not be fulfilled until the later stages of education and ultimately when they are full group members. And as the character of such education is passive, and the group is constituted by a hierarchical culture, the students demand to be made passive, to participate in a monologue, and ultimately to have truth presented to them as fixed and beyond question. It is a peculiar, paradoxical demand by the students which asks for education to take place by already being done for them.

The character of this demand extends to the other students as well. They too must demand that the other students act in accordance with the standards of the group, and that they too remain passive as they absorb the educational content. It is a demand for the serialization and atomization of the students, for their own removal from the process of education, and more generally for the absence of a collective orientation toward truth and the process of obtaining it. From this point of view, to be an institutionalized student is to fulfill the educational demands established by the sovereign and to extend them by placing them on both the teacher and the other students. Furthermore, the age of the students is less significant in defining and placing demands on the group. Of course, the demands can develop or become clearer as the students advance in the educational process. However, instead of an increased consciousness and understanding of the relation between the demand and freedom, the students constrict the demand in order to ensure that the knowledge obtained is exactly what is needed by the group and for their future life in it. Rather than a movement toward freedom to be carried out in the future of the group, there is a movement toward inertia, toward depersonalization, in order to assimilate as much as possible with the ideal of identification and complete coincidence with the group. This demand endures throughout the educational process, at some points potentially being more or less implicit or explicit, but it is constant in demanding the necessary education for life in the group, even if this demand is only articulated later in the educational process and applied retroactively.

The students, as thirds in the group, paradoxically regulate the pedagogy of the teacher in passively accepting the knowledge transmitted. Their contribution to the class, its atmosphere, and culture, is to de-totalize themselves in their process of totalizing the teacher's act and the process of education. Their contribution to the pedagogical experience, in other words, is largely to remove themselves from it. Their presence to the group and its educational process is their absence from it. They reflect the role of the teacher in this regard. They too, in their presence-absence, make possible the necessary educational atmosphere. They contribute to the monologue of the educational process, and do not themselves establish relations of knowledge and ignorance, situate their own understanding of a subject in relation to that of the other students, but ascribe a priority to the individual relation between themselves and the teacher fulfilled in the act of passively listening and absorbing content. The relations between the students, which are atomized and serialized, are initially established by the teacher and then maintained by the students themselves. There is a peculiar manner in which, though collectively objectified by the look of the teacher, each student maintains a singular orientation toward them. This occurs despite the fact that the teacher addresses the class as a whole and with indifference to the subjectivity of the students. Relations of knowledge and ignorance are therefore first established by the teacher, and subsequently continued by the students. There is no collective totalization of the knowledge and ignorance in the classroom, but rather an individual totalization of the material presented in order for it to be internalized in the right way.

There are additional component parts to the educational acts of the students, namely, that of analysis and synthesis. Each student carries out a unique synthesis of themselves and the teacher, and founds a unique, binary pedagogical relationship. But this synthesis also synthesizes and excludes the rest of the students. There is an analytic whole wherein nothing emerges that was not previously implicit in the context established by the teacher and which transcends the material presented. And yet the student must synthesize the other students in order to exclude them as a whole. The inherent, analytic relation of a teacher to a student is therefore continued through the exclusionary synthetic act of the individual student. The seriality of the classroom is perpetuated by the synthesizing isolation of each student. The synthetic acts of the students continue and perfectly conform to the serializing-serialized atmosphere established by the look of the teacher. There is a one-sided, fragmented, collective educational act on the part of institutionalized students. There is, moreover, a sanctioned mediation between the teacher and the student, one which is meant to approximate immediacy as much as possible, precisely because the ideal is the transmission of knowledge directly from the teacher to the student in the absence of interpretation. Any possible mediation from other students is itself repressed insofar as they can serve to interrupt, corrupt, and possibly even lead to a collective orientation toward the knowledge presented. The students, in this regard, are seen as a threat insofar as the possibility of collective, educational *praxis* would disrupt the process and culture of the group. Immediacy and mediation are in constant tension in such education, and the students contribute to it by maintaining the unity of presence and absence in their relations to one another and the content taught.

The students collectively in their isolation totalize the teacher in their singularity. The teacher is totalized by each student, put in relation to each student and the class collectively, but such totalization establishes an individual relation with each student and an anonymous relation with the class as a whole. This peculiar lack of reciprocity, or, perhaps better, such a degraded form of it, further modifies the character of the students' *praxis*. The *praxis* of each student, which is in truth a process of passively conforming to the culture of the group, establishes corresponding educational relations with the other students. In this case, however, the relations are exclusionary, being established between all of the students in order to keep them cut off from the individual student's education and therewith to establish a reciprocity with the teacher alone. Reciprocity in this group, it follows, is ultimately a lack of reciprocity. As such, the relations between the students, or the atomized constellation of the students, is static. It does not develop over the course of a semester, year, and so on. The foundational relations that comprise the educational process do not change with the knowledge and ignorance of the class. Such relations continue, paradoxically, both in accordance with the character of each student, and by preserving the static, serialized character of such relations. The reciprocity remains a basis for the future education of the students and their life in the group, but it does so by maintaining the absence of genuine reciprocity and their seriality as group members.

The static relations of reciprocity give rise to an additional, peculiar character of the unity of this group form. Like committed education, the group is never complete. It necessarily develops with the knowledge obtained. It is a unity of atomized subjects, a plurality of indifferent relations. However, it is also complete, fixed, and static. It is a continuous process of reflection in accordance with the sovereign. As such, it requires the continuous institutionalization throughout the process of education, the passivizing, indifference, and atomizing of the students. It is, more generally, a constant process of perception in order for the process of education to form a unified, perceptual whole, which deepens the processes of perception for the sake of continued acceptance. It is both a totalization with a totalizer and "a totalization without a totalizer" (Sartre 2004a, 805). On the one hand, the process is ultimately totalized by the sovereign, and their will is totalized as extended in and through the task of the teacher. The students also serve as various extensions of the will of the sovereign as they are integrated into the group through education. On the other hand, all of the students, together with the teacher, totalize a process which, much as it attempts to eliminate subjectivity, relies on the individual *praxes* of all of the group members and is therefore irreducible to any one of them. The process is therefore totalized-totalizing, a unity of a single act and a plurality of acts, all of which contribute to the anonymity of the process of education which, as it also involves serialization and the repression of the imagination, is a process of depersonalization. Education is a process of the group that belongs both to the group and the group members, but in such a way that their totalization is totalized in advance by the sovereign and consistent with it. As a result of the form of this totalization, the educational process of depersonalization is never complete, but continues throughout the formal period of education, and translates into the appropriate life in the group.

However, what happens to both the teacher and the students once this stage of education, that is, this stage of depersonalization, is complete? As the contradictory opposite of the committed teacher, this teacher teaches in order to never be surpassed, in order for the students, at best, to reach their level of knowledge, but never to transcend it in maintaining the hierarchical order of the group. The teacher teaches to depersonalize and therefore to keep the students immanent to the group. Knowledge is not a point of departure, but the end of a process and a restriction on the individual. As much as the teachers have the task of no longer having an explicit role in the lives of the students in the future, they are meant to maintain a presence in the lives of the students in reducing them as much as possible to group members. As part of the memory of the students, the teachers are meant to be remembered, regardless of the extent to which they are also meant to be forgotten. And this is due to the fact that the teacher represents the sovereign, and determines the past of the students as that of the sovereign. As such, the teacher as sovereign is meant to continue to limit the students. They are therefore a permanent third, defined by a constant, implicit presence. Their educational life in the group may continue, and regarding their task and function for a designated period the teacher is also temporary. But given their task of depersonalization and the accomplishment of it, they remain present in the lives of the students as a restriction on their subjectivity. The teachers have, as a result, transcended the present in helping produce the necessary future, but are themselves locked within immanence, confined to it by the transcendence of the sovereign, and therefore fall back into the educational process to continue to fulfill their predominantly permanent task in the life of the group as a whole.

The students, as the other side of the totalization of the teacher and the sovereign, continue to integrate what was learned into their lives in the group, but do so by never truly surpassing the life that the teacher made possible. The teacher will be remembered and integrated as a limit, as a constraint, as ultimately unsurpassable insofar as their continued life in the group is dependent on and reducible to the knowledge obtained. As the students continue to progress through the group, as they continue to assimilate, and as they continue to perceive, the teacher, as an incarnation of the memory of the group, is integrated into the collective perception of the group. The permanent totalization of this third therefore continues to regulate the perception of the students and, to the extent to which it is present, their instrumentalized and depersonalized imagination. The students continue to integrate the teacher into the group insofar as their future action is continuous with the education received. The teacher's immediate task of teaching is continuously fulfilled with greater degrees of mediation or temporal mediacy across the life of the group as the students fulfill their tasks and functions as full group members.

NOTES

1. See Sartre (1968, 8–17, 28–34).
2. Such unity is of course impossible for Sartre. For discussions on this point, see Sartre (2004a, 581). For a related analysis of individuality, see Horkheimer (1947, 139–43).
3. This view is contradicted later by Roquentin's own reflections. See Sartre (1964, 84, 94). A similar point is made in *Existentialism Is a Humanism.* See Sartre (2007, 49).
4. As justified in its existence and privileging inertia over growth, institutionalized education is also anti-dialectical. It does not allow for the free, spontaneous development of the group or the group members, but rather attempts to preserve the group as it was. In this regard, it is a peculiar instance of Sartre's description of the for-itself as "*est été*" insofar as it attempts to collapse the distinction between *is* and *was,* preserving its *past being* as its present (Sartre 1943, 57).
5. For an analysis of "the serious man," see Beauvoir (1976, 45–65). See also Hayim (1996, 58–61).
6. For a clear statement of the nature of impure reflection, see Sartre (1984, 224).
7. For a related discussion, see Marrou (1956, 306).
8. Also see Sartre's discussion in Sartre (2004a, 579).
9. In fact, in his discussion of "other-direction" in the chapter on the Institution Sartre writes: "But this is not really possible unless the serial individual has been

produced from childhood as other-directed. It has recently been shown, in fact, that in infant schools in America (and, of course, throughout the child's education), everyone learns to be the expression of all the others and thereby of his whole social milieu, so that the slightest exterior serial change returns to him and conditions him from outside in alterity" (Sartre 2004a, 651).

10. The account here is more consistent with Sartre's analysis in *The Family Idiot* insofar as it explains Flaubert's flight from reality, choice of the imaginary, and failure.

11. This, in certain respects, is consistent with the early formulations of the relation between perception and the imagination in Sartre's thought. See Sartre (2004b, 12, 186). For his later views, see Rybalka, Pucciani, Gruenheck (1981, 23).

12. In this regard, though perception and the imagination posit their objects differently, they *accept* them as given in the same way.

13. This alters the concept of education as the schema and third thing necessary for the group to properly relate to and understand itself. In truth, it is a "fourth thing," insofar the reflection of the group on itself is accomplished by the sovereign. There is, therefore, an additional term in this relation. And as a result, the teacher not only participates in the group as both reflecting and reflected-on, but in the act of the individual who carries out such reflection. Thus, the teacher is the third term insofar as they serve as a moment of the group's reflection on itself, but a fourth term insofar as they are an extension or component part of the reflection of the individual responsible for the group reflecting on itself. The teacher, therefore, must be "homogenous" with the sovereign on the one hand, and the group on the other, giving them a tense, mediating status as the "fourth thing" required by the group for its education (Kant 1998, 272).

14. In institutionalized education, the teacher is an instance of "the alienating third" (Flynn 1973, 4–10).

15. See Bugental (1978, 36).

16. In this regard, and as a complement to the analyses of Martinot, within the context of education, the institutionalized look is a condition for a *monologue*. See Martinot (2005, 43–61).

17. This is another instance of the claim that "*Esse est percipi*," which Sartre discussed and criticized in *Being and Nothingness* (Sartre 1984, 9–24). In this form of education, essence is reduced to its educational phenomenality.

18. In this case, the reduction is used to *oppress* rather than *liberate*, and attempts to keep the students in a serious or "solemn" attitude (Sartre 2007, 49).

19. This raises an interesting question regarding Sartre's critique of Husserl's phenomenological reduction. Here, the danger is not in bracketing the reality of the independently existing, external object in order to describe it purely as it appears and to bring it to intuition, but in bracketing *all other realities and interpretations* to reduce the content taught to a *single reality*. Of course, as an empirical suspension, whose goal is not uncovering transcendental subjectivity, it is of a different character than the phenomenological reduction. However, it still acknowledges the essential

reality of the object, but does so by reducing it to its single, educational appearance. On Sartre's critique of Husserl, see Detmer (2008, 55).

20. Interestingly, at the close of his article on the different ways in which Sartre used Husserl's phenomenological reduction, Busch writes: "What Sartre shares with Husserl is this use of phenomenological tools—in particular the reduction—to recover from an alienated state our individual lives and social institutions, and return them to the human" (Busch 1980, 29). In the analysis I am providing here, I am showing the manner in which the reduction can be used to alienate subjectivity and institutions, and to continue to do so, rather than to "return them to the human" (Busch 1980, 29).

Chapter 5

The Temporality of Institutionalized Education

In the previous chapter, I provided an account of the Institution and the form of education appropriate to it. As was the case in my analysis of committed education, I devoted particular attention to the theme of reflection, but in this case the analysis was complicated by the presence and role of the sovereign. The reflection of the sovereign, I showed, determines the direction of the group, and in so doing determines its form of education, the content taught, and the relations between the teacher and the students. The theme of reflection, as I showed in chapter 2, is intrinsically linked to the theme of time, and as the Institution represents a form of impure reflection, its temporalization possesses many of the characteristics of psychic time and the psychic object.[1] As discussed in chapter 1, the institutional sovereign is concerned with *preserving* the group, and therefore ascribes a priority to the past. In order to provide the temporal counterpart to the analyses of chapter 1, and to introduce the form of genetic phenomenology appropriate to an oppressive form of education, I will incorporate a distorted form of synchronic and diachronic temporality into the institutionalized group and explain the presence of the sovereign in such temporality.

The temporality of the Institution and its education has the unique quality of being reducible to the temporality of a single individual. The sovereign temporalizes the group through their reflective determination on both the synchronic and diachronic levels and constitutes all of the temporal relations and experiences in the group with varying degrees of immediacy and mediation. The present, lived, temporal phenomenological experience occurs within the temporal framework established by the sovereign and in accordance with the rhythm of their temporalization. Regarding the diachronic temporalization of the group, it is the result of the present sovereign, as well as the history of sovereignty. And this, as I will show, requires the reinterpretation of Sartre's notion of "microtemporalization," which, in the case of Flaubert, involved his totalizing his era in advance.[2] Here, it is true that a single individual totalizes the temporal process in advance, but rather than a part that is *internal* to it and living it in advance, the sovereign is a peculiar internal-external moment that imposes their own temporality on that of the group. As a result, the objective, historical unification of the group is accomplished by the present sovereign for the other group members on the basis of generations of sovereign unifications.

In order to account for these two levels of time in education, I will provide an analysis of the diachronic relations in the group, emphasizing the look and demands of previous generations, as well as the relations between education and the practico-inert. I will then provide a phenomenological account of the lived-time of education in the teacher and the students, showing how such time, as well as the temporal relations between the teacher and the students, the students among themselves, and between both and the content taught, are mediated to varying degrees by the sovereign. Through an analysis of these two levels of temporality, I will demonstrate the temporalization of passivity and assimilation produced in institutionalized education. Throughout the chapter, I will stress the manner in which such education coheres with, and acquiesces to, the past of the group and its traditions, accepts the group in its present reality, and further cultivates perception while limiting the imagination. Education as a form of passive acceptance, therefore, temporally appears in the group on the basis of the sovereign and their corresponding culture. Temporality, therefore, in its institutionalized, educational dimension, as itself situated within the conditions of need, scarcity, and the practico-inert, necessarily unfolds in accordance with such conditions, harmonizes with them, and perpetuates them in order for their manifestation in an oppressive approach to education to continue.

THE DIACHRONIC TEMPORALIZATION OF INSTITUTIONALIZED EDUCATION

The diachronic temporality of institutionalized education involves the integration and overlapping of several temporalizations which bear upon the unity and identity of the group. As was the case in organized education, the theme of diachronic temporality is intrinsically linked to the question of education across generations within the group. However, in this case, the account of generations is complicated by the presence of the sovereign. Rather than a free unification of past generations brought about through the process of education, a forced unification of the group is realized through the imposition of an educational form both determined by the sovereign and consistent with the history of sovereignty. In this regard, there are generations within generations in the group, that is, generations which can be considered primary because they are determining in their reflection, and generations which can be considered secondary because they are determined by such reflection. There are primary and secondary processes of temporalization in the Institution, and they individually and collectively contribute to its overarching diachronic temporalization. There is the same conflict of generations, the conflict of past forms of education and educational demands, but such conflict is now operative on several levels. The present, sovereign, essential generation conflicts in certain respects with its own past generations, as well as the past and present generations of inessential group members. The present, inessential generation is itself in conflict in various respects with its own past generations, and the past and present of the sovereign.

The generational conflicts introduced here are themselves complicated when taken in relation to the development of the *Critique.* This generational conflict, like this group itself, is a degraded form of what was discussed in part 1, and therefore is in a novel sense in conflict with the prior, free, and non-alienated generational forms in the previous groups. It is in conflict with the previous group forms insofar as it no longer contributes to free individual and collective *praxis*, but rather the establishment of a hierarchy wherein the temporal determination of one part is determinative of the whole. Moreover, this inter- and intra-generational conflict raises the question of the particular educational form of the practico-inert in the institutionalized group. Following the logic of the *Critique*, the practico-inert of the Institution has its origins in the group in fusion, the statutory group, and the Organization. Education is therefore practico-inert concerning these three prior group forms as well as the generations within the Institution itself. Not only is the Institution comprised of prior generations of non-group members, it is also itself a qualitatively different group form insofar as it conflicts with the continuous development of free *praxis* seen in the previous groups. In a dual sense, then, the previous generations of non-group members serve as a condition for the present. As such group members, they are a condition of possibility of their respective groups and the subsequent groups that develop out of them. Their initial condition of possibility of the freedom of the Organization changes sign over the course of the history of groups and becomes a condition of possibility of alienation and ossification. Moreover, as of different educational forms, these past generations are in conflict with the present. They conflict with the previous generations of the Institution and their systems of education insofar as they serve as a basis for the present, degraded system of education.

This account of the multidimensional diachronic temporalization of institutionalized education leads to a corresponding concept of the practico-inert. And this concept is more consistent with the explicit analyses one finds in the *Critique.*[3] In this respect, the practico-inert is understood negatively, as an oppressive weight that dominates the group members. The ossification of past educational *praxis* imposes on the group in such a way that it is weighed down by it and incapable of developing freely. However, the negative weight of the practico-inert weighs differently on the different generations. First, the inertial form of the system of education is meant to benefit the sovereign and to allow it to continue to determine the group. Secondly, it inhibits the genuine educational development of the students and further forces them to conform to the content, expectations, and traditions of education. While it is the case that the practico-inert distorts free *praxis*, ossifying it and returning it in an altered form, in this case the *praxis* of the students requires them to harmonize with the practico-inert education, and to continue and remain consistent with them. In this regard, education as practico-inert has the character of being a burden on the group members and contributes to the imposition of unity on the group accomplished by the sovereign. It is ultimately of dual significance insofar as it is positive for the sovereign, but negative for the other group members. And of course, this concept of "positivity" must be properly understood as benefiting the sovereign, as allowing them to continue to oppress the group.[4] Such a form of the practico-inert continues to serve as the condition of possibility of life in the group for some, and of the impossibility of life for others.

Moreover, this dual status of the practico-inert is further complicated when it is connected to the theme of culture and its demands. With two distinct generations, there are also two sets of cultural demands, and these demands are themselves temporalized differently by each generation individually and in relation to the other. One of them, the temporalization of the sovereign, is primary, dominant, and determining. It is both "microcosmic" and "macrocosmic" insofar as it is the temporalization of a single individual, a peculiar, external, untranscendable part of the whole, and yet the temporalization *of* the group as a whole (Sartre 1993, 407–8). It guides the temporality of the other group members, which, as inessential and secondary, flows in accordance with the standards and culture of the sovereign. As the result of past *praxis*, the culture of the Institution is paradoxically established and maintained by one generation both for itself and the other. Furthermore, these demands need to be reanimated in order to avoid ossifying into the practico-inert. However, in this case, only one side of the group is re-enlivening its culture, and therefore it remains positive for part of it, while weighing negatively on the other. Paradoxically, while reanimated, demands are simultaneously inertial, alienated, and oppressive. The present temporalizing of the past demands by the sovereign results in the free temporalizing of one part of the group and the temporalized-temporalization of the other.

There is, within the Institution, corresponding forms of both "une éducation-faite" and "une education-à-faire" (Sartre 1972, 58). In this case, however, the two forms of generations respond to these aspects of education differently. Concerning the sovereign generation, it inherits the éducation-faite, which was established for its benefit, as a positive, self-serving educational form whose essential characteristics it has the task of maintaining. The education-à-faire, as continuing the educational system already established, requires the sovereign to appropriately blend the past and present for the present, historical moment of the group. The manner in which the Institution diachronically temporalizes itself is accomplished by maintaining a static genesis that prevents an immanent development that would reconfigure the relations between generations. Rather, it is largely preestablished and prescribed by previous generations of sovereignty and subsequently developed as needed by the present sovereign. The present sovereign generation, in personalizing itself in the group, also *personalizes its past* as sovereign in bringing the past educational forms into the present and allowing them to continue to personalize and depersonalize the group. From the point of view of the other group members, however, both the éducation-faite and the éducation-à-faire are determined for them, and do not require any meaningful contribution on their part. To the contrary, their task is to passively accept it, to view the éducation-à-faire of the group as an imperative for what must be done in order for them to become full group members. In so doing, they remain consistent with the tradition of inessential generations of which they are the present incarnation. They do not personalize the past through their education, but rather have such personalization done for them through the sovereign. Thus, their diachronic, educational temporalization is in truth a form of de-temporalization and depersonalization insofar as they continue the tradition of inessentiality to passively accept the education of the present sovereign.

On the basis of their historical primacy in the group, the past generations of sovereignty place corresponding demands on both present generations. They demand that the present sovereign generation continue the educational past of the group, and that the other group members continue to comply with it. From the inessential past there is a demand for its own present generation to remain inessential, and for the present sovereign generation to continue to organize the Institution in accordance with the past and present standards of sovereignty. The present generations therefore bestow upon the past of the group a meaning in the present for the generational duality of the group. As a result, the synchronically treated educational tasks of the previous chapter are diachronically temporalized and the teacher and students now have the responsibility of fulfilling present tasks that are placed on them by past generations. The sovereign past, in placing a burden on the present sovereign, demands that it provide the resources for an educational culture. However, as this culture is split, that entails providing the resources for the depersonalization of the non-sovereign group members. The demands of past sovereign generations are therefore for the depersonalization of the present, non-sovereign group members or, perhaps more generally, a culture of depersonalization. Therefore, the present sovereign generation has the task of enlivening education as a part of its culture in order for the necessary duality of generations and the values, norms, standards, and so on, of the group to be maintained as both positive and negative. The educational response to the imperatives of the Objective Spirit involves the unification of two independent, yet interwoven continua, such that the one generation inherits and imposes the imperative, and the other inherits and submits to it. This demand has the further quality of being mediated for the inessential generation and immediate for the sovereign, insofar as it is implemented for the group as a whole *through* the sovereign generation. As a result, certain group members can only access and fulfill the educational, cultural demands of the past through other members, and not immediately simply as group members inheriting the past of the group.

There is a further element embedded in the relation of the educational demands of the past to the present. The past *praxis* of the group, in its solidity, in its inscription in the in-itself, condenses into *a single*, *collective look* that objectifies the different group members in distinct ways. Moreover, in placing demands in relation to the two present generations, the past sovereign generation has the significance of a regulating third party whose look continues to bear upon and objectify the present.[5] This look, however, does not establish the present plurality of individuals of the sovereign generation as an "us-object," as a unity which can sustain itself through an objectifying look, but rather as part of its "we," as the modern incarnation and culmination of past, sovereign generations with which it is continuous (Sartre 1984, 537).[6] As a past third with a dual look, the sovereign past of the group as a demand objectifies the two generations, the two sides, and demands that they fulfill their educational tasks in accordance with their role in the group. In this sense, the look of the past as a demand is a transcendental condition for the education of the present. And yet, paradoxically, this condition is itself fulfilled and completed by the sovereign generation taking over its past and personalizing it in order to develop it as needed to preserve the Institution as it was. Even in "surpassing" its past forms, the emphasis is on the continuity with them insofar as the Institution is concerned with harmonizing with them, the practico-inert in its dual significance, and the traditional culture of the group.

Regarding the development of the *Critique*, there are several points concerning the look of past groups that need to be addressed. The previous groups do not all look at the Institution in the same way, as the group in fusion and the statutory group looked at the Organization.[7] Although they are their own respective groups with their own structures, cultures, and histories, the group in fusion and the statutory group both look at the Organization as a continuation of individual and collective freedom. As a degraded Organization and therefore having its roots in freedom, the Institution attempts to block the looks of the previous groups as they are part of a tradition of the development of freedom in groups. Moreover, the previous groups place a burden of freedom on the Organization to provide a form of education that will promote individual and collective freedom and resistance. Accordingly, in blocking such looks, the Institution alters and distorts the ultimate educational demand that is placed on it by previous generations in previous group forms. It therefore creates its own academic demand, its own academic culture, but one that is at odds with the previous demands and cultures of the previous groups and consistent with those of the history of the institutionalized group. In recognizing the meaning of the previous looks, it attempts to either conceal its origins in freedom through its educational apparatus or culture to continue to function as an Institution, or to create the illusion of the fulfillment of the demands of freedom established by prior group forms.

In the case of the Institution, there is only a single look that is valued, namely, that of the previous generations within the Institution itself. The individual generations of the Institution bestow their own looks on the present, and do so in accordance with their generational form. However, the looks of the past sovereign generations, whose individual looks place an identical demand on the present, coalesce into a single, collective look of the past which dominates the looks of the previous, inessential generations and their unification. The look, then, which demands that the present maintain the hierarchy and established order of the group is the only one that is valued and maintains a meaningful presence in the group. Thus, the identity of the look of the Institution is exclusive of any difference, a homogenizing look, and a look which is ultimately a personalization which also depersonalizes the group. As a result of such a dominating look, there is a priority of the diachronic temporalization of one past generation, of one temporalizing demand, and therefore of one educational form over all others. The diachronic temporalization of the look of the past sovereign generations represses the diachronic temporalization of the looks of the previous group forms, and consequently represses an open, free, and creative temporality for the sake of an imposed, sovereign, and linear temporal development. The temporality of sovereignty, it follows, represses both the temporality of past group forms and that of the non-sovereign generations within the Institution itself.

On the basis of this situation concerning generations, it is necessary to newly raise and pose the question of how the educational demands of the past can be integrated into the present of the group. Is it the case that the transition between past and present generations is smooth, that there is a seamless transition from one generation to another within the Institution? Is it not rather the case that, regardless of any consistency across the diachrony of the group, there is also discontinuity, or potentially inconsistent, if not inassimilable, elements? The diachronic flow of the group involves multidimensional conflicts and discontinuities as much as it establishes a multidimensional continuum. As much as the various past appear in the group through education and their respective demands, they do not all do so in the same way, either within a single generation or across all of them (Sartre 2004a, 54). Such generational relations involve the manner in which the demands of the past and present are incarnated in the group through the material taught, the various subjects, the teaching style and methods, and so on.[8] Each of these themes can serve as a point of departure, as a transitional point between past and present, and therefore as a point of both continuity and discontinuity, unity and conflict, that serves as a basis for the present and future life in the group. There is a necessary development of education across generations, but such development of the the meaning of a certain content taught may not be perfectly continuous, and may even involve various forms of conflict. And this conflict has the aim of preserving the freedom of some, and the oppression of others. It is therefore a modification of the whole of the group by a part and the conflict is predominantly between the generations of sovereignty, their respective views on education, and the needs of the group. There may be a form or degree of conflict with the inessential generation, or within the inessential generation itself, but insofar as it does not meaningfully contribute to the modification of the group, such conflict is secondary and ultimately inconsequential.

In addition, part of what it means to modify the group and the system of education as needed is to appropriately cultivate perception and instrumentalize the imagination. Thus, while certain of the demands of the past are constant, and the present responds by continuing them, the methods of teaching, the manner in which the content is presented, and the very meaning of what it is to perceive and to imagine can alter across generations. This reconsideration of what it means to educate the present group members is part of the way in which the present looks back at the past, objectifies it, sees it as a point of departure and modifies it as needed. There is, furthermore, a dual look backward. The look of the sovereign generation is continuous with the look of the past. Though there may be conflict and discontinuity, in objectifying the sovereign past that objectifies it, it maintains the demands and form of the group established by the previous generations. It is therefore a reciprocal look. The inessential generation also looks back. Their objectifying look, however, is secondary and inconsequential, coincides with the look of the sovereign, and serves to continue the culture of sovereignty and its history. Within the diachronic present of the group, there is therefore a synchronic plurality of looks, each of which is in conflict with others in varying respects, has a different significance within the group, and establishes a peculiar dialogue in which the look and modification accomplished by the present sovereign are dominant.

The relations of diachrony and synchrony established through the look lead to the question of how past generations relate to the teacher and the students. At this point, and expanding on the analyses of chapter 4, one can ask: How do the teacher and the students keep the past generations in the present of the group? How do they personalize, and therefore depersonalize, the history of the group? How does the synchronic temporalization of the teacher and the students relate to the diachronic temporalization of the group whose direction and orientation are determined by the reflection of the sovereign? In general, the process of educational inheritance and personalization is twofold insofar as it serves one generation while oppressing the other. Both the teacher and the students inherit the traditions of the past differently, but again the situation is made more complicated by the presence of the sovereign. The teacher, in this case inheriting a history that is in part blocked, is in truth not so much in several groups at once, *as in several generations at once.* The teacher belongs to their own generation, in many ways now past, that of the students, and in a peculiar, incomplete sense, to that of the sovereign. The teacher contributes to the self-understanding of the present as a group member who is both past and present. However, the present they help articulate is that of the sovereign. The present historical moment of the group that they are a part of, and that their synchronic temporalization belongs to, is that of the sovereign and their generation, reinforcing and continuing the inessentiality of the non-sovereign generation for the temporalization of the group.

The institutionalized teacher is caught in an additional transcendence-immanence tension insofar as their education is specific to a previous generation, they have been personalized as depersonalized accordingly, and continue various traditions of the past in the present. They are transcendent to the present generation as partially belonging to the past, their own generation as partially belonging to the present, yet immanent to the overarching temporalization of the transcendent sovereign whose transcendence they cannot surpass. They are therefore a third between past and present generations, as well as present generations themselves, making them both transcendent and immanent in various ways to all of the generations. They are, through the will of the sovereign, a partially transcendent element to the present generation who serves as a condition of possibility of their future life in the group. The teacher condenses the diachronic temporalization of the past of the group through their unique role and therefore keeps it present. Thus, the teacher only properly belongs to "half" of the group they are responsible for articulating and handing down to subsequent generations. They are a paradoxical sign which is both collective and individual, a historical sign of the collective past *but this past is split in both the generations and their respective temporalizations.* The past continues to totalize itself through the teacher and the education of the students, and aims to do so as seamlessly as possible by ensuring that any personalization of the teacher remains a form of depersonalization and any pedagogical developments remain consistent with the structure and sovereign demands of the group. Of course, to an extent this depends on the age of the teacher in that they may belong to the generation of the "older brothers" or the more distant past, but regardless of the distance from the present, they are in an unstable position insofar as they articulate a group to whose generations they partially belong in various ways (Sartre 1993, 33).

The teacher, in their generational status within the group, is a diachronic-synchronic third regulating the relations between the diachronic and synchronic generations through their teaching. And it is here that the look of the teacher takes on particular significance, insofar as they constitute the relations between the various generations through their objectifying, that is, institutionalizing, look. The inter-generational look of the teacher unifies the multidimensional continuum of the group. However, the look of the teacher is not wholly present insofar as they can only look at the students from the perspective of their own, past generation. Their look is therefore a dual past-present look which can never be wholly present insofar as it is necessarily infused with a past dimension. In linking the generations, in recognizing the students as group members who will never be capable of being fully integrated into the group as sovereign group members, the teacher creates the educational present of the group and the students and yet is necessarily at a distance from it. They create a temporal present to which they do not belong insofar as it is the present of the students. The temporal objectification of the look of the teacher is therefore that of the sovereign who continues to determine the direction of the temporalization of the group through their presence and reflection. The look of the teacher is historicizing, temporally placing the students in the group in their relation to previous generations, but the truth of this historicizing look is the transcendent sovereign.

The synthetic look of the teacher, as a correlate to the depth of their own life, inscribes the lives of the students in the past of the group, but does so by simultaneously bringing them into the group, determining them in their generational character, and cutting them off from the rest of the group, the sovereign generation, and by extension the group itself. The temporal depth of the students' lives itself only partially belongs to "half" of the past of the group. They do not, and in principle cannot, fully belong to the past of the culture and group of which they are in the process of becoming members. And all of the relations of knowledge and ignorance, of the material taught, and of the students to the educational apparatus, are accordingly temporalized insofar as they are explicitly placed in relation to the past and present life of the group. Through their temporalizing look and pedagogy, the teacher allows the group to maintain its identity across any generational differences. The demands of the past generations are fulfilled in the present by the teacher as a present-past group member who maintains the identity of the group through their individual-collective temporalization. It is such temporalization that allows the past of the group to appear in the present of education. The diachronic temporality of the group, itself split into a single temporalization of two generations, reaches its limit in a present which continues the separation of generations but involves a discontinuity in the present forms of education. The teacher therefore stands as a unique member of the group who both serves as a continuous synthesis of the multiplicity of inter- and intra-generational temporalizations which serve as a condition for the present and, through their teaching, hands down the inherited temporality, its rhythms, and the knowledge of the group to the students.

As themselves inheritors of the past of the group, what is the relation between the students and its diachronic temporalization? The students, as in the process of becoming group members, as a blend of belonging and not belonging to the group, inherit the previous generational demands and imperatives in a number of different ways. And they do so as the complementary opposite of the teacher, as group members who are grounded in the present, will be future group members, and will continue to move into the future and therefore farther away from the prior and subsequent generations. The teacher, on the other hand, is grounded in the past, part of the present, and will continue to move into the past as the group moves into the future. Moreover, as in the process of becoming group members, their diachronic place in the group and their synchronic temporalization are still indeterminate and to be filled out. They have not yet been fully diachronically personalized as depersonalized, and are in the process of becoming depersonalized group members continuous with the past of depersonalized generations and thus incapable of becoming full group members. The diachronic demand to become educated is ultimately a demand to become inessential, to continue the history and tradition of inessentiality, and to passively accept both what is taught and their place in the group.

The students are accordingly before and after the group. They are before the group insofar as they have not yet entered it, and will continue to fashion it after doing so. However, as inheritors of the group, they come after it, and will continue it as they develop it in the future. The look of the past makes them such continuous-discontinuous group members, and their future action in the group is both an extension and completion of the look of the past. As discussed earlier, this past look situates them in the present, and as a result, given their place in the group, they become historical thirds of the present moment who temporally totalize their academic relations to one another, yet are not fully regulating thirds insofar as they are not yet full group members. This past, historical look, however, also makes their status as thirds possible, establishes the variety of temporal relations in education, temporalizes the process and, as I will show in the next section, the content taught, and further makes their own present, generational look possible. They become institutionalized group members in part because of this look from the past, and as a plurality of generational, individual looks themselves, derivatively temporalize the relations between the sovereign and non-sovereign generations, the teacher, the past and present, and the material taught. This present, backward-facing look continues the diachronic temporalizing look from the side of the present and continues to ascribe a temporal location to the past generations in the present. Despite their incomplete character, the students are necessary thirds who continue to articulate the diachronic process of the group in their synchronic totalization. As initially and continuously brought into the group by the look of the past, they continue to bring the past into the present through their present look. The original temporal look of the past serves as a sketch of the educational life of the students as well as their future life in the group, and the reciprocated look toward the past further makes possible the fulfillment of the diachronic demand placed on them. The students as partial thirds help keep the past of education present. Their synchronic educational process therefore personalizes the sovereign diachronic relations and depersonalizes the non-sovereign diachronic relations of the group. The students are able to do so by recognizing the diachronic temporalization of the group as the necessary, continuously present transcendental condition for their education and life in the group.

THE SYNCHRONIC TEMPORALIZATION OF INSTITUTIONALIZED EDUCATION

The analysis of the diachronic temporality of education has led to the question of the synchronic lived-temporality of education in the present. The previous analyses accounted for the manner in which institutionalized education temporalizes itself across the different generations in the group, while also acknowledging the synchronic component of such temporalization. Moreover, I emphasized that such "objective" time was determined by the sovereign, and that their individual temporalization served to temporalize the other group members and education in general. On the basis of such a single temporalization, one can now ask how the microtemporalization of the sovereign determines the lived-experience of the temporality of education for both the teacher and the students. In the following section, I will provide an eidetic analysis of the lived-time of the teacher in the institutionalized group. I will show the manner in which the presence of the sovereign makes their temporalization a de-temporalization in a manner analogous to that in which I showed that personalization is a form of depersonalization.

As discussed in the previous section, the teacher is in several generations at once and inherits the diachronic, educational demand from the past generations of the group. In their lived-teaching, however, one may wonder: How does their multigenerational status bear upon the act of teaching? The teacher is in several generations at once, and therefore both symbolizes and synthesizes multiple temporalities and their rhythms in their teaching. Concerning their synchronic temporalization, the teacher has the paradoxical, twofold demand of cohering with the practico-inert, need, scarcity, and the additional aspects that led to the particular, present historical form of the group, but also of adapting them to maintain them in the present. The temporal weight of the practico-inert therefore guides the teacher in the act of teaching in its negative significance. However, as needing to be developed and extended, the practico-inert does not have the positive significance it did in committed education. It now takes on a third form that is ultimately negative, but makes use of certain parts of its "positive character" as well, above all its ability to serve as a point of departure. The teacher, then, caught between multiple temporalizations and forms of the practico-inert, is in a multidimensional temporal tension in which they have to consistently maintain and develop. Moreover, as subject to the will of the sovereign, the teacher's temporalization of the academic content has to harmonize with them as well. The teacher continues the traditions of the sovereign and non-sovereign generations in their teaching, temporalizing the content in accordance with the dominant temporalization of the one, and the dominated temporalization of the other. They present the content in its present and historical significance in such a way that it preserves the rhythms, forms, and methods of the previous generations in order to maintain the structure and hierarchy of the group.

However, in addition to being caught between the various pasts of the group, the teacher is also caught between various futures. In a sense, they are caught between the character of the temporalization of past generations and future generations, that is, their rhythms, rate, relation to the other aspects of the group, and so on.[9] They are also in a tension with the future of a generation that has not yet been fully integrated into the group. The future is further complicated insofar as it too is dominated by the sovereign past. The future of the group that the teacher stands before is that of a future-past which will be continuous with the past history of the group. "It *is* already" (Sartre 1984, 230). The educational future of the group is an extension of, in certain respects a repetition of, its educational past. The teacher is therefore caught between a past-future and a future-past, or an identity of pasts and futures in both the future and the past. The teacher begins and carries out the present act of teaching as a synthesis and tension of synchronic and diachronic temporalizations with significance for the present. Again, as in committed education, the teacher inherits a cultural and temporal rhythm from the past of the group. However, in this case, they inherit cultural and temporal rhythms from two distinct generations, which serve to comprise the temporality and culture of the group as a whole. As such, the eidetic structure of the temporalization of the teacher is comprised by a tension between a plurality of pasts and futures to which they do not fully belong, which they are responsible for enlivening and making possible, and depersonalizes their own temporalization in reducing it to that of sovereignty.

As discussed in chapter 2, each previous generation and group had its own rhythm toward its long-term goals, its immediate concerns, and so on. The Institution, however, is unique in a few respects. First, it inherits previous generational rhythms, but attempts to block the rhythms, as well as the values, educational content, and so on, of the previous, free and liberating groups. Whereas previously there was openness to the development of the rhythms of the different group forms, here the previous, non-alienated group forms and their rhythms are blocked from entering and affecting the Institution. The institutionalized group therefore inherits rhythms from past generations, but not from past groups. The collective rhythm of the group, first determined by the sovereign, and implemented by the teacher, determines the manner in which the students are temporally oriented toward their academic tasks and functions. The teacher has to find the correct way to introduce such a rhythm to the present generation of the students. In so doing, the teacher *brackets time itself to impose one form of time while excluding all others*. The temporal bracketing of the institutionalized teacher, as part of the establishing of the necessary temporal atmosphere, necessarily excludes previous and possible temporalizations that will conflict with that of the group. In order for temporality as a form of de-temporality to appear in education, it is necessary for the teacher to implement an exclusionary suspension which is the single and necessary transcendental condition of the de-temporalization of education. Therefore, as depersonalized, the teacher continues the educational traditions of the past, not only regarding the images produced, or the material of a particular subject, but also regarding the very process of temporalization. The teacher accordingly re-temporalizes past content, establishes an appropriate temporal context, and in so doing re-temporalizes past generations in bringing them into the present to guide it. In this regard, the images created, the speed of the lesson, the time for questions, and so on, will all contribute to the internalization of the temporal rhythm necessary for the group. And again, these aspects are already been predetermined and pre-temporalized by the present and past of sovereignty.[10] The synchronic act of teaching is therefore itself multidimensional insofar as it is a single, polythetic, temporal act of a single teacher layered with the temporalizations of past teachers, generations, and the sovereign.

The teacher's approach to teaching, the manner in which they present the material taught and respond to the students, accords with the sovereign's demand that they present content as complete and to be absorbed. In this regard, the act of teaching and the educational process it gives rise to establish a linear and mechanical temporal rhythm. The teacher presents content as complete, the students passively accept it as such, and the temporal process of perception and the restricted imagination continue throughout the educational process with an emphasis on immediacy and efficiency. It is defined by the rigid, "empty form before-after" (Sartre 1984, 236).[11] In a given lesson, there is a series of content provided, specific to the subject, age of the students, and so on, which leads to an uninterrupted succession of necessary content and serves as a basis for what will come later in the particular course, the subsequent stages of education, and ultimately the future life of the students. There is a preestablished amount of time allotted to each subject, lesson, unit, and so on, and once the given requirements for the subject have been met, the class then moves on to the next topic, which is then completed in the same way, and so on. The mechanism of this time comes from the lack, if not the total absence of, spontaneity, the predictability of the process, and the manner in which the material is presented and received. The rhythm of teaching is a continuous, linear temporalization of the presentation of content in an atmosphere wherein it is passively absorbed.

The time of institutionalized education, concerning the contribution of both the teacher and the students, is also discontinuous. It is continuously created by the teacher in the teaching of certain content, of bits of information with preestablished, institutionalized relations and meanings, and begins and ends with such content. The discrete character of the lessons corresponds to and helps create a discontinuous, linear, and mechanical form of time. And, paradoxically, the discontinuity of the pedagogy of the teacher constitutes the continuity of the lesson and the expectations of the students. Each portion of the content presented follows necessarily from the previous stage and leads into the next, with an internal necessity that excludes variation in the rhythm of its presentation and unique engagement with it by the students. In a further, paradoxical sense, in simply *letting the content be*, allowing it to present itself as it has been determined by the group, the necessity of the form and content of the act of teaching confines it within a foreign, external temporal order. Together, both the temporalization of the presentation and its content form the contradictory unity of a *discrete continuum*, one wherein time itself is shattered in order for the academic content to be absorbed as a unitary whole with a single meaning.

The qualities of linearity, mechanism, and discontinuity lead to the temporal repetition unique to institutionalized education. The temporalization of the teacher and the content is always experienced in the same way, with the same expectations, as part of the same educational process of the individual class and the system of education as a whole. The form of the presentation of content, the expectations of the teacher and the students, and the very experience of time itself continuously comprise a process of repetition. The lived-temporal rhythm of education is therefore a continuous, successive series of repetition which, while experienced diffferently in certain respects with the age of the students, particular class, and subject-matter, continues to repeat as familiar, accepted, and predictable. Of course, the content in the process of being taught is new to the students, *but the temporality of education is not.* Regardless of the novelty of the content or subject-matter, the temporalization proper to education is a priori understood and familiar, and therefore the students continue to assimilate themselves throughout the process of education on the basis of their previous, pre-delineated and constantly pre-delineating experiences. In institutionalized education, it is as if *time itself has grown old*, is nothing but "more of the same," a peculiar linear process which has always already reached its end. The interweaving of discontinuity and repetition constitutes this form of temporality as a process of growth which has already grown old and in which its very experience is dated. The rhythm of education is therefore temporalized in advance by the teacher, received, and ultimately experienced as such by the students.

And yet, the linearity of this process is further complicated when the theme of past generations is taken into account. As I mentioned, the teacher is a multigenerational temporalization. As such, the future is itself a further repetition of the process insofar as it is continuous with the past sovereign generations across the present. The teacher therefore teaches the present for a future which is already past, for a future of the group that coincides with its past. As a result, the repetitive dimension of the linearity of time also has a cyclical character as the past generations are continuously brought back into the present from the past as the group progresses for the sake of a particular future-past. The temporal continuum of education is further layered in this regard and the repetition of time is in part a product of constantly bringing the past back into the present and concomitantly determining the future so that both can remain past. The future itself is therefore already old in being predetermined by the past sovereign generations of the group. The synchronic temporalization of the teacher, as comprised of a synthesis of rhythms, involves the recognition of the need and application of the traditional educational rhythms of the group. As discussed in the previous section, this all occurs within the overarching diachronic temporalization of the group, and the present act of teaching is dominated by the past.[12] The teacher accordingly needs to comprehend the rhythm of the culture of the Institution in the present and, with whatever minimal differences might exist in comparison with past generations, determine how best to instill the necessary rhythms for the students to complete their present tasks as students and their future tasks as future group members.

A few additional points need to be recognized here. First, as much as possible, the teacher attempts to maintain the educational rhythms of the past in the present. There is, in this case, a peculiar coincidence in the synchronic and the diachronic in the continuity of temporal educational rhythms across the different generations in the group. Secondly, and as a complement to this point, the teacher represses any genuine, spontaneous, and freely developed rhythm on the part of the students individually and collectively. The unique temporalization of the material presented and the possibility of a free, collective temporalization is repressed, that is, de-temporalized and "de-rhythmic" insofar as it prevents a spontaneous and unique rhythmic connection to the material and imposes a single temporal rhythm and orientation. The linear temporal continuum is therefore a way of preventing a rhythm and temporalization that could in any way problematize, threaten, or ultimately destabilize the hierarchical order of the group. In contrast to committed education, then, different developments of culture, such as that of technology, are used to preserve, as much as possible, the previous temporal rate of the group. The lessons will accordingly be taught in such a way that the absorption of the content coheres with the traditional models of education. The relation of the content to the present, as past, will keep both the content and present past, and the teacher will make use of whatever technology and media will serve to ensure this. In addition to the content of the lesson, a particular orientation toward the content is itself learned and internalized. For example, referencing reading a text, as much as possible, the methods used in accessing it and the expectations of the students will coincide with those of the past. The way in which material was traditionally introduced, with the content that was presented and emphasized, will temporally coincide. The process, for example, of explaining a concept, a historical event, engaging a text, and so on, will preserve as much as possible the form and content of previous education. Again, there may be minimal differences or adjustments to be made, but the act of reading, the manner of relating to and interpreting a text, will cohere with past traditions, and continue to ossify the group over the course of its education.

The analysis of the temporal rhythm of institutionalized education further leads to the questions of the relation between temporality and the transcendence-immanence tension specific to this form of education as well as that between temporality and knowledge. The teacher, through their knowledge, is transcendent to the collection of students they help constitute and at a necessary distance from it. However, as part of the process of education, regardless of how minimal, they are part of the immanence of the group of students. Moreover, as a present member of the group, the teacher has a unique, dual past. As part of the past of the group, and one way in which it is inherited, the act of teaching itself is connected with its own immediate, lived, temporal past as well as that of previous generations. It is therefore a single act with a dual past insofar as it is continuous with the subjective past of teaching and the objective past of the group. And each dimension bears upon the teacher's synchronic temporalization in different ways. The diachronic temporalization sets the stage for the synchronic act of teaching. The latter, however, continues to contextualize, inform, and constitute the present educational experience. The lived-time of teaching has its own past specific to the lesson for the day, the portion of the lecture already delivered, and even of the previous semester or previous period of education insofar as it directly relates to the immediate experience of education. The past of the act of teaching, it follows, is immediately continuous with the lived educational time of teaching and mediately continuous with its historical basis. And as part of the temporalization of the present sovereign and the past sovereign generations, *the past of the teacher is not properly their own.* Rather, it is its *own past as other*, an incarnation of the life of past generations and the present sovereign. In its synchronic temporalization, therefore, the teacher is constituted, weighed down, and directed by the totality of sovereignty in its temporalization.

There is an additional component part of the temporal context that needs to be addressed, namely, that of the objective aspect of the lived-time of the educational process. The teacher is forced to temporalize themselves and the content while creating a temporal atmosphere in accordance with the objective temporal framework established by the sovereign. This bears upon the duration of each stage of education, the amount of time spent on the different subjects, units, the time allotted to assignments, as well as the amount of time the teacher can devote to a certain topic in the classroom. The temporality of the teacher, it follows, is regulated by the sovereign as a present-absent third. The latter prescribes a priori limits to teaching that by definition exclude spontaneity, for example, an educational temporalization of the content based on the interest of the students, the various responses to questions posed by the teacher, and so on. There is a set length to each aspect of the process, and in this regard, education is *pre*-temporalized. This varies in certain respects with the level of education, subject-matter, and so on, but rather than serving as a point of departure, the temporal limits on education constrict the process. The teacher is not guided by the content, or the dialogue with the students, but by the temporal order imposed by the sovereign. There is a certain, "correct" amount of time necessary to internalize the academic content, to take from it and the lesson what is necessary for the group, and to incorporate it into future lessons. Their lived-time is in truth that of the sovereign, and the time of education in all of its aspects begins and ends with the latter. The objective time imposed is meant to eliminate or repress the subjective temporality of the teacher and the students, and to replace it, in the corresponding, necessary manner, with the time allotted by the sovereign to the educational process and its different aspects. There is a single temporalization of the group, but, in a sense, it splits up into the different stages and aspects of education, determining their limits, the content, and the manner in which it is understood. These limits, moreover, ensure that the institutionalized teacher fulfills their function as needed. The manipulation and rigid determination of time have the additional aspect of forcing the teacher to continue to reinforce their depersonalization by ruling out any part of their teaching that does not cohere with the a priori requirements of institutionalized temporality.

THE SERIALIZED TEMPORALIZATION OF INSTITUTIONALIZED EDUCATION

The analyses carried out thus far have focused on the manner in which the teacher and the sovereign temporalize the process of education. However, the students also temporalize education synchronously and live through the sovereign's determination of the temporalization of education. What, one may ask, is the student's lived temporal relation to truth and knowledge, the teacher, and one another? The teacher, as the realization of the will of the sovereign, begins the temporal process of education for the students. To begin, then, the students are dependent upon the establishment of a temporal context by the teacher. Their temporalization, understood both individually and collectively, is dependent on this context, but also on how the teacher temporalizes the content and the process of teaching through the act of teaching. The depersonalization of the students in their lived, educational temporality, begins with the depersonalization of the teacher and the manner in which they continue it through their teaching. Initially, then, the students' contribution to the lived-time of education is simply to accept the temporal framework the teacher has established and their temporalization of the content. Their relation to time is therefore passive, it is received, as is the manner in which they continue and live through it. Both the temporal rate of the process of education and the way in which they are oriented toward it are entirely determined for them.

The entire temporal experience of the students, from the beginning of the temporal process in the classroom, involves a unique form of the transcendence-immanence tension. They are not full, temporalizing members of the group insofar as they have not yet been fully integrated into it. They are, however, "before" the temporality of the group concerning its different generations, and therefore stand before the split time of the group, though they will only be integrated into one of them. Their tension therefore inheres in their relation to the different, past generations in the group, as well as the corresponding forms of these generations to come in the future. They are accordingly transcendent to multiple pasts and multiple futures as they remain in the immanence of the educational process. Concerning the group as a whole, in its diachronic temporalization, they are "after" the one side of it, and "before" the other. The students form a temporally ambiguous, presently historicizing generation which lives its inheritance through the content taught as it orients itself toward its future life in the group. They are both transcendent and immanent, outside of the temporalization of the group as they are brought into it, and within the temporalization of the group as they transcend it to become group members.[13] They are, moreover, building their relation to the past insofar as the content taught meaningfully connects them to it. Their immanence-transcendence tension involves them being between several different generations in the group, as not yet fully belonging to one or many, and is the lived-tension of the present as both inheriting the past and being directed toward the future.

On the basis of this ambiguity, the students have an unstable and indeterminate temporal location in the group. Their tasks and functions as students, however, begin to ascribe them an educational place in the group, and this continues to develop as they absorb the necessary academic content and temporal rhythms. Their passive totalization, in other words, continues to bring them into the group across the lived-time of education. And this passivity, which begins with the act of the teacher, is followed by the inheritance of the past. In this process, however, each student individualizes in an identical way, that is, simultaneously both individually and collectively, the past of the group. The material presented, in this regard, situates them in the history of the group. As such, it makes the immediately lived present continuous with the past, or the synchronic present continuous with the diachronic past. The retention of the student, in living through the experience of education, in its temporal significance in the group on the basis of the content immediately taught, opens them to the past that made the present possible. As of yet, the students do not have a temporal, educational or, more generally, a generational rhythm. Their passive orientation to their education and the group begins to address this and leads to the internalization of the rhythm necessary for the group. The temporal orientation toward truth and knowledge instilled in the students is, in a paradoxical sense, static, insofar as the content is presented as complete, the students absorb it as such, and then move on to the next topic, lesson, and so on, as part of the linear, predictable continuum.

There is a further factor which serves to orient the temporal experience of the students, and this involves the temporality of the object of knowledge. There is no recognition and appreciation of the intrinsic temporality of the subject studied.[14] There is, it follows, a single, predetermined temporal experience for the students which correlates to the time imposed on and by the educational object as well as the teacher's act of teaching. The rate of the educational process is therefore in part developed by virtue of the temporality imposed on the educational object. And this rate, the manner in which the future is continuously realized in the present, does not adapt itself to the unique character of the object. Rather, the object and its temporality are standardized. There must, however, be a minimal recognition of it, insofar as the time allotted to it has its roots in a particular understanding of it. This understanding, however, based on a certain study of the object and sanctioned by the sovereign, ultimately neglects and represses the object, and reduces it to its educational appearance. Not only, then, is "*esse percipi*," but essence is what is a temporalized *percipi* (Sartre 1984, 9). As a result, there is a particular adequation, in truth an "equality," between the object studied and the temporal process of studying it, insofar as *the object as studied* is reducible to the knowledge of it.[15] Its being is mere appearance because the latter is the sanctioned knowledge of it. The rate, again, is not that intrinsic to the object, but rather a result of the imposition of an objective order onto the educational object which corresponds to the sanctioned, objective time of the educational process itself. The rate of the temporalization of education is therefore imposed on the students, and while ultimately a result of the reflective determination of the sovereign, is immediately experienced through the teacher's pedagogical acts and the manner in which they integrate the imposed temporality of the object into the lived, temporal experience of education. Thus there is a distorted *temporal equality*, but not a *temporal adequation* between the teacher, students, and the object studied.

In addition to the temporal relations established by the teacher and the object of study, the students also form temporal relations among themselves in the classroom. How, exactly, in light of all the restrictions on them, do they do so? The students are isolated in their temporal experience in the classroom. However, as passively involved in the process of education, in the absorption of content, they passively constitute the other students as educational thirds. They isolate the other students in their academic experience, and yet this isolation does not allow for each student to uniquely engage with the material, but rather for each student to internalize the content in the same way as all the others. There is, it follows, a plurality of individual temporalizations, which are isolated and identical and which, as the temporalizations of third parties, continue and reinforce the seriality of education. The students as temporalizing thirds regulate one another by locking each other in place and prevent the emergence of a creative and unique temporalization by continuing to impose the temporality of the sovereign, the teacher, and the object. As such, the students regulate the *de-temporalization* of education by regulating each other in such a way that the passivity necessary for this form of education is maintained. As a result, the process that begins with the teacher is continued by the students in their perpetuation of the passivity of the group. They form a collective temporal process of serialized, isolated, and passive temporality constituted through their passive totalization as regulating thirds. There is, it follows, a plurality of de-temporalizations subordinate to an overarching temporalization in which the students form a false unity. Again, the isolated character of this temporal experience makes it identical to all others, as a kind of collective, but one whose collective temporality is isolated and fragmented. Everyone is therefore totalized as not belonging to the process of which they are a part and as absorbing content they have no part in creating.

Throughout this process, there is, paradoxically, both a plurality and a singularity of the temporal dimensions, an overlapping and coincidence in the isolated temporalizations. The past of each student is lived by each student, but to the extent that all of the pasts are determined by the temporal rhythm and content of teaching, they form a collective, homogenous past. The past of each student is that of the individual student and all the others, identical in its rhythm, orientation, and content in forming the past of the particular student. The plurality of pasts constitutes a single past whose different elements are intrinsically separate and externally related. The life of education in the group is temporally lived by each student as the same as all others. Each past is therefore its own and that of the Other, and the collective past is the past of the Other as the students' own. The orientation toward the object, it follows, and the temporality of the educational object, cannot themselves serve as points of unification insofar as the orientation of each student is defined by isolation and seriality. The students cannot, in other words, form a unity in being directed toward the same object because they do so in isolation and continue to impose this isolation through their totalizations as regulating thirds. The same is the case for the present insofar as the lived-present is that of each student and all others, situated within the temporality of the teacher, and isolated as the same in being lived through. The temporalization of the students is therefore defined by an a priori coincidence and non-coincidence, an impersonal, collective isolation.

Despite the overlapping and separation of all three temporal dimensions, the future has a particularly significant status. It too is collective and individualized insofar as the future of each student is reduced to that of the class. As such, and as part of a linear continuum, it is determined in advance, a priori determinable and accessible, and therefore a form of repetition. As I discussed earlier, it is already old. The future of the teacher, it follows, in their teaching, presentation of content, and so on, prescribes the future of the students, and therefore how and when they will achieve the truth of the lesson. The future is determined by the teacher as well as the individual and collective passivity of the students, and is ultimately a truth that they are directed toward without their active involvement. In its lived-experience, the future is given in advance and received by the students, and as a result is not their future, but that of the teacher, the sovereign, and the group. Whether related to the immediate future of a lesson presently underway, the next class, or more distant topics and assignments, the future belongs to the group and is inherited by the students. It accordingly has a peculiar immanence insofar as it *is* already. The only somewhat indeterminate aspect of the future is the content to be taught, but the form is already given, and with the process already established and the content rigidly determined in accordance with the standards and culture of the Institution, it is itself largely determined.

The isolated, collective orientation toward the future is simply the reverse of the past.[16] The students are therefore wholly immanent to the process, and wholly transcendent to one another, regulating each other as the temporality of the teacher directs them and their temporal experience to the future. And again, as such, they form a quasi-collective transcendence toward the future insofar as they are directed beyond the present to the content to be passively accepted as true. Reduced to the educational process, the truth of their individual futures is that of the collective. Their immanence-transcendence tension is in part absorbed by the educational process insofar as their synchronically lived-time is determined by the teacher, and in part heightened insofar as they are transcendent to each other in their isolation. And this immanence-transcendence tension is complicated by the fact that the truth of their temporal experience of each temporal dimension is that of the collective. In their individual-collective temporal orientation, the students further contribute to the determinate and predictable process of education. There is an absolute reciprocity insofar as the students can only mediate and regulate each other in accordance with the demands of the group, and a corresponding lack of reciprocity, that is, a limited, restricted reciprocity in the relation between the teacher and the students. The students reflect one another in their reciprocal isolation as a collective of harmoniously related disparate elements. In contrast with committed education, what this absolute reciprocity gives rise to is an absence of conflict in the group, an absence of asymmetry, which is a result of, and continues to contribute to, the oppression of the students. The absence of conflict in this case is due to the passivity and acceptance of the established order, of the culture of education, and of the isolation and seriality of the students. The individual temporalizations of the students do not conflict, their lived-relations to the content do not involve a conflict of rhythms, but rather the passive and ingrained temporal orientations lead to their harmonious functioning. The preestablished harmony of the group, as a condition for the absence of conflict, is also a condition for the oppression of the students. There is, therefore, a collective temporalization as de-temporalization of the content, the individual student, their relation to the other students, and to education in general.

NOTES

1. For the complete analysis, see Sartre (1984, 223–37).
2. See Sartre (1993, 406–10), and Sartre (1972, 440–43). Also see Barnes (1981, 290).
3. See, for example, Aronson (1980, 258–63). For a negative account of the practico-inert and its relation to education see Papastephanou (2009, 451–70). Also see the analyses in chapter 2, pp. 4–5.
4. In truth, the "positive" character of the practico-inert for the sovereign is also negative insofar as it maintains the structures of oppression in the group. As such, it needs to be kept distinct from the genuinely positive character of the practico-inert I discussed in part 1, wherein it served as a basis for the freedom and imagination of the group.
5. The non-sovereign, inessential generations are also third parties, but they are primarily "regulated" rather than "regulating." In fact, they are only "regulating" insofar as they cohere with the regulation proper to the essential, sovereign generation.
6. For a relevant discussion of the "us-object" and the third in *Being and Nothingness*, see Flynn (1973, 8–10).
7. Of course, these looks were not identical insofar as they were relative to the particular group forms. However, as the concern was the development and perpetuation of the freedom of the individual and the group, their looks ultimately coincide.
8. Interestingly, in this regard, in addition to the possibility of sedimentation and an original forgetting, traditions are formed on the basis of an initial recognition, and subsequent repression. In certain cases, the original intentions of various traditions, as they turn into their opposites through their own dialectical development, are not forgotten, but rather *repressed in memory* in order for the present generation, the last, in this respect, in a series of intentional modifications, to preserve itself as its own tradition. From this point of view, the tradition of Western philosophy, which assumes an origin in Ancient Greece and Rome, is not only defined by forgetting or mistranslation, but *a primary repression* of the "pre"-history of this tradition and its own conditions of possibility. On this point, see Husserl (1970, 16–18, 360–62) and Heidegger (1962, 19–24).
9. There are multiple future generations in accordance with the level of education and the system of education taken as a whole, as well as the students the teacher has already educated. However, for my purposes here, I will only focus on the teachers and the class they are currently teaching.

10. For the relation between the claims here and the relevant aspects of Sartre's notion of programmation, see Sartre (1993, 408).

11. Again, I am drawing a comparison between the degraded time of the psyche and this form of education. In this regard, the complete passage further demonstrates the character of this temporality: "As such psychic time can be constituted only with the past, and the future can be only as a past which will come after the present past; that is, the empty form before-after is hypostasized, and it orders the relations between objects equally past" (Sartre 1984, 236).

12. This also further extends the status of the phrase "*est été*" insofar as it concerns the different temporalizations operative in the Institution (Sartre 1943, 57). In this case, the institutionalized group *is*, as it *was*, and there is an attempted temporal coincidence between past and present, such that it is not accurate to say it "has been," but rather that it "is been" as it continues in the present. For a discussion of the various translations of the original French, see Flynn (1984, 211). See also Barnes's remarks in her footnote to the phrase in Sartre (1984, 57).

13. It must be remembered that this is not a genuine form of transcendence, but a forced, imposed, "going beyond" insofar as the students remain within the immanence of the group. Their transcendence, in other words, is reducible to their facticity.

14. Again to invoke Nietzsche, there is no recognition of the intrinsic requirements of understanding the educational objects. See Nietzsche (1997, 5).

15. This notion of the equality between the study of an object and the object studied further relates to Carruthers's analyses of *adequation* and *aequatio* as they were understood in the Middle Ages. Most relevant to my account here is the following description of *aequatio:* "*Aequatio* and its adjective, *aequalis*, convey the notion of iteration, 'equal,' identity of a formal, quantifiable sort. *Aequalitas* is an absolute and necessary state of affairs" (Carruthers 2008, 28–29). In this form of education, the relation to the object of knowledge is best illustrated "with an equal sign," rather than through an approximation, or an approaching toward . . . , insofar as the object is reduced to what is known about it, and therefore the knowledge obtained "equals" the object (Carruthers 2008, 29). However, as such equivalence is imposed, it is also false, and therefore the equal sign is in truth a sign of a *décalage,* a temporal non-coincidence between the object studied, the process of studying it, and the knowledge obtained. However, it is also possible that the knowledge gained of the object would be present in a general understanding of it as well, but besides the difference in process, the presence of other interpretations and the view of knowledge as *ad-equate* and not *equal* would differentiate the two forms of understanding.

16. In the *Die "Bernauer Manuskripte,"* the future in Husserl's analyses is described as the past "turned on its head." Protention, that is, is characterized as "umgestülpte Retention" (Husserl 2001a, 17).

Chapter 6

Institutionalized Culture as Perpetual Depersonalization

In the previous two chapters, I provided an account of the nature of education in the institutionalized group and the temporal character of such education. In so doing, I demonstrated the manner in which institutionalized education is the complementary opposite of committed education, as well as its unique qualities. Chapter 4 was devoted to an analysis of the nature of this form of education, its role as a task in such a group, as well as the presence and role of the sovereign in the educational experience of the teacher and the students. Chapter 5 extended these analyses by reinterpreting them through the lens of time appropriate to this group form. This involved an account of the "objective," diachronic temporalization of the group in accordance with its different generations, as well as a phenomenological account of the synchronic, lived-temporality of education. On the basis of the previous two chapters, the following questions present themselves, namely: How does such a form of education translate itself into an alienated and oppressed form of collective action? What type of culture is produced and maintained through such education? And lastly, what kind of literature does it give rise to, what, in other words, is the nature of institutionalized literature, an oppressive and passive literature, which serves as the diametrical opposite of committed literature?

In order to respond to these questions, I will again take up several themes from part 1 and invert them while adding the aspects unique to the Institution. First, I will discuss the kind of group members produced by such a form of education, their imaginative and temporal orientation toward their tasks and functions, the role of perception in such an orientation, as well as the continued and constantly felt presence of the sovereign in their lives. To adequately articulate the form of the imagination in this group, I will also develop the concept of the institutionalized, individual image. This will demonstrate how the oppression and instrumentalization of the imagination lead to the restriction of tasks and functions and the reducibility of the individual group member to them.

This analysis will lead into section II and the discussion of a second, central theme, namely, that of the continued education of the group members once the period of formal education has been completed. It will be guided by the following question: What does it mean to consider education a perennial task in the Institution, and how does such continued education bear upon the tasks and functions of the group members? This latter task will further involve the reconceptualization of the relation between perception and the imagination, as well as between both themes and the sovereign.[1] In order to provide an account of the cultural context within which this happens, I will draw an institutionalized equivalent of Sartre's notion of "the objective neurosis" in *The Family Idiot.* In addition, as a correlate to the discussions in chapter 3, I will provide an institutionalized interpretation of the public imaginary, and show how perception is interwoven with it in this particular group form.

These two themes lead to the analysis of the status of literature in the institutionalized group in the third and final section. Through a reinterpretation of the concept of committed literature, I will develop the complementary opposite form of literature and explain its role in this group. This will also involve a reconsideration of the relation between this text and the *Critique*, showing the manner in which the chronologically subsequent text, in its account of sovereignty and oppressive forms of media, complements the prior through making possible the development of the concept of institutionalized, oppressive literature. In addition, through such an analysis, I will show how institutionalized literature contributes to the intelligibility of this particular form of group action. Finally, I will develop the concept of the institutionalized, collective image, which, though produced by literature, has the paradoxical quality of extending to the group as a whole while remaining the image of a single individual.

THE ORACLE OF THE INSTITUTION AND ITS IMAGINARY

The analyses of the previous two chapters lead to the question of the effects of education in the institutionalized group. Moreover, they lead to the general question of continued education in the group. As addressed in chapters 1 and 4 concerning the respective forms of education, education is a perennial task. What, however, does it mean for institutionalized group members to continue to educate themselves? In addition, what is the context within which such continued education and life in the group take place, and how, given this group form, does the relation between the teacher and the students in an academic setting translate into action in the group and contribute to its intelligibility? And lastly, what is the relation between perception and the imagination in the institutionalized group?

To begin, the Institution establishes a culture of perception and the public imaginary that allows it to sustain its hierarchical order. In order to do so, it creates a two-fold public culture of perception and the imagination.[2] In fact, and as I will show throughout this chapter, the two terms of perception and the imagination reciprocally determine, guide, and limit each other. Each serves as a context for the other, and dialectical interplay between them in part determines the various tensions in the lives of the group members. In a negative sense, such a culture is the correlate of Sartre's notion of "the objective neurosis."[3] I have already introduced this concept in chapter 3 and will not discuss it extensively in this chapter as well. However, of particular significance for my purposes here are the "attitudes of detachment, solitude, and derealization" and I will situate them within the Institution (Flynn 2014, 400). Moreover, I will demonstrate their educational significance by showing how they contribute to the perpetual task of education in the institutionalized group. Throughout this chapter, I will also draw a parallel with the oracular character of Flaubert and show the way in which the circumstances he found himself in, both concerning his father and the general culture, are reflected in the Institution.[4]

The students are "prophetic" in their own right, but in a sense different from that in which Sartre describes Flaubert (Sartre 1993, 452). First, as students, these group members were caught between perception and the imagination, as well as their education as individuals and the demands of the teacher and sovereign. Their education was imposed on them, their imagination instrumentalized and restricted, and their subjectivity repressed. From their point of view as students, they are themselves prophetic insofar as the tensions they lived through, the imposition of content, and their temporalization by the teacher and the sovereign, all "foresee" or serve as signs of their life to come in the group. The situation they find themselves in as students, in general their depersonalization, indicates the kind of life they will lead, as well as their general situation and orientation in the group. As a parallel to the manner in which the teacher has lived their life before them in the knowledge they possess and their own, past depersonalization, the group members as students lived their own life in the group before themselves because the limits of education become the limits of the group and its culture. The continuity between education and life in the group both extends and prepares the students to maintain its hierarchical order. Although education is preparation for life as full group members, and the fulfillment of tasks and functions is the students' fulfillment as group members, the structure, form, and relation between their ability to perceive and imagine has largely been determined and alters minimally, if at all, after the period of formal education comes to an end.

In a different, indirect way, the teacher is also oracular both regarding the content taught and their role as a teacher. As the committed teacher was a model of resistance through imagining, the institutionalized teacher is a model of assimilation through the act of teaching. Both the material presented and the form of its presentation are absorbed both consciously and unconsciously by the students. The teacher's orientation in the classroom, their monologue and minimal interaction with the students, serve as indications of the way the students will approach their lives in the group. For example, such an approach both conditions and foreshadows how the students will read, process the images of different media, as well as how they will behave and adapt themselves to the general life of the group. The teacher, in carrying out the will of the sovereign, instills the tension between perception and the imagination through the cultivation of the one and the repression of the other, and produces the students as oracular instances of themselves, whose oracle will be fulfilled through the fulfillment of their tasks and functions. Lastly, as caught between the sovereign and the students, and the present of the students and their future, the teacher represents the tension they will find themselves in as group members whose *individual lives* are determined by, and find their truth in, the sovereign and the culture of the group. As simultaneously between various factors in the group, the teacher serves as a sign of the comparable situation the students will find themselves in when they fully enter the group.

There is an additional sense in which the oracular character of Flaubert is at work in this group form, and this concerns the past generations of the group. The previous generations, both in their past, independent existence, as well as in their existence in the present, anticipated in various ways the lives the students would lead and how they would contribute to the present culture. Again, the generations as split need to be understood in this regard. The students enter a context weighed down by the past, one which is still largely determined by the past, and for which their education prepared them. With varying degrees of immediacy and mediation, and with varying degrees of accuracy, which can vary, for example, with the distance from technological advancements, the prior generations themselves prophesied what life in the group would be like. They too were defined by a split in the generations, a hierarchy, a tension between perception and the imagination, and as constitutive of this particular group form, perpetuated in part through education, the past serves as a prophecy for the future. The culture of the sovereign, the institutionalized image of the sovereign, is constant, perpetually determinative, and in its several generational forms continues to guide the group while making it increasingly difficult to change, meaningfully respond to, or resist as it continues and accumulates throughout the generations. The new generation, then, finds itself in a historically laden context which, as such, is limiting, stultifying, and weighed down, rather than a point of departure for free, spontaneous *praxis*. The present moment of the group continues the restrictions begun during the process of education, and therefore continues to narrow the subjectivity of the group members as the oracle of the past and present of the group is fulfilled. The new group members inherited a prophesied culture which is fractured in its generations and constituted by a tension between perception and the imagination, and for which their prior educational experience serves as the archetype.

This multidimensional cultural context takes on particular significance concerning the imagination understood as a collective phenomenon. There are, accordingly, concepts of the "social image" and a "social imagination" which correspond to the Institution. There is, therefore, a social imaginary—restricted though it may be in this case—which the group members enter and operate within throughout their lives in the group. The limits on the act of imagining, as well as on the nature of the image, have been historically established through the oracular character of past generations as well as the period of formal education. There is a continuity in the character of images across past and present in the Institution. There is, to state it somewhat differently, *a schema for the imagination itself*, that is, educational, historical, and cultural determinations which delimit it while making it possible. As a result, the transcendental condition of the ability to imagine is also its restriction, and not concerning the a priori forms and limits to finite, human knowledge, but concerning the demands of the sovereign and the culture of the group.

This schematism of the imagination takes two forms. First, the educational process has placed a limit on the ability to imagine. This was due to both the content taught, the pedagogy of the teacher, as well as the educational atmosphere created in the classroom. The imagination of the students and ultimately of the group members has led them to conform to, and remain consistent with, their prior educational history as well as the standards of the group. And as it was the case for education, so is it for the subsequent life of the group, that the imagination is ultimately meant to serve perception, that is, the group in its present reality. Moreover, institutionalized perception has the additional act-character of *acceptance*, of positing reality as to-be-accepted. As was the case in the Organization, there are short- and long-term aims and an image that the group has of itself. The issue here, however, is that this image is that of the sovereign, and the aims of the group are in truth a singular objective that is common in its fulfillment but neither in its origins nor its determination. Such an image is degraded because it is the work and image of one individual, imposed on the group members, fashioning and limiting their lives as they fulfill their tasks and functions. Limited by the context within which it operates, the imagination of the group members is perpetually degraded throughout their lives in the group.

Secondly, and as a complement to this first point, the work of imagining has already largely been done by the group both in its education of the group members as well as in its present cultural standards and expectations. In addition to the ability to imagine, what can be understood as the form of an imagining act, the content that can be imagined is restricted as well, and in this case largely because what can be imagined, what images an individual can create, have already been produced by the group. This is a further result of the act-character of perception since, if reality were not perceived as to-be-accepted, the imagination would orient itself with the freedom to modify the content presented. The collective image of the group, which has the paradoxical quality of being that of an individual, guides the group members in their imaginative acts. And again, part of the meaning of such acts of the imagination and the images they create is that they reinforce the structure and hierarchy of the group. The social imaginary of the institutionalized group, it follows, *is* the individual imaginary in preceding it, repressing it and making it possible, and determining its meaning in advance.[5] Combined with the claims made earlier, it is now clear that the Institution, with its initial, formal and now subsequent period of education, with its images, memories, and expectations, serves as its own schematism. Or, perhaps better, the Institution simply is a cultural, historical, and educational schematism of the imagination. The public imaginary of the Institution, in its subservience to the sovereign, is a false imaginary for the group. It is an objective, false imaginary insofar as it is not comprised of the individual, free acts of the individual group members, but rather the result of an oppressive form of education and the culture of the group which dictates what images can be produced and how to produce them. In so doing, the group not only limits them, but ultimately has already produced them insofar as what will be "imagined" coincides with both the past and present reality of the group.

There is an additional quality of the institutionalized imagination which needs to be emphasized and which greatly restricts its use by the group members. Given the limitations placed on it by education and the sovereign, *the imagination is always of an identity.* It is a form of preserving the order of the group *as it is*, which is to say *as it was and will be*, and as such is exclusive of any meaningful difference. As mentioned earlier, any possible change, modification, or difference, must be approved by the sovereign, and, in being so approved, it is absorbed into the identity of the group. *The imagination is confined to reality*, and this is necessarily the case because the reality of the group, in both its past and present, bounds the imagination such that whatever images are produced cohere with it across all of the temporal dimensions. This further modifies and preserves the nature of the act of imagining as the derealization of a prior reality. There is, therefore, a primacy of the real.[6] However, given the restraints on the imagination, the derealization of a prior reality produces images that are consistent with the prior realized content and coincide with it. And this consistency bears upon the content of the image produced, the subjective act of imagining, as well as the value or meaning it has for the group. The transcendent image, the creation of an irreal content, in this case, is reducible to the prior reality from which it emerged. As peculiar imaginary-perceiving group members, as belonging to a group with the same peculiar unity, their imaginative acts derealize a reality only to return to it in and through the imagined content.[7] The logic of the imagination is therefore preserved insofar as it is a derealization of a prior reality, but it is modified insofar as the derealized content is constrained by the real and ultimately returns to it insofar as what is "new," what is produced, is perfectly consistent with what is perceived. The imaginary therefore returns to perception, and the derealized reality is not fully derealized but a sanctioned modification that preserves the reality derealized. As a result, the imaginary loses its character of being a "contestation," a challenge to the real, and instead is continuous with it, and ultimately subordinate to it (Sartre 1971a, 595).

Moreover, as mentioned earlier, the value of what is imagined is consistent with the real as well. This is due to the fact that it coheres with the sovereign, contributes to the collective functioning of the group, and is a translation of the imagination cultivated during the period of formal education into the life of the group. Whatever value it has, therefore, is due to its being in the service of the present reality. In general, in the institutionalized imagination, it is the case that the imagination is in the service of perception and images are in the service of the real. In a sense, then, as the institutionalized complement of the question "Why Write?," and in anticipation of the institutionalized response to this question in the next section, the question "Why imagine?" is answered: "*in order to perceive.*" Again, as discussed earlier, there is an arch-image of the group that contextualizes the images produced and perception because they both occur within the self-understanding that this image provides. In one sense, the images produced are consistent with the perceived reality as derealizations of it, but in another sense, the perception of the institutionalized group members is bounded by the imagination insofar as the images produced reinforce and further determine it. The over-arching image of the group serves to determine and limit perception such that what is perceived coheres with the self-understanding established through the image of the sovereign.

There is a further, two-fold significance to the context within which life in the group is fulfilled. First, there is an origin in perception, a beginning in the perceived reality of the present, which is continuous with, and an extension of, the past of the group. The past, of course, is remembered in the present, but it is also *perceived* insofar as the present structure and order of the group are identical to those of the past.[8] Secondly, however, and as a complement, there is the image the group has of itself. Such content is both connected to its aims and a *reflective*, *epistemological* origin insofar as it provides an understanding of the group in its essential reality. The new group members enter the group by entering an image and perceive the present and past reality within the context of this image. Concerning priority, then, there is a constant, necessary tension between the imagination and perception, between the derealization of content and the return to perception, and the image of the group and the perception that occurs within it. The culture of the group is defined by a constant, unresolved dialectic between the imagination and perception in which each overcomes and returns to the other. There is not, it follows, a necessary progression in the dialectical development, nor a regression to a former stage, but a paradoxical dialectic of *stasis* which involves the constant overcoming and return of each to the other in order for the institutionalized group to preserve itself. In this sense, the institutionalized group blurs the line between the imagination and perception, and does so in order to keep the functioning of the group, understood on both a collective and an individual level, in a static dialectic, or an analytic genesis. Within the confines of such a dialectic, the very meaning of what it is to be a group member involves the lived-tension between perception and the imagination, and contributing to the constant reversal, overcoming, and return which plays out between them.

One additional theme which has not been sufficiently addressed thus far is the relation between the images produced in the present and those of the past. The images, as produced in the present, are not entirely new, but rather continuous with the images previously produced. Said somewhat differently, the images of the present are in part defined as mere repetitions of the images of the past and, in this sense, establish a structural form of repetition within the group. Of course, in accordance with the present of the group, technological advancements, and so on, the content and variety of images may change in various ways. Nevertheless, in cohering with the past of the group, being situated within the present, over-arching image of the group, and in general being bounded by its structure, there is nothing in the present that was not implicit in the past, and ultimately determined by the past and present. To adapt the language of Kant, in the Institution, there is nothing combined in the present image that was not already combined by the past and sovereign image of the group.[9] Regarding the nature and hierarchy of this group form, there is nothing in the image that had not already been present in the group, nothing, that is, in the imagination, that was not first present and combined in perception. Repetition, therefore, is a structural component of the act of imagining in such a group form, and extends to the images produced as well, making them not only bounded by perception, but peculiar contents that are already old.

The image is, as I stated above, bounded by the arch-image of the group but, as such, is also an image of an image, a reproduced content that varies the content of this image in its identity and in so doing continues to reproduce the group. As a result, in a paradoxical sense, the reproductions keep the group new insofar as they maintain the group in its structure in the present, keep it current, while also keeping it old insofar as the imagination has lost the ability to produce original, novel content. Each individual act of the imagination, therefore, repeats and reproduces the group as a whole, and each content is the product of a new act that has already been schematized. Such imagined content reflects the group, serves as a mirror of it, and regardless of the form it may take, is ultimately determined by the culture and education of the group and can be traced back to them. Concerning the imagination in this group, *continuity with the past is repetition.*[10] And this repetition of the imagination is itself multidimensional insofar as it does not only repeat the content, the past, and structure of the group, but also its values, standards, and expectations. As a result, taken comprehensively, each image, as a repetition, is a synthesis of the group as a whole. The image produced by the institutionalized group member, it follows, is in truth an image of an image, but one which, because it is such, contains the whole of the group in it. It is an image of an image which is the image of the sovereign, one way in which the sovereign maintains their presence in the group and continues to permeate it. Individual acts of the imagination, therefore, create individual images which are iterations of the collective image of the group which is that of the sovereign.

THE INSTITUTIONALIZED DIALECTIC OF PERCEPTION AND THE IMAGINATION

The previous section explained the culture of the institutionalized group that the students enter after the period of formal education and the manner in which it continues to confine them in their lives in the group. Moreover, I explained the institutionalized concepts of perception and the imagination, the relations between them, and the limitation that each places on the other. However, there was an additional quality that I discussed only briefly, and is in need of deeper analysis, namely, the instrumentalization of the imagination. What does it mean, in this group form, to instrumentalize the imagination? First, it has the two-fold significance of serving both the sovereign and perception. In being used to serve the sovereign, it is oppressed and exploited for the sake of the perception and continuity of the present reality. As I will show, the instrumentalization of the imagination is particularly significant in the way in which it orients the group members toward their tasks and functions *as they are* and allows them to develop as needed to preserve the group *as it is*. As a result of its education, the group produces group members who either, as a limit case, cannot imagine, or are severely limited in their ability to do so. After such education, the capacity to imagine is not a realization of transcendental freedom, but rather the realization of the will of the sovereign. By having an educational system and a curriculum that do not emphasize and cultivate the imagination, as well as inheriting a particular culture of the imagination and perception, to use Kant's language, the work of transcendental constitution is already done. The group members passively receive, accept, and reinforce the reality of the group as they continue to assimilate themselves to it.

As new group members, they perceive and accept the essential, fixed character of their tasks and functions, as well as their ability to fulfill them. There is, in fact, a limitation on both the side of the subject and the object. Both are accepted simply as they are and, regardless of any possible developments, preserve the same essential structure, form, and role in the group. Each, therefore, is related to the other as a fixed point, and despite any development in the group, maintains the same structural relations to the rest of the group. If the group member modifies a task, it follows, the task continues to maintain its relations to the other tasks. And from the side of the task, if the group member modifies their orientation toward it, they still preserve their role in the group and their relation to all of the other roles in the group. The tasks and functions are viewed as complete, necessarily being what they are, and prescribing the necessary orientation toward them. They impose, both individually and collectively, the necessary relations to themselves and the general life in the group. The tasks and functions, conceived as the object pole of life in the group, as that for which the group members are prepared, determine and continue to determine the lives of the group members. In this sense the objects extend the previous process of education, are continuous with it, and continue to reinforce and perpetuate it. And yet, paradoxically, this educational value limits future, genuine education. The object demands an orientation and continuous education, but simultaneously, in order to remain the object that it is, it blocks any other education, prevents and represses it, making the condition of possibility of continued education its impossibility. As such educational objects, they continue to impose the established order of the group.

As I mentioned, however, there is also a subjective correlate to this domination by the object. As a result of the patterns instilled through the process of education, the group members come to accept themselves and their abilities as being what they are, as largely determined, and as admitting of little, if any, further development. At best, any change will be perfectly consistent with the education and order of the group and will simply be a slight improvement to what was already taught and in place. The group members have accepted themselves as institutionalized subjects, and now demand that the object conform to their institutionalization. In this regard, the group members dominate the object, and do so by imposing their previous education on it. The object itself is reduced to simply being what it is, and yet paradoxically is not itself allowed to be what it is because it is reduced to a single form and has its own, intrinsic possibilities repressed. The process of institutionalization, it follows, produces group members who dominate their tasks and functions, *depersonalize them*, and in so doing force them to continue to conform to the past and present of the group. The group members continue to educate themselves in continuing to impose their education on the object, and yet again, paradoxically, limit their ability to do so. The condition of possibility for their continued education becomes its own impossibility insofar as a new, inconsistent, and unexpected education is in principle ruled out. They therefore block their own continued education by reinforcing the education they received and serve as their own conditions of impossibility by reducing themselves to a single possibility.

This reciprocal imposition involves a tension between the subject and the object. It lacks genuine correspondence, and instead contains an inherent tension in the correlation between them. As educating, each is in a certain tense relation to the other, and yet they correspond to one another within the present of the group. The object prescribes an orientation and limits the subject, and the subject imposes its previous education and limits the object. Each prevents the other from fully being what it is and does so because each is only what it is. The object demands that the group member conform to it, and the subject demands that the object conform to its education, and, paradoxically, by each imposing on the other, they attain the same result, while repressing their own possibilities and those of the other. This tension involves a peculiar correspondence which ensures the fulfillment of the tasks and functions as they were meant to be fulfilled. Furthermore, subject and object form a paradoxical, *asymmetrical symmetry* insofar as their relationship is founded on reciprocal repression. Therefore, as an extension of what I described earlier regarding perception and the imagination, there is here a tense dialectic between subject and object wherein each overcomes and returns to the other through the repression of possibilities in order for the particular task to be fulfilled.

This tense relation between the object perceived and the act of perception takes on an additional layer, an additional complexity, when the theme of the imagination is emphasized. The subject and object are not only in a perceptual, dialectical tension, but one which involves the imagination as well. Thus, on the basis of what I have just discussed, the following question presents itself: What is the imaginary orientation toward tasks and functions on the part of the subject, and what is the imaginative response of the object as the correlate and complementary opposite of the subject? First, in contrast with the Organization and from the side of the subject, the nature of the images alters in character. They are, in this group, and because of the prior education, screen images.[11] Although ultimately oriented toward the object-pole as the intentional correlate to be modified through the imagination, the images are blocked, suppressed, false or distorting. As discussed earlier, the imagination is schematized by the culture of the group and its education. The imaginative approach to the tasks and functions is therefore itself schematized and bounded by the group, meaning that the orientation toward the object, the imaginative modification of it, and the images formed are determined by the group such that the individual group member, in the act of imagining, never truly makes contact with the object.[12] The images produced prevent the group member from truly accessing the object and relating to it as a correlate of their unique subjectivity. Rather, in producing an institutionalized image, the group member is cut off from the object, disconnected from it in the act of relating to it. The images therefore serve as screens insofar as they block a genuinely subjective relation to the object on the part of the subject, and instead present the object as previously determined by the sovereign. In a paradoxical sense, the image, as an opening to the object, blocks the relation to it, prevents a genuine engagement with it, and replaces such a genuinely individual orientation with that of the group. As a screen, the image limited by the group reinforces the institutionalized order and continues to separate the subject from it.

This, however, is not to say that every conceivable image had itself already been imagined or exhaustively thought through, but rather that the meaning, value, and limits of what can be imagined were already prescribed. Regardless of any variation in the individual, the images produced will allow the tasks and functions to be completed as they were intended to be completed by the group. Intersubjectively understood, then, the screens play off of and harmonize with one another insofar as they all make possible the fulfillment of tasks and functions by blocking genuine access to them. And as such, there is a constellation of images produced which preserve their order and relations and continue to ensure the collective orientation toward tasks and functions in so doing. In this regard, each image is a fixed point in a constellation of images, or that around which the others revolve in order to maintain the coherence of the imaginary life of the group. The culture of images, in this group, is a culture of screens, blocking entry into the group as the condition of possibility of entering it. Such a culture is accordingly a preestablished harmony of group members, which is in part defined as the preestablished harmony of screen images which harmonize the group in repressing it.

Similar to the case of perception, the object in its imaginary character demands its own imaginative orientation toward it. As an object with a certain structure, which appears in the group on the basis of its culture and education, it demands a certain imaginative orientation toward it in order to be fulfilled. In this regard, the tasks and functions serve as analoga of themselves, as objects that indicate their own possible, future modification in order for them to remain what they are in the group. They outline their own imaginary variation, and in so doing outline the limits of the subjective acts of imagining that correspond to them. As perceptual, the object prescribes the limits of its own derealization and imaginative modification. As an analogon of itself, it dictates the necessary, imaginative approach to it. As "the bearer of its own perceptual intention," it is "the bearer of its own imaginative intention," and therefore there is nothing in the image produced by the act of the subject that was not previously outlined, indicated, or pre-analogized by the object (Husserl 2001b, 310). And in so pre-analogizing the subject, the object also continues to reinforce the education obtained by continuing to instrumentalize their imagination. As perceptual, the object is no more than it is. However, as possessing an imaginative dimension, it serves as an analogon of itself which indicates how it can be modified in order to be more than it is at present, but precisely so that it will be no more than it is. The imaginative indications intrinsic to the object allow it to develop statically so that it can keep its designated place within the overall functioning of the group. It is therefore an analogon of itself in order to preserve the necessary, prescribed relations to the other tasks and functions, and to preserve itself as a point of reference in the group. As did the screen images, so too do the imaginative indications of the objects play off of and harmonize with one another to maintain the order and relations of the group through and because of any possible change.

The perceptual and imaginary dimensions of the object give rise to a further tense dialectic between subject and object. The subject imaginatively orients themselves to the object to adjust it to the group as needed, and the object outlines its own possibilities to be fulfilled by the subject. In so doing, however, each is constrained by the other. Each therefore represses the other for the sake of itself, and not only does not allow the other to be what it is, but also for it to be no more than it is. The reciprocity between subject and object is therefore the basis for their mutual repression, and this tense, unresolved dialectic allows the group to continue to function through the imposition of preestablished demands. Each object, then, is a tension between perception and imagination, between what it is and what it imaginatively indicates it could be. The subject, too, is a peculiar blend of perception and the imagination insofar as the two orientations toward the object overlap and conflict. In this complex dialectic of perception and the imagination, it also needs to be remembered that, because the images produced are preceded by the arch-image of the group, they are themselves images of this image, or, in its plurality and the previous images created on its basis, images of images. As a result, the imaginative orientation toward tasks and functions is *intrinsically imitative.* The group members imitate the necessary orientation toward objects in replicating the images of the group as they produce them in fulfilling their tasks and functions. The images produced, therefore, in addition to being limited by the culture of the group and its education, have the additional quality of being imitations, or images of images, and these particular images are demanded by the tasks and functions themselves in their fulfillment. Such an imaginative orientation, it follows, is also an imitation of the ways in which tasks had been previously fulfilled, and the corresponding imagining acts of the group members themselves have the further act-character of being imitative.

The limitations placed on the imagination by the group and its serialized functioning have an additional, temporal component. The temporalization of both the subject and the object in this group is in truth a form of de-temporalization. The conceptually limited and bounded imaginary confines the individual group member and the fulfillment of their tasks and functions to the past and present. It is, however, a forced present. As I have discussed, the individual roles in the group are not allowed to develop freely. They are fixed, reduced to being solely what they are in the group. As a result, there is an identity in the three temporal dimensions. The group members are locked in the present and cut off from a genuine, new future. The role is also fulfilled—as much as possible—as it had been in the past, and therefore in imposing the imaginary on the group the sovereign imposes the past on it and attempts to maintain an identity between past and future. Moreover, the sovereign attempts to do so concerning the "two sorts of future" Sartre described in *The Imaginary*, which in this case correspond to the immediate future as the fulfillment of the task of the group member, and the future understood as the general future of the group against which such fulfillment is completed (Sartre 2004b, 182). The future too, as perfectly continuous with the present, is identical to the past, and the imaginative orientation toward the present, the prescribed immanence of such an orientation, is simultaneously an orientation to the past and future, *but as coinciding with the present.* The image, as blocked, as a screen, as an opening to tasks and functions, also opens the group members to all three dimensions of time, but it reduces the transcendence of the past and the future to the immanence of the present. However, as I discussed, development is sanctioned by the sovereign as needed, and therefore the instrumentalization of the imagination does potentially open the group members to a novel future. This future, despite such minimal novelty, remains an extension of the preestablished harmony of the group, a way of maintaining it in all of the relations that comprise it through the addition of a new element. Despite any novelty in the image, the linear order of time is preserved, and, with the exception of the variation brought about through the instrumentalized images produced, the continuity of the form of time in the group, its experience, and the orientation toward it, are preserved.

In addition to being restricted to the present through the culture of the group, both the objects themselves as well as the group members contribute to the limitation to the present dimension of the group. As I showed above, the object in its imaginary dimension indicates its possible modification, and therefore contains an intrinsic orientation toward the future, the not-yet, a possibility to be actualized through the appropriate steps. What, however, is the temporality of such an analogizing indication? What, in other words, is the institutionalized temporality of the object, and how does it contribute to the temporal rhythm both of the fulfillment of the individual task and the collective functioning of the group? There is a single, imposed temporal form on the task to which both the object and the individual group member are meant to conform. Rather than an open temporality, one which is itself flexible, determining its own rate in accordance with the circumstances of the group, a single rate and linear temporal process are imposed on the object in order for it to be fulfilled in the allotted time. The object has a temporal layer forced upon it, and, as a result, demands the corresponding approach on the part of the group member. As such, the object in its temporal dimension further limits the processes of perception and the imagination, and their various interrelations, insofar as it bounds each, confining it to the pace designated by the group. In this regard, the object is *pre*-temporalized, and such pre-temporalization, due to the fact that it is a result of the sovereign, possesses the "speed, rhythm, and duration" of their microtemporalization (Sartre 1993, 408). At most, there may be slight modifications, or minimal alterations, in the demands of the object if they will contribute to fulfilling the task more efficiently. But in this case, the aim is to continue to have the object determined by an "external temporality," and to adjust it in order for it to remain what it is and to maintain its place in the group.

Such temporal imposition extends itself to the various parts of the task that serve to comprise it as a whole. In the case of institutionalized tasks, time is imposed on the necessary sub-tasks as well. Each step temporally leads into the other insofar as it has had its temporal work already done for it, has already been planned out in advance, and only requires the corresponding acts of the group member for its completion. The different stages of the completion of the process are temporally *fixed*, and the fulfillment of the task is the temporal fulfillment of the stages in accordance with their designated temporalization. Through the sovereign, the object serves as a unity in a multiplicity of standardized temporalizations which determine the action of the group member. As a standardized temporal whole, the object is the point around which the group member revolves, and as such, requires a minimum, and as an ideal the total lack of, spontaneous and individual temporalizations. There is a preestablished harmony of the object which does not recognize the intrinsic nature of the object, but at most, and again only minimally, will take such a nature into account in order to more efficiently detail its completion. The object is taken outside of itself, turned inside out, and is subject to the microtemporalization of the sovereign, which may attend to certain of its features, but places the completion of the process in the designated time period ahead of its intrinsic character and the corresponding process of its fulfillment. And this uniform temporality of the object in all of its phases is further meant to maintain the constellational, intersubjective temporalization of all of the other tasks and functions of the institutionalized group as a whole. The overarching temporal unity and process of the group as a whole, it follows, is comprised of the reciprocal, determined, and standardized temporalizations of all of the tasks and functions in the group. The uniform, linear, standardized temporalization of the aims of the group is the result of the imposition of fixed temporal relations on the lives of the group members and their tasks.

The group member too, with their designated role, possesses a characteristic temporality that locates them in the group and corresponds to their task. In this sense, there is a temporal harmony between the object and the subject insofar as the subject recognizes and fulfills the temporal demand placed on them by the object. They recognize the object, therefore, but do so on the basis of its prior determination. As a correlate to the static temporality of the object, the group member views their own role as *permanently situated* within the group through its designated temporality. They have been temporalized in advance through the microtemporalization of the sovereign and the temporalization of the object. As much as possible, the group member does not reflect on their task, more appropriate ways to complete it, and so on, but accepts their role as it is given and attempts to maintain it. There is, it follows, no room for a possible new rate for the fulfillment of the task, or a possible reworking of the steps, but a single, direct process necessary for its fulfillment. In this regard, the understanding of their own role in the temporalization of their lives is determined by the sovereign and the culture of the group. And they accordingly ensure the correct temporal approach to the task in order for it to maintain the appropriate relation to the temporal demand made on it.

In a sense, the group members and their task comprise two identical sides to the same temporal process. Each is fixed, with a demand on the other to fulfill its designated task in the group and requires that each conform to the temporality of the other. As a result, the lived-time of the subject is a reflection of the temporality set for the object. The rhythm of the subject lies in the object, and that of the object in the subject. There is a mutual temporalization on the basis of the repression of the internal temporalization of both terms of the process which results in the group member only doing what is asked of them in the appropriate time, and of the object being fixed in place for its own continuous, static fulfillment. There is therefore a further, temporal asymmetrical symmetry insofar as each represses itself and the other in order for both of them to be what they are in the group. To supplement, and complete, the initial characterization of the temporalization of the group I provided above, the temporalization of the institutionalized group can be defined in the following way: it is a product of the repression of the temporality of both the object and the subject, and maintains itself through the imposition of a uniform, standardized, linear order in which all of the tasks and group members preserve the form and structure of their symmetrical relations throughout their lives in the group.

INSTITUTIONALIZED LITERATURE AS COLLECTIVE DEPERSONALIZATION

The first two sections of this chapter discussed the culture of the Institution after the period of formal education and the group members' orientation toward tasks and functions on the basis of the education they received. There was, however, a certain, necessary limitation to this analysis, which I am now in a position to address, namely, that the images produced by the group members were *individual*, relative to the fulfillment of their particular roles in the group. However, as discussed in chapter 3, the group also produces *collective images* of itself, which allow it to further reflect on itself, grasp the present, and develop as needed. As I showed there, one source of collective images in the group is literature. It is through literature, broadly construed, that the group produces collective images and guides its development through the dialogue between author and reader. In the case of committed literature, images are intersubjectively and imaginatively constituted through the freedom of the author and the reader. The literature of the institutionalized group, however, also produces such collective images to articulate itself, but does so in order to continue the depersonalization and oppression of the group members.

On the basis of an oppressive literature in a degraded group form, a number of questions present themselves. First, what is the nature of a collective image in the institutionalized group? Secondly, what exactly is the form of literature that corresponds to the institutionalized group? Thirdly, and as a complement to these questions, what is the nature of the act of reading in such a group? And finally, how do the restricted imaginary and its corresponding de-temporalization contribute to the unique folding of the static dialectic of the Institution? In order to adequately respond to these questions, I will divide this section into two parts. First, I will discuss the relation between reading and the imagination in the institutionalized group. Secondly, I will discuss the temporality of reading and the imagination and the manner in which they orient and develop the dialectic of the group.

Institutionalized Reading

As I showed in the first section of this chapter, the individual images of the group members are dominated by the collective image of the group. In addition to being schematized, they are subject to the over-arching image of the sovereign. Paradoxically, however, even the collective image of the group ultimately has an individual character insofar as it is the image the sovereign has determined for themselves and the group. The collective images produced through literature, which bear upon the group as a whole, extend to all tasks, functions, and generations, and therefore, with varying degrees of immediacy and mediation, contribute to the reproduction of the group in its present form. Similar to the dialectic between perception and the imagination, there is a further dialectic of the image in the act of reading in the institutionalized group. The different kinds of images, which are ultimately reducible to one another, and which, as I will show, overcome and return to one another, produce the dialectic of the image as a tense dialectic between the individual and collective images in both their individual and collective dimensions.

A few further comments are necessary regarding the structure of the consciousness of the author and the reader. First, and regarding the author, in addition to the consciousness they have of themselves and the group, the institutionalized authors also contains the sovereign as a structure of their consciousness. In order, then, to produce the images necessary for the group, the authors require a three-fold intentional structure comprised of the consciousness of themselves, the intentional object, and the sovereign. The author, as having such a three-fold intentional structure, produces literature consistent with the sovereign and as subject to them. And as the complement to this, the readers too are defined by a three-fold intentional structure of themselves, their respective objects, and the sovereign. The authors, moreover, on this basis, through a blend of activity and passivity, of passively accepting the standards and demands of the sovereign, actively produces literary images sanctioned by them. And again, the reader passively accepts the literature presented, its respective images, and its significance in the group. Both author and reader are oriented toward the same collective object, in this case the literary image, which is reached on the basis of the appropriate engagement with the book, symphony, and so on. In different ways, both author and reader, individually and collectively, are oriented toward the same intentional object.

There is a further nuance in this intentional relation to the object which complicates the lived-experience of the noetic-noematic correlation and the comprehension of the object in its various profiles. In a peculiar sense, there is an intentional object below the presented content, which is only capable of being reached and absorbed through the latter. The truth of the particular literary work, in this case, is "beneath the surface," accessible through the image, established on its basis, but ultimately with a depth lacking to the image.[13] In institutionalized reading, the truth of the image, of literature comprehensively understood, is the sovereign and the form of the group. From their respective sides, therefore, the truth of the book produced by the author, and read through the imagination by the reader, is interwoven with its content and the foundation of it. In being reciprocally, intentionally related to the literary work, both author and reader are ultimately directed toward the sovereign, the group, and its culture. The truth, it follows, is not inaccessible in its immediate, literal form, but rather the object-pole of an intentional act which accesses and assimilates it through the various images produced. In a sense, then, there is an image *of* the group, and the group reached through such an image is the truth of it which is communicated through the image while also remaining its support and foundation. The object in its manner of appearing is sustained by a truth, which is ultimately intended in the act of reading and accepted through the particular image. Such a truth adds a layer to intentional experience, a "thing in itself" which is a condition for appearance which, in a paradoxical sense, both appears and remains invisible in the image. The truth of the image does not appear as it is not an immediate part of the object, work, or image produced. However, as an incarnation of the sovereign, it appears *in and through* the object as interwoven with it and as its ground.

This relation between surface and depth, and visibility and invisibility, is more than just a difference between background and foreground, appearance and thing-in-itself. It is true that the group is the background against which the book is intended as the foreground, and that the sovereign is a *permanent background* to the life of the group as a whole. However, as what the literary text is ultimately about, as what the author is attempting to reproduce, and the group member will themselves accept and reproduce through their life in the group, the literary work is an intentional object which indicates another object that serves as its ground. Again, this ground is a blend of presence and absence, appearance and thing-in-itself, which permeates the text and its images while also holding back in being irreducible to its particular manifestation. Paradoxically, there is "a transphenomenality of the being of the sovereign" insofar as they are the foundation of the literary phenomena produced which is both irreducible to any single phenomenon and the condition for all of them (Sartre 1984, 9). The primary truth of the book is the sovereign, the form of the group, and its culture. There is, however, a second truth, a derivative truth, one pertaining to the text itself, the meaning specific to it, what it is "about," the story, for example, of the novel, and so on. There are, therefore, two fundamental forms of imagined truth in the institutionalized group, which are interwoven and irreducible to one another, though accessible through the appropriate imaginative acts. The truth of the sovereign, as the truth of the group and all of its literary manifestations, is the ultimate truth of the literary image, though this latter, in being lived-through and comprehended, has its own, immediate, corresponding form of truth. Institutionalized literature therefore plays on both of these levels, the explicit and the implicit, the manifest and the latent, and thus the immediate intentional, noematic correlate is not *the ultimate intentional correlate of the act of consciousness*. The literary image is accordingly a point of departure, but as the truth of that image is the sovereign, in the act of reading, the group member is ultimately oriented toward an intentional object which is "preceded by" another object, or has another object "in front of it," for which it serves as its truth and condition of possibility.

In its multidimensional character, institutionalized literature has a central and unique pedagogical function. It provides the necessary, sanctioned images of the group that allow it to properly relate to itself and develop as needed. As Sartre defined it in *What Is Literature?*, committed literature is a form of "directed creation" (Sartre 1988, 53). As such, it is a model for how a free and spontaneous group can reflect on itself, articulate its present, and act on that basis. However, as committed, there are certain assumptions, or perhaps an appropriate interpretation, of the terms "directed" and "creation," which apply to both the author and the reader, and which change signs in the institutionalized group. The free creation of committed reading, in this case, becomes a paradoxical unity of several opposing or even contradictory qualities. It is a form of "passive creation," an "imposed creation," but one in which the act of creation has in truth already been completed, and what is necessary is acceptance, imitation, and repetition. As a form of imitation and repetition, the reader lives their understanding of the group and the images produced by literature as already having been completed by the group. As the teachers have lived the life of the students before them, so here the authors, as an incarnation of the sovereign, have lived the life of the group members before them, and presents them with an image of the group which has already been lived through both before and after it has been lived through by the group members. In this respect, the work of imagining and, to that exact extent, the act of living in the group, has already been done for the group members. They are presented with content that is understood as complete, for which further, active imaginative engagement is not necessary, and which continues the process of education as the passive acceptance of content.

There is an additional element in the relation between author and reader, which fashions both the experience and expectations of reading and writing, namely, the demands of literature. In varying respects, and for different reasons, both sides place demands on the other. Again, in *What Is Literature?*, Sartre writes: "Thus, reading is a pact of generosity between author and reader. Each one trusts the other; each one counts on the other, demands of the other as much as he demands of himself" (Sartre 1988, 61). The first question, then, is of the nature of the demand in such circumstances. First, and building on the quotation just cited, the sovereign permeates and mediates the relation between author and reader. As stated above, the style, content, and so on, of the author are consistent with and ultimately determined by the sovereign. In addition, the demand that the author makes on the reader and the particular form the demand takes are similarly determined by the sovereign. It is not the author alone, then, who places such a demand on the reader, *but the author as guided by the sovereign*. The demand, in this respect, is twofold insofar as it follows from the author and their demand that the reader engage the content, understand the story, and articulate the present of the group through the various images. It is, however, also informed by, and saturated with, the will of the sovereign. The demand is therefore a peculiar blend of the demand of the text and that of the group.

The literary demand immediately bears upon the content of the literary work, and the required act of reading on the part of the reader to appropriately engage it. As a correlate to the act of the author, this demand requires the necessary imaginative engagement for the readers to take from the text what is required of them. However, as also containing the demands of the sovereign it is the demand that the group members understand the image as it relates to the necessary present form of the group. It is therefore a single demand for the appropriate engagement with the image, but also, and as its ultimate truth, for the appropriate form of life in the group. Whereas Sartre claims that both author and reader reciprocally demand more from one another through the dialogue of reading, in this case the author, as an extension of the sovereign, demands that the reader fulfill the literary demand, but, simultaneously as a fulfillment and a restriction, *only fulfill the literary demand.*[14] The reader is only meant to take so much from the text, and to exhaust their understanding in what was intended by the author. This results in the reader remaining locked within the immanence of the circumstances of the group. They are not able to transcend the text or the circumstances because of the repression of the imagination and acceptance of what is given. There is a further symmetry between the text and the engagement of the reader, which adds an additional imperative to the literary situation, namely, that the reader accept the text in all of its dimensions. The reader, in receiving the text as a priori true, accepts the text as it is, which also means *as it ought to be*, and in so doing completes the act of reading in being reduced to it. The act of reading, therefore, is further composed of an act-character which infuses the content read with the character of *necessity.* The form, content, and experience of literature make a demand on the reader, which involves viewing the contingency of a present form as intrinsically necessary, and making what is the case appear as *what ought to be the case.*

This demand on the part of the author, which is guided by the sovereign, has its complement on the side of the reader, which also involves a particular role of the sovereign. As a result of the previous process of education, the readers only demand so much from the author. In the act of reading, they demand that the content be presented in such a way that it is understood as complete, fixed, and necessary. Moreover, the reader demands that it be accessible, which is to say that the previously established uses of perception and the imagination are all that are needed to understand and internalize the text. There is therefore a demand, which can be made with varying degrees of explicitness and implicitness, that the text remain consistent with the process of education and the previous experience of life in the group. The demand from the readers are not a demand which challenges the author and the text, which attempt to glean more from the text as they continue to engage with it. In this case, Sartre's claim that "the literary object has no other substance than the reader's subjectivity" reverses itself, and is comprised of the readers' anonymity, the repression of their subjectivity, and the continuous process of depersonalizing themselves (Sartre 1988, 53). The reader's subjectivity is replaced by anonymity, and the demand that began in freedom changes into the demand for passive engagement, a minimum of intentional constitution, and that the text remain consistent with the group. The demand from the reader is that *the writer only be a writer, that the text only be a text,* that neither be more than itself, and that literature and its engagement reduce themselves to the immanence of the group.[15]

There is a further modification in institutionalized literature of one of the central ways in which Sartre describes the relation between the author and the reader. In *What Is Literature?*, he describes it as "a pact of generosity" (Sartre 1988, 61). What, in the institutionalized group, is the equivalent of the "pact of generosity" of committed literature (Sartre 1988, 61)? First, as an extension of the previous discussion, it further modifies the demand that each makes on the other. In this case, the appeal to the freedom of the reader from the author, and from the reader to that of the author, completely alters. It is no longer the freedom of each side that is being appealed to, but rather their role in the group, the stasis of the group, and the limited, institutionalized functioning of perception and the imagination. It is, in this sense, "a pact of continued depersonalization," insofar as each, in the appeal to the other, through the mediation of the sovereign, ensures the continuous depersonalization of the group members as they engage with literature and its images. As much as possible, the author does not appeal to the reader as an individual, and neither does the reader appeal to the author as an individual, but they both appeal to one another as rigidly bounded group members whose individuality and identity coincide with their lives in the group. The pact between the two is a pact between depersonalized and continuously depersonalizing group members who continue to repress their own subjectivity as well as that of the other as they continue to read, write, perceive, and imagine. The dialectic of reading is therefore not the free literary engagement of two free subjectivities, but rather the imposed, pre-delineated engagement of two depersonalized group members. There is repressed contact between the author and reader as individuals in order for them to make contact as group members. As a result, the acts of writing and reading become manifestations of the institutionalized culture and expectations of the group. In this sense, the group itself, previously and continuously, reads and writes, perceives and imagines for the group members and, in so doing, continues the process of collective depersonalization.

There is a further, essential aspect to the act of reading in the institutionalized group, namely, its particular form of seriality. The isolation of the experience in the classroom translates into the isolation of the future group members. As they are kept isolated and disconnected as they passively accept content, so are they isolated and disconnected in the act and experience of reading. The individual character of reading in the organized group contributed to the continuous unification of the group, and served as a moment of reflection which was consistent with the functioning of the group. In this case, the seriality of literature contributes to the continuation of seriality within the group, to the disconnect between the group members or, said somewhat differently, to the general discontinuity within the group. In the engagement with literature, the imaginings of the group members never unify into a collective, imagining *praxis*. The images of literature are consumed individually, reading occurs in isolation, and there is no ultimate unification achieved through such engagement. Reading becomes not only a solitary activity, but an isolated and isolating one. Moreover, it is isolating not only in the act of being carried out, but in its effects on the group as well. It does not lead to a further, collective orientation toward the life of the group, but rather begins and ends with the individual. It prevents any possible, future transcendence. It confines the group member to their life in the group, to their designated role and status. Reading, and literature in general, articulate the present of the group for the group members to further situate themselves within it in isolation and to conform their lives to it. Reading, therefore, reinforces isolation, and attempts to preserve the isolated, constellational relations as they exist at present.

The isolation of literature, however, further involves the question of the transcendence of the author and the immanence of the reader, as well as that of the serialized relations of the readers. The author, confined to the immanence of the group by the sovereign, remains transcendent to the immanence of the experience of the reader, and is not pulled into the experience as a group member who will contribute to the collective action of the group. They remain external to the act of reading, and therefore to this dimension of life in the group. The author produces a work, and subsequently withdraws from it and the experience of the reader. The author, rather, creates the space for the "collective immanence" of the readers, but does not further engage with them. The readers, within the individual immanence of the act of reading and the collective immanence shared with all of the other readers, remain, in a paradoxical sense, transcendent to one another. Each is locked within their own immanence, transcendent to all of the others, and disconnected from them as they collectively absorb the same content. There is, then, a collective immanence, with a collective-individual transcendence, in which each reader is cut off from all of the others. There is therefore a minimal immanence-transcendence tension of the group insofar as it is comprised of blends of both, and the author and the reader are confined within the immanence of the sovereign and do not attempt to transcend it.

The De-Temporalization of Literature

There is a further aspect of the manner in which the act of reading is determined by the sovereign and the culture of the group. In addition to schematizing and instrumentalizing the imagination, they also de-temporalize it and provide it with a temporal direction. The act of reading, therefore, is not a temporal process which unfolds in accordance with its own rhythm. Rather, it is a predetermined, micro-temporalized, and pre-temporalized temporalization. Just as the rate of the group and its rhythm are determined by the sovereign, so too is the direction of the temporalization of reading (Sartre 2004a, 391). Time itself, therefore, is externally situated within this particular group, and does not have an intrinsic direction, orientation, or harmony among its different dimensions. In a sense, it moves "forward," and necessarily does so as long as the particular form of the group is maintained and continues and as long as the group members fulfill their tasks and functions. However, this forward movement is *imposed, external, and foreign,* and thus neither its rate of unfolding nor its direction are rooted in the nature of temporality itself.

In the act of reading as the continued reinforcement of the culture of the group, the temporalization of the imagination is uniquely oriented to each of the three temporal dimensions. Again, however, in accordance with the microtemporalization of the group, there is a priority of the past. In this case, the imagination is dominated by the past and present, and minimally oriented toward the future. The imagination is predominantly directed toward the past through both the particular presentation of the content, and the way in which it is absorbed. The reading in images occurs in such a way that, regardless of the novelty of the form of the present and its content, it is ultimately past-directed. Reading attempts to have the past and present coincide as much as possible in order to preserve the form, structure, and culture of the group. In other words, what is presented as new is a reforming of certain aspects of the group in its past and present in order to perpetuate it as it was and still is. The perception at the basis of reading is a form of repetition of what has already been perceived, as is the imagined content, and the degraded derealizing act of the imagination is a repetition of previous, institutionalized imagining acts. As a result, the dialectic of perceiving and imagining in the act of reading is a temporalization that moves, paradoxically, in two directions, insofar as it moves into the "future" of the past by stretching into the past and the present as the replication of their images.

On the basis of the two-dimensional emphasis in the temporalization of reading, a further constituent element comes to qualify the imagination. The derealizing act of the imagination, concerning the content derealized, is a form of reimagining, a reforming of the "matter" of the group which, as much as possible, is meant to be preserved in its original form. As a result, the character of irreality that infuses imaginative acts is complemented by a corresponding, in truth an opposing, quality of "already was." Thus, as the condition for an institutionalized act of the imagination involves the perception of reality as to-be-realized, so does it also involve an imaginatively and temporally interwoven "already" and "not-yet." However, in this case, the irreality of the object is the result of a derealizing act which posits the image as "already present in the group" and "to be repeated." These are the additional, degraded, oppressive act-characters of the imagination as it temporalizes itself in and through the act of reading in the institutionalized group. The institutionalized, collective image of literature is thereby meant to direct the imagination to the past of the group, to take its inspiration from the group as it was, but also to imagine in a way that is itself—as much as possible—a repetition of the previous individual and collective acts of imagining and their correlates.

This imaginative-temporal repetition leads to the further repetition of generations insofar as there is a coincidence in both the form and content of imagining. The imagining in the act of reading, as a form of reimagining, is one which, as a form of repetition, begins to take on certain of the characteristics of memory. The schema of the imagination is that of the past, and is bounded by it to prevent its unexpected, creative use. As the group is a movement "backward" and "forward," and its temporalization de-temporalization, it is also a re-temporalization in accordance with an older temporal rhythm. Reimagining is a process of re-temporalization which continues the de-temporalization and therefore the depersonalization of the group members. As so dominated by the past, the present itself is not allowed to be a proper present, a unique moment, but is instead seen as an extension of the past and continuous with it. The act of reading in the present, as also concerned with the present of the group, creates a present that is meant to be a repetition of the past. The present, paradoxically, is only ever present to itself *as past*, as a form of the past, and leading to a future which will coincide with both previous temporal dimensions. Regardless of the novelty of the literary image, its end is to stimulate the imagination in such a way that the image presented is viewed as complete, familiar, and at best as what is old in a new form. It is to be accepted as a representation of how the group ought to be in its present *because* it represents how it was in its past. In this sense, the image splits the imagination, directing it toward the past, instrumentalizing it in the present, and limiting the future.

This emphasis on the past-directed character of the imagination involves a reconsideration of the role of the past in Sartre's thought, which, in this case, is the complementary opposite of the future as it is discussed in *The Imaginary.* In this early text, and as cited above, Sartre acknowledges a more explicitly determined and general concept of the future. Here, there is the past as the general background against which reading takes place, as well as the particular, remembered content of the past. There is both the overarching context of the past of the group and the particular, individual pasts of the different generations, events in the group, and group members. When reading, and appropriately relating to the image presented, the concrete, particular past, that, for example, of a particular historical form of the group, becomes the specific content of the determinate future situated within the horizon of the future in general. The act of reading, then, occurs against both a general background of the past and future, and with attention given to a particular past, which is mirrored by a particular future. The past, in both its general and particular dimensions, determines not only the present in its imposed coincidence with it, but also the future, in both its general and particular dimensions. The present therefore becomes a peculiar point of transition between past and future because it is a transition from a past which has been to a past which will be and to a future which is a reflection of the past image of the group. The present accordingly becomes a repetition of the past of the group as a memory which will become the image of the group as it is when it is realized in the future. The act-character of the imagining act is simultaneously a positing of its content as irreal and the repositing of the past of the group as its present and the future it will be. Imagining, in this case, is therefore comprised by a moment of memory. As instrumentalized, it reproduces past images of the group as its memory while being directed toward the past in the forward movement of the group accomplished through reading and its continuous functioning.[16]

As a result of this dialectic of time and images, reality becomes a play of pasts and futures, of images and memories, of various positings of content as no-longer and not-yet, and necessarily such because they are both posited as existing in the present as the repetition and reproduction of the group through literature. The de-temporalization of the imagination, then, is a result of the imposition of the order of the group and is oriented toward the past as the group continues into the future. It is a forced, collective temporalization which manifests itself in the individual, imagining acts of the group members whose individual acts have collective significance. The temporalization of the imagination therefore occurs across all three temporal dimensions, but in such a way that the past and future coincide in the present and the future is a mere reflection. The temporalization of the act of reading is ultimately a process which reduces itself to its past in repressing the present and denies a future by having it reflect the past. It is a past-oriented, future-directed process which, in its present, repeats the past. The temporalization of the group is reduced to itself in its self-reflection, and fashioned into a process that moves in two directions in and through its constraints. The instrumentalization of the imagination, then, allows for the replication of the past in and as the future, and prevents a genuine future from emerging in the group.

From the above analyses, it follows that the truth of the group, as found in literature, reading, and the imagination, is a temporalized, more specifically, a pre-temporalized truth. It has already been thought through and produced in advance in accordance with the culture and expectations of the group. Truth is not a temporalizing process in and of the group, but a temporalized object which only needs to be passively absorbed by the group members. The institutionalized group is temporalized by its images and does not produce anything genuinely new as part of a future-directed, imagining process. It temporalizes itself as temporalized and in order to be temporalized. It is a tension between temporalizing action and a temporalized past, but in attempting to maintain itself as it was it temporalizes itself in the present and future as already temporalized in the past. As continuing to temporalize in its being temporalized, the past culminates in a present to which, as much as possible, it is identical, or with which it coincides. Furthermore, the present is an extension and reflection of the past. As a mirror of the past, it does not present or anticipate a genuine future, but rather, as a temporalized-temporalizing, the present reveals the group as a fixed entity that continues to develop itself by limiting itself. It is also a temporalizing-temporalized, a process whose end is already reached, a development toward what is, the movement of a circle. The process of temporalization as de-temporalization in the institutionalized group is oriented by the instrumentalization of the imagination and institutionalized literature. It itself is not allowed to flow freely, or to be what it is, *precisely because it is reduced to being no more than what it is*, and the group itself functions in accordance with such an imposed temporal rhythm.

NOTES

1. This will supplement the discussions in part 1 wherein I addressed the development of the relation between perception and the imagination from *The Imaginary* to *The Family Idiot.* In this case, while "realizing and irrealizing theses" may interrelate, I will argue that the two are in certain respects reducible to one another (Rybalka, Pucciani, Gruenheck 1981, 47). It is not, then, a question of how perception and the imagination are interwoven rather than distinct, but how, through an oppressive education and in an oppressive group, they alter in character and are not able to fully be what they are. The relations between the two, in other words, are forced, and the mode of positing proper to the one is limited by, and to an extent confused by, the positing of the other. Thus, the "inclusion of the imaginary in perception" is, in this case, a result of oppression (Rybalka, Pucciani, Gruenheck 1981, 47).

2. For an account of the seriality of institutional culture, see Gordon and Gordon (1995, 65–70).

3. For further discussion of this topic, see Catalano (2010, 192–94). Barnes also provides a helpful summary. See Barnes (1981, 278).

4. For the family situation, particularly the standing and view of the father, see Catalano (2010, 3–20). For the role of Flaubert's father and his older brother in his development, see Barnes (1981, 39–53). For an account of the family in his "'choice' of the imaginary," its role in the process of personalization, and the conflicting ideologies Flaubert was subject to, see Flynn (1997, 180–86).

5. Although in a different context, this also relates to the claim made by Horkheimer and Adorno in *Dialectic of Enlightenment* that the schematism in Kant has been replaced by mass culture in modern, industrialized societies. See Horkheimer and Adorno (2002, 98). In a sense, I am adding an additional layer to this analysis in claiming that education schematizes the imagination, and that the act of imagining has largely been carried out in advance by the group.

6. For a brief discussion of the question of the primacy of the real or the imaginary, see Flynn (2014, 408).

7. This claim has interesting relations to Sartre's criticism of surrealism in *What Is Literature?* He there writes: "For the proletariat, engaged in struggle, must at every moment, in order to bring its undertaking to a successful conclusion, distinguish the past from the future, the real from the imaginary, and life from death" (Sartre 1988, 156). In the context here, the repression of the imagination, and the reducibility of the image to a prior reality, have the effect of depersonalizing and oppressing the individual group members. In other words, though I am not claiming that the institutionalized context forms a strict parallel to surrealism, it shares, from a Sartrean point of view, a distorted understanding of the relations between perception and the imagination, and the real and the irreal, which produces a culture of assimilation. For an account

of Sartre's views on surrealism in his early short stories and *What Is Literature?*, see Plank (1981, 1–58).

8. Moreover, as perception is interwoven with the imagination, or perceptions with images, it is at least in principle possible that memory can interweave with the perception of the present reality. Thus, the positing of an object as "*given-now as passed*" in memory can overlap with the experience of the object of perception as "posited as existing" (Sartre 2004b, 12, 181). The positings coincide in various respects in the experience of the identity of the object with its past in the present.

9. In the Transcendental Deduction, Kant writes: "we can represent nothing as combined in the object without having previously combined it ourselves" (Kant 1998, 245).

10. The concept of continuity here serves to expand on Aristotle's definition of it in the *Metaphysics.* He there writes: "The *continuous* is a species of the contiguous; two things are called continuous when the limits of each, with which they touch and are kept together, become one and the same, so that plainly the continuous is found in the things out of which a unity naturally arises by virtue of their contact" (Aristotle 1984a, 1688). In this case, the form of contact with the institutionalized past is a result of the repetition across the diachronic temporality of the group.

11. The concept I am developing here is a present, future-directed correlate of the concept of screen memories developed by Freud. See, for example, Freud (1966, 248). See also Freud (1965, 62–73).

12. Again modifying Aristotle's definition of continuity, the subject and object are not in contact with one another in this case insofar as the contact that is made is not genuine (Aristotle 1984a, 1688). That is, as restricted, the images of the group members do not meaningfully affect the object, and are therefore perfectly continuous with it through such false contact insofar as they are reducible to the object as determined by the group.

13. There is a further parallel with Freud here and his distinction between the manifest content and laten thoughts of dreams. In particular, see Freud (1966, 147). Here, there are two levels to waking, conscious life, and though the content beneath the surface is the truth of the literature produced, it is accessed, but not fully *recognized or understood* in its truth as a form of oppression.

14. For the complete discussion, see Sartre (1988, 58).

15. This extends the notion of bad faith as it has been traditionally discussed insofar as it does not involve an attempt to conceal one's own freedom, or to deny that of others, but rather the repression of an object. In this sense, the object, as more than it is, irreducible to itself in its transphenomenality, is reduced to a single profile. I would therefore add this particular form of bad faith in the orientation toward objects to "the manifestations of bad faith" in Barnes (1959, 66). For the complete discussion, see Barnes (1959, 48–154).

16. On the basis of my analysis here, just as there was a refashioning of the relations between perception and the imagination in Sartre's thought, there is a corresponding reconsideration of the relations between memory and the imagination. See Sartre (2004b, 181). Because of their education and the constraints of the group, there are various moments of coincidence between memories of the group and its past

images. Moreover, the positings specific to them overlap in certain respects, such that one moment of the positing of the irreal can involve the concomitant positing of it as "having been."

Conclusion

Biography and Prophecy

In the analyses of this book, I developed two distinct phenomenological orientations to education implicit in Sartre's work which correspond to the Organization and the Institution as they are analyzed in the *Critique.* In order to accomplish this task, I educationally reinterpreted several core Sartrean themes, such as the imagination, temporality, and the third. In so doing, I demonstrated the importance of his thought for phenomenological analyses of education, complemented philosophies of education grounded in Sartre's thought, and added a new dimension to the traditional accounts of his work.[1] As stated in the introduction, I had to be selective in my choice of texts, focusing on what was essential to my task in this work. I was, however, largely guided by the themes of the imagination, its relation to perception, subjectivity, and alterity, and the levels of time. Moreover, each of these themes, as well as their corresponding analyses, understood in their dialectical significance, served as a condition of possibility of two opposing, but internally related, phenomenological descriptions of education. In addition, by making use of texts from all of the periods of Sartre's philosophy, and incorporating late interviews, I also attempted to extend the range of Sartre's work and introduce texts that are generally ignored outside the world of Sartre scholarship.

The text began with an account of a genuine Sartrean phenomenology of education which involved properly interpreting the Organization as both the first group form in the *Critique* capable of establishing and sustaining a system of education, as well as the group form appropriate for committed education. In the first chapter, I reconceived of Sartre's notion of the third in educational terms, reconsidered the relation between the imagination and perception in such an educational group, and developed a new, imaginative concept of the phenomenological epoché and reduction. These opening analyses were largely static, but implicitly contained a genetic, temporal dimension.

The analysis of committed education in the classroom, that is, led to the temporal character of this group, which was treated in chapter 2. The temporality of the group, moreover, contained both diachronic and synchronic levels, requiring the appropriate analyses. Thus, I explained the temporality of education in its objective, diachronic character, as it bears upon past generations in the group and the various demands they make on the present generation. As the necessary complement, I provided a phenomenological account of the lived-time of education from the side of the teacher and the students. In chapter 3, I analyzed the consequences of committed education for the organized group, with particular attention to the theme of culture. I developed the concept of a culture of the imaginary, demonstrating the manner in which the group members were imaginatively oriented toward their tasks and functions, as well as how the images of literature continued to educate and fashion the group. Lastly, I showed the multiplicity of dialectics running off simultaneously in the Organization, and that the dialectical development of the group as a whole is guided, sustained, and oriented by the imagination.

The three chapters of part 1 articulated a genuinely Sartrean analysis of education. The analyses of these chapters individually, and part 1 taken as a whole, also allowed for their own dialectical reinterpretation and the corresponding analyses. And this was the overarching aim of part 2, which established the complementary opposite approach to education described in part 1, what I termed "institutionalized education." I made use of the same texts and concepts, while incorporating the additional elements specific to the Institution. To begin, then, I provided an account of education in this group form, the concepts of the teacher and the students, their status as thirds, and the form of the phenomenological epoché and reduction appropriate to an oppressive system of education. Again, these analyses were largely static, pointing the way to their temporal reinterpretation, which I provided in chapter 4. As a reflection of chapter 2, I began with an analysis of the diachronic temporality of the group, clarifying how the sovereign and non-sovereign generations are differently temporalized across the life of the group through educational demands. I then turned to the synchronic, lived-time of education, and provided a phenomenological description of the temporality of the teacher and the students. What was of central significance here was that the lived-time of education was not temporalized on its own terms, but rather in accordance with the temporality of the sovereign. In chapter 6, I described the culture that such education produced, and the role of perception and the imagination in such a culture. I showed how the institutionalized group members are oriented toward their tasks and functions, and what an oppressive form of literature looks like. I further showed the different dialectics operative in the institutionalized group, and that it ultimately forms a static dialectic, or an analytic genesis.

As a conclusion to this book, through a reflection on its analyses and the current state of Sartre scholarship, I would like to devote a few words to the relations between Sartre, phenomenology, and education, with an emphasis on the imagination, and indicate directions of future research into Sartre and education. I would also like to discuss the educational significance of Sartre's biographies and autobiography in general. In particular, I will provide a brief comparison of the aspects of Sartre's text on Flaubert with John Stuart Mill's autobiography. I intend to demonstrate the presently situated, oracular character of both texts, their similar prophetic temporalizations, and the lessons, ignored if not forgotten, to be gleaned from both texts.

PHENOMENOLOGIES OF THE IMAGINATION

Through the analyses of this text, I hope to have shown the importance of Sartre's thought for education and a new approach to his philosophical work. There are, however, a few potential dangers in the accounts of the imagination I have provided, and in my use of the phenomenological epoché and reduction, which I would like to address here. First, I have argued both for the appeal to the imagination as a necessary component part of any genuine form of education as well as that one of the aims of education is to cultivate the imagination and make possible its future use. It is, in this regard, both part of the process of education and its ultimate end. Furthermore, through such education, it is hoped that the students will have learned *how to continue to cultivate their imaginations* through the various aspects of their lives. It is important, however, to address a potential issue within any account of education with such methods and aims, and that is the danger of essentializing or homogenizing the imagination itself.[2] It is true that there are certain essential aspects of the imagination in Sartre's treatment of it, and arguably in general, but this should not lead to a reductive understanding of its character and limits. For example, in *The Imaginary*, the imagining acts of consciousness are described as positing their objects as absent, "outside the real," and so on (Sartre 2004b, 192). Moreover, throughout the text on Flaubert, the imagination is described as the derealization of the real, as a way of surpassing the given through the derealization of a prior reality. To a certain extent, and part of both phenomenological and existential-psychoanalytic analyses, such accounts uncover and describe certain of the essential qualities of images and the experience of imagining and should not be thought to be conceptually lacking in light of the proposed tasks of both works.

On these various accounts, it is necessary to recognize that the imagination *is not only the imagination* in a few different senses. First, one of the essential aims of committed education is to integrate the imagination into the educational process, and that necessarily means recognizing its role in the educational acts of both the teacher and the students. Moreover, this raises a paradoxical state of affairs. The students, within a given class and at the beginning of the educational process, possess various "levels" of the imagination in accordance with the uses they have previously made of it. They do not begin, in other words, in the total absence of the imagination, but rather with an imagination that has already begun to be developed, which as of yet has not been educationally fashioned and cultivated. Thus, in this sense, there is a reality which is a blend of actuality and potentially in the state of the imagination at the beginning and throughout the educational process. The imaginations of the students, however, are not all identical, regardless of what the eidetic qualities they necessarily have in common, nor are their particular uses of them. Moreover, depending on the classes they are taking, the material taught, and so on, the individual character of both the imagination and the images formed is further complicated by this academic "third thing" that serves to further inspire and cultivate it. And this multidimensional state of affairs regarding the imagination has to be appropriately recognized and empathetically understood by the teacher throughout their lesson plans. The imagination of the students, then, especially early on in the process, needs to be understood in its individual character and largely as a point of departure. In addition, there is not necessarily, and I would argue there largely is not, a preestablished harmony or a priori symmetry in the relations between the imagination of the teacher and that of the individual students. The teacher, then, depending on the situation, previous experience, and culture of the classroom, needs to reflexively grasp their imagination, and come to understand the appropriate way to create images in appealing to the varieties of the imagination in the students.

As a blend of actuality and potentiality throughout the educational process, there is a further element that needs to be addressed. While it is true that the imagination remains such a blend, and most importantly, always admits of more potential and actualization, the movement from its early, incipient state to its later, educated forms, is not a single, linear, predetermined or even predeterminable process. The cultivation of the imagination has to be understood as an open process whose "fulfillment" is never absolute and does not admit of a fixed sequence of stages which measure or account for its progress. Rather, it is an intrinsically unstable blend of actuality and potentially, and in appealing to it, the particular actuality achieved, with the particular potentialities that dwell within it, need to be appreciated and properly addressed. And as can be seen from these descriptions, the "actuality" of the imagination is not the single form of fulfillment of an identical capacity shared by all subjects. It is not the case, then, that the imagination, at the beginning of the process, contains everything it will be at the end of the process, and in reaching such a stage fulfills what it was meant to be. It is a paradoxical unity of a capacity which can always be further fashioned, and whose fulfillment is always incomplete. It can be said, however, that the imagination of the students needs to reach various levels throughout the educational process, and that a student of a later stage of education should have cultivated the imagination to a further extent than that of a student at an earlier stage. One would hope, for example, that in a subject such as ethics, the moral imagination of the student would have advanced across a college career, and that therefore the approach to moral questions and the possibility of a more informed and defensible decision, would be different after years of study. Again, however, there is a danger in recognizing a necessary form of "progress" in educating the imagination insofar as it runs the risk of not appreciating, if not dismissing altogether, the imagination of students in the earlier stages of formal education.[3]

The very concept of educating the imagination, what I have constantly referred to as "cultivating" the imagination, has to be understood as an appeal, inspiration, and encouragement of the individual imagination as individual. However, and as I stressed throughout part 1, part of such an educational process is to harmonize the plurality of imaginations, and therefore to have the students understand their own imaginative capacities as both individual and collective. As much, then, as the individual character of the student's imagination needs to be appealed to, it also needs to be understood by the student as, at least regarding the process of education and the ultimate culture it gives rise to, incomplete when considered in isolation and therefore *intrinsically intersubjective*. There is, then, a blend of actuality and potentiality in the case of each individual understood as both individual and collective, and therefore part of the cultivation of the imagination is recognizing the unique interrelations within its individual and collective character.

An additional issue emerges when the imagination is conceived as corresponding in various ways to the different levels of education, and concerning the particular subjects being studied. It cannot be understood on the model of other subjects, that is, of being "acquired" as can an understanding of historical events, the laws of nature, and so on. When dealing with an understanding, for example, of a historical event, it is possible to conceive of a symmetry between the teacher and the students. In this case, the teacher possesses knowledge of an event or a period of history, which the student did not until the completion of the lesson. There is, it follows, a correlation between the initial ignorance and knowledge, as well as the subsequent knowledge on both sides, such that the knowledge acquired eliminates the initial ignorance. However, in the case of the imagination, the goal is not for the students to be able to imagine as does the teacher, or for the student to reach the "level" of the imagination of the teacher. It is not the simple acquisition of a skill or an ability which can be understood as analogous to the knowledge the teacher possesses of a historical event before and after the lesson. It is not the case, however, that the use of the imagination should be, or can be, completely without order, an anarchy of images conceived of as a form of freedom without restraint.[4] However, there is no limiting imperative in the student's imagining, such that they should imagine in the same way the teacher does. The blend of actuality and potentiality, of the imagination as an incomplete reality, is not fulfilled when the student, for example, repeats images provided by the teacher, or approaches all aspects of a subject-matter as the teacher does. The student does, nevertheless, improve the use of the imagination, "acquire" new abilities, but it is precisely insofar as it is an ability, individually and collectively understood and exercised, that the individual imagination does not find its fulfillment in the imaginative capacity of the teacher. The student, in learning, continues to learn *how to imagine*, and this will complement the content taught while remaining irreducible to it.

As a correlate to the danger of essentializing the imagination, of reducing it to a single form, there is a similar danger in the use of the phenomenological epoché and reduction. As there is not a single, operative concept of the imagination in education, so is there also not a single form or use of the epoché and reduction. Again, as analogous to the situation of the imagination, there are certain eidetic qualities of this method, such as the suspension of content, the appeal to the imagination, and so on. However, the form of the suspension to present content, the images used, and the other subjects and content that are present in such a reduction, will vary. The epoché and reduction are themselves situated and will incorporate past content throughout the educational process. The imaginative reduction itself, in developing throughout the educational process and integrating what was previously taught and learned, will also be flexible, multidimensional, making possible the further manifestation of the truth and knowledge of a particular subject. The imaginative reduction can accommodate various pedagogies and systems of education. Such an act of suspension is a condition of possibility of the incorporation of the content of one subject into that of another in an appropriate way. For example, in a lesson on math presented in accordance with the epoché and reduction, it will be possible, as relevant to the given topic, to introduce aesthetics, music, concepts of harmony and proportion that involve math yet are also central to discussions of beauty and art more generally. This will allow for the various relations between the subjects to be appropriately introduced into the lesson and properly understood. Moreover, such a use and version of the phenomenological method preserves the reality of the content suspended, and accordingly allows for the prior assumptions regarding the subjects and their relations to be put in brackets while the positing of the reality of the content is maintained. It is therefore necessary to find a form of committed education appropriate for each subject, in truth a phenomenology and an imagination for each subject, in order for the subject-matter, the imagination, and teaching and learning themselves to be more than their particular manifestations in the present educational circumstances. It is, therefore, equally important that the imaginative reduction itself not be standardized, lest as at least one possible consequence, it will standardize the imagination of the students and the general process of education.

MILL AND FLAUBERT: THE SCYLLA AND CHARYBDIS OF EDUCATION

After having discussed certain of the dangers which dwell within my discussions of the imagination in part 1 of this book and the appropriate way of responding to them, I would like to turn to the theme of the educational significance of two seemingly unrelated texts, namely Sartre's existential biography of Gustave Flaubert and John Stuart Mill's autobiography. More generally, I would like to raise the question of biography and autobiography for an understanding of education, issues it may potentially face, and certain ways to address them. As such, I would like to pose as an educational, hermeneutic, and existential-psychoanalytic task the reading of biographies and autobiographies, embedded as they are in their historical context, in order to illuminate education for contemporary educators of all levels, subjects, approaches, and so on. Moreover, I would like to inquire into the different ways in which biographies and autobiographies as such can be considered prophetic, and therefore intrinsically possessing their own mictrotemporalizations, lending them an import which will continue to bear upon education. It is also important to note that Sartre wrote several biographies, as well as an autobiography, wherein the theme of education is discussed, or which at least have educational significance.[5] It is accordingly necessary to continue to raise the question of the educational significance of biography, and the manner in which such a form of writing continues to situate itself, temporalize itself in advance as part of its oracular character, and re-temporalize itself through its generational reinterpretations.

As an additional component, I would also like to draw a brief comparison between the aspects of Flaubert's personalization, the role of his formal education in it, and his family situation, and the personalization of John Stuart Mill as it was discussed in *The Autobiography of John Stuart Mill.* In his recounting of his early childhood, the family structure, his education, and relation to his father, much would seem to place him in diametrical opposition to Flaubert. For example, he was instilled with the value of hard work, dedication, and the dangers of idleness and even of vacation. In the *Autobiography* he writes: "No holidays were allowed, lest the habit of work should be broken and a taste for idleness acquired" (Mill 1909, 28). He was not overly cared for as was Flaubert by his mother, but rather, at the age of three, began studying Ancient Greek, and within a few years, had read Aesop, the dialogues of Plato, Herodotus, Xenophon, and so on. Thus, at ages when Gustave was struggling to learn how to read, and words appeared to him as fixed, with predetermined meanings that would "make themselves speak through him," Mill had not only learned to read and write, but had done so in a foreign language, one which would have required the additional exertion seemingly made impossible by virtue of Flaubert's passive constitution (Sartre 1981, 39).

As an additional, significant difference, Mill was the eldest of nine children, responsible for educating and caring for them, and was very close with his father. For example, he recalls with fondness and admiration the days he spent as a young child studying in the same room with his father while he worked on his book on the history of England and its relation to India, and the character the father showed in constantly "interrupting" his own work to explain the meaning of Greek words Mill did not know (Mill 1909, 10).[6] In this respect, the contrast in relations to the father could not be starker, and the desire to be taken in by "the black Lord," the resentment toward a preferred, older brother, were entirely absent (Sartre 1981, 439). In addition to working at the same desk, John Stuart Mill and his father took walks together wherein they discussed what Mill was studying, his father provided "discourses," and as Mill grew older, his father began to rely on him for editing his own work, for helping with his own research, and so on (Mill 1909, 10).[7] In this regard, Mill and Flaubert had entirely opposed relations to language, knowledge, their role in the family, and, as was to be determining in different ways for both of them, different relationships with their fathers.

Despite these obvious differences in their life situations and educational experiences, there is a single commonality in their fathers that ultimately led both to find a distinctive value in the imagination itself and as an antidote to the worldview they had inherited. Flaubert's father, in addition to being a unique, contradictory unity of a self-made man and a member of the nobility, was imbued with analytic rationality, the spirit of analysis, and the general value of utility and science.[8] He was, moreover, the atheistic counterpart to Flaubert's mother, and hoped Flaubert would pursue a career in law, and fulfill what was destined for him as a Flaubert and second son. James Mill, though of a different background, was also imbued with the same spirit, a friend and supporter of the utilitarian philosophy of Jeremy Bentham, and a proponent of the associationist school of psychology. Thus, rather than being caught between different classes and aspects of a developing culture, James Mill was in various respects consistent with them, and even contributed to them through his various publications and professional life. Such an emphasis on analytic reason, the accompanying psychology, and utilitarian calculation led him to provide an education for Mill that was dominated by these various orientations. Furthermore, he valued pure intellectual development over an education that would have also appealed to feelings, the imagination, or a creative, artist outlook that would have had the additional benefit of serving as a complement to the spirit of analysis.

It was, in fact, as a result of such an education, and of such a cultural orientation, that Mill eventually reached what he called "A Crisis in my Mental History" (Mill 1909, 88).[9] There are several aspects to this crisis, but I would like to focus on two of them. First, he asked himself, on the basis of the education he received and the worldview he inherited and continued, if he would be happy if all of his wishes were fulfilled and all of his hopes for social progress were realized. He writes:

> In this frame of mind it occurred to me to put the question directly to myself: "Suppose that all your objects in life were realized; that all the changes in institutions and opinions which you are looking forward to, could be completely effected at this very instant: would this be a great joy and happiness to you?" And an irrepressible self-consciousness distinctly answered, "No!" At this my heart sank within me: the whole foundation on which my life was constructed fell down. (Mill 1909, 89)

In this regard, the attainment of happiness alone, both individually and collectively, and through the use of the proper, ethical means, was seen as *insufficient* for a meaningful life.[10] Something, though it may not yet have been entirely clear, was felt to be lacking, and the goal of a pure, efficient realization of happiness was without support.[11] Happiness alone, that is, without struggle, without suffering, without hardship, seemed an empty ideal, one which failed to meet what later philosophy would term deeper, existential aspects of life.[12] A perfectly calculated happiness, that is, one which seemed to address every issue, to check every box, left him with a feeling of incompletion, of unfulfillment, which appeared paradoxical, and inconsistent with the aims he was pursing and the education he had received.

The second point, which follows from the foundations of his education and is the more important of the two for my purposes, is that his feelings, emotions, and imagination had been entirely left out of his education. It is true that he was trained in classics, that he was reading literature and history from a very young age, and that he went on to complement these studies through pursuits in math and science. However, what was notably lacking, what ultimately caught up with him, was the total neglect of this entire side of life, of what now, in educational terms, is part of the approach of the humanities and is the complement to the present, cultural orientation toward the sciences and technology. In fact, he describes his situation as follows:

> My education, I thought, had failed to create these feelings in sufficient strength to resist the dissolving influence of analysis, while the whole course of my intellectual cultivation had made precocious and premature analysis the inveterate habit of my mind. I was thus, as I said to myself, left stranded at the commencement of my voyage, with a well-equipped ship and a rudder, but no sail; without any real desire for the ends which I had been so carefully fitted out to work for, no delight in virtue, or the general good, but also just as little in anything else. (Mill 1909, 92)

In this regard, with an overly analytically oriented father, Mill found himself in a situation comparable to that of Flaubert. And although his crisis precedes Flaubert's by nearly two decades—with Flaubert's prophetic fall coming in 1844, and Mill's crisis in the winter of 1826–1827—I would like to treat them as largely contemporary in their respective responses to the scientific spirit of the age. Moreover, as he discusses in detail, it was by turning to these other aspects of life, first and foremost through the poetry of the Romantics, that Mill began to emerge from the depression he found himself in because of the educational and existential shortcomings he faced. Thus, while Flaubert derealized himself and chose himself as *un homme imaginaire* to respond to his family situation and the analytic rationality of his father and culture, Mill turned to the imagination and poetry in order to more appropriately embed himself in reality and to fill the void created by his overly analytic, calculative education. Thus, as a first point of comparison, I would simply like to state that both, responding to an extreme view held by their fathers and present in the culture, found a solution through turning to precisely what had been repressed in their experience. As a result, in both cases, Flaubert, because of his attempt to flee the real through the imagination, and Mill in his initial emphasis on the philosophy and worldview of his father and Jeremy Bentham, serve as twin poles of a single cultural phenomenon and as an object lesson for education and its various manifestations.

Now, I have chosen this comparison with Mill to complement Sartre's analyses because in many ways he is the identical opposite of Flaubert, and yet came to an appreciation of feeling, poetry, and aesthetics more generally. However, I have also chosen him because he too was oracular, both regarding the development of education and his own life. Mill too, I am arguing, felt himself caught between extremes, the one being the analytic rationality of his father which he shared with Flaubert, and the other a lack he did not fully *understand* or appreciate until later in life. In a peculiar sense, Mill was prophetic of his own life insofar as he was ahead of himself in the particular lack which only manifested consciously and in its full force later. He was not, then, as was Flaubert, explicitly caught between science and religion, or the spirit of analysis and the arts, but between analytic rationality and *the lack of the arts, poetry, and feeling.* He too serves as a microtemporalization, but under different circumstances and for different reasons. Whereas Flaubert suffered in advance the contradictions of his period throughout his life and underwent a crisis to become a writer, Mill, *on the surface,* harmonized with the conditions of his time, consciously inherited them, and continued to extend them. He was educationally, philosophically, and existentially consistent with the general outlook he found himself in, or in Sartre's language, with his facticity. In this regard, his transcendence was always the transcendence of the given *in accordance with the given,* that is, *on its own terms.* It was not until much later that the lack which was present from the beginning manifested and led to his crisis.

On the basis of Mill's unique personalization, and by extending Sartre's concept of microtemporalization, I would like to argue that *Mill had microtemporalized himself but* had done so in such a manner that his microtemporalization was *delayed,* that it did not become fully manifest until much later, and in such a way that he was not prepared for it. In this regard, Mill temporalized himself in advance without full consciousness of doing so, and only later, after the fact, came to realize the manner in which such a tension had always been implicit and lived through. Said somewhat differently, given the singular emphasis on analytic rationality in his personalization, Mill, through the approach of his father, was prophetic of his own life insofar as such a crisis was inevitable. He could not, in other words, continue to live in the absence of feeling, imagination, and as I showed above, struggle. And because these aspects had been missing, such a conflict, that between utilitarianism and Romanticism, between science and the humanities, was "fated," and thc only indeterminate aspect of it was when exactly it would come to pass. In this regard, in his initial state, regardless of the uniqueness of his upbringing and education, as he grew up he was macrotemporalized in his microtemporalization. The culture was "ahead of" him, providing both the context and the aim of his educational and professional efforts. However, such cultural macrotemporalization did not completely repress or eliminate the microtemporalization operative within it, and once the latter presented itself to Mill, in full consciousness and knowledge, his break with it and eventual crisis necessarily ensued. In this sense, once Mill, after having previously temporalized himself in accordance with the spirit of the age, "caught up with himself," and finally coincided more fully with his own temporalization, he experienced the crisis he details in his autobiography.[13]

As a result of his process of personalization, in particular the form of rationality present within it, Mill possesses a unique oracular character which slightly diverges from Sartre's analyses. While exceptionally situated in his circumstances, I would like to extend Mill's oracular character beyond nineteenth-century England and its immediate future. In order to do so, I would like to extend the concept of microtemporalization by combining it with a material eidetics, which results in this particular microtemporalization taking on the character of an instance of a general possibility, but with the accompanying nuance of prophesying a necessary future state of affairs as such, regardless of how much the concrete, historical circumstances may vary. As an extension of Sartre's concept of prophecy, Mill becomes both a microtemporalization of his particular historical circumstances and a perennial temporalization, an eternal temporalization continuously re-temporalized, insofar as he serves as the realization of an eidetic type both in his own personal history and concerning the future of such a history. Once educationally situated, that is, he becomes an oracle of the outcome of any educational process as such, any system of education as such, that emphasizes analytic rationality and the development of the intellect *to the exclusion* of feeling, emotion, poetry, and the arts in general. Through following the steps of his individual circumstances, and his eventual crisis, which I am here claiming was a priori necessary because of the repression of the other "half" of life, he serves as a historically situated eidetic figure, the *essential* corresponding form of the universal singular, whose prophecy is perennially valid for education to the extent that it takes such a reductive form. Mill, in this regard, is the other side of Flaubert's personalization, insofar as he did not respond to the scientism of his father, but embraced it, and ultimately through so doing was forced to break with it, reflect on it, and complement it with the imagination, in his case that of the Romantic poets. Mill, himself then, is a perennial oracle who may be forgotten or deliberately repressed in education, but his unique personalization and temporalization continue to serve as the sign of the consequences of an overly scientific, technological, mechanistic, and efficient education.

NOTES

1. The analyses are relevant to the philosophy of education understood in accordance with both the objective and subjective genitive. On this point, see Papastephanou (2009, 2).

2. Such essentialization or homogenization would be yet another form of bad faith, reducing a capacity to a single form despite its inherent multiplicity, in order for it to be what it is.

3. One response to such a state of affairs is the increased awareness of the philosophical thinking of children and the area of contemporary philosophy generally referred to as "philosophy for children."

4. On this point, concerning both memory and the imagination, see Newman (1982, 106).

5. For a brief discussion of the *The Words* and its relation to education see Gordon (1985, 49).

6. For a summary statement that emphasizes the contrast between the two, see Mill (1909, 10–11).

7. For a detailed description of their walks, see Mill (1909, 10–11).

8. See Barnes (1981, 39–41) and Catalano (2010, 6–8).

9. The full title of chapter 5 is "A Crisis in my Mental History. One Stage Onward." For the complete discussion see Mill (1909, 88–110).

10. On this point, see Adam Etinson's article in the *New York Times* titled "Is a Life without Struggle Worth Living?"

11. For Mill's revised views of happiness, see Mill (1909, 94).

12. See, for example, part 1 of Dostoevsky's *Notes from Underground.* He writes: "As far as my own personal opinion is concerned, to love only well-being is somehow even indecent. Whether good or bad, it is sometimes also very pleasant to demolish something. After all, I'm not standing up for . . . my own whim and for its being guaranteed to me whenever necessary. For instance, suffering is not permitted in vaudevilles, that I know. It's also inconceivable in the crystal palace; suffering is doubt and negation. What sort of crystal palace would it be if any doubt were allowed? Yes, I'm convinced that man will never renounce real suffering, that is, destruction and chaos. After all, suffering is the sole cause of consciousness. Although I stated earlier that in my opinion consciousness is man's greatest misfortune, still I know that man loves it and would not exchange it for any other sort of satisfaction. Consciousness, for example, is infinitely higher that two times two" (Dostoevsky 2001, 25). Interesting in this regard, in the textbook *Philosophy from Plato to Derrida*, in the second chapter of Mill's *Utilitarianism*, the editor has included two pictures of the crystal palace Dostoevsky refers to, with the following, telling caption: "*Interior, Crystal Palace.* The palace was a shrine to science, industrialization, and progress. The architectural marvel represented in concrete form Mill's optimism when he spoke of the 'wisdom of society' and the 'progress of science which holds out a promise for the future'" (Mill 2011, 933). I would also like to extend the notion of microtemporalization as it is being discussed here to fictional characters, in particular to the character of Bazarov from Ivan Turgenev's *Fathers and Children.* The logical development of his nihilistic and overly scientific attitude also serves as a perennial temporalization which demonstrates the untenability and self-destructiveness of such a view.

13. I am not suggesting that Mill fully coincided with himself as does the in-itself, but rather that he experienced his temporalization as his own, and not solely as that of the familial and cultural situation he found himself in.

Bibliography

Aristotle. 1984a. *Metaphysics.* Translated by W. D. Ross. Princeton, NJ: Princeton University Press.

———. 1984b. *On the Soul.* Translated by W. D. Ross. Princeton, NJ: Princeton University Press.

Aronson, Ronald. 1980. *Jean-Paul Sartre—Philosophy in the World.* London: NLB.

Barnes, Hazel E. 1959. *The Literature of Possibility.* Lincoln, University of Nebraska Press.

———. 1967. *An Existentialist Ethics.* New York: Alfred A. Knopf.

———. 1973. *Sartre.* Philadelphia: J. B. Lippincott Company.

———. 1981. *Sartre and Flaubert.* Chicago: The University of Chicago Press.

de Beauvoir, Simone. 1976. *The Ethics of Ambiguity.* Translated by Bernard Frechtman. Citadel Press.

———. 2004. "Literature and Metaphysics." In *Philosophical Writings,* edited by Margaret A. Simons et al., 269–77. Urbana: University of Illinois Press.

Blenkinsop, Sean. 2012. "From Waiting for the Bus to Storming the Bastille: From Sartrean Seriality to the Relationships That Form Classroom Communities." *Educational Philosophy and Theory* 44(2): 183–95.

Buber, Martin. 1979. *I and Thou.* Translated by Walter Kaufmann. New York: Simon and Shuster.

Bugental, James F. T. 1978. *Psychotherapy and Process: The Fundamentals of an Existential-Humanistic Approach.* New York: McGraw-Hill, Inc.

———. 1987. *The Art of the Psychotherapist.* New York: W.W. Norton & Company.

Busch, Thomas W. 1980. "*Sartre's Use of the Reduction: Being and Nothingness Reconsidered.*" In *Jean-Paul Sartre: Contemporary Approaches to His Philosophy,* edited by Hugh J. Silverman and Frederick A. Ellison, 17–29. Pittsburgh: Duquesne University Press.

Camus, Albert. 1991. *The Myth of Sisyphus and Other Essays.* Translated by Justin O'Brien. New York: Vintage International.

Carruthers, Mary. 2008. *The Book of Memory.* Cambridge University Press.

Casey, Edward S. 1981. "Sartre on Imagination." In *The Philosophy of Jean-Paul Sartre,* edited by Paul Arthur Schilpp, 139–66. La Salle: Open Court.

———. 2000. *Imagining: A Phenomenological Study.* Bloomington: Indiana University Press.

Catalano, Joseph S. 1986. *A Commentary on Jean-Paul Sartre's "Critique of Dialectical Reason": Theory of Practical Ensembles.* Volume 1. Chicago: The University of Chicago Press.

———. 2010. *Reading Sartre.* Cambridge University Press.

Contat, M., and M. Rybalka. 1977. "Un Entretien avec J.-P. Sartre." *Le Monde des livres*, May 14.

Cormann, Grégory. 2020. "The Historical Origins of Sartre's Account of Temporality." In *The Sartrean Mind,* edited by Matthew C. Eshleman and Constance L. Mui. 198–211. London: Routledge.

Degenhardt, M. 1975. "Sartre, Imagination and Education." *Proceedings of the Philosophy of Education Society of Great Britain* 9(9): 72–92.

Detmer, David. 2005. "Sartre on Freedom and Education." *Sartre Studies International* 11(1/2): 78–90.

———. 2008. *Sartre Explained: From Bad Faith to Authenticity.* Chicago, Illinois: Open Court.

Dort, Bernard. 1981. "Sartre on Theatre: Politics and the Imagination." *Canadian Theatre Review* 32: 32–43.

Dostoevsky, Fyodor. 2001. *Notes from Underground.* Translated by Michael R. Katz. New York: W. W. Norton & Company.

Dufourcq, Annabelle. 2014. "De la Chair à la Révolte: L'activité Passive dans *L'Idiot de la Famille.*" *Horizon* 3(2): 55–70.

Etinson, Adam. October 2, 2017. "Is a Life without Struggle Worth Living." *New York Times.* https://www.nytimes.com/2017/10/02/opinion/js-mill-happiness-anxiety.html.

Flynn, Thomas. 1973. "The Alienating and the Mediating Third in the Social Philosophy of Jean-Paul Sartre." In *Heirs and Ancestors,* edited by John K. Ryan, 3–38. Catholic University of America Press.

———. 1975. "The Role of the Image in Sartre's Aesthetic." *The Journal of Aesthetics and Art Criticism* 33(4): 431–42.

———. 1980. "Sartre-Flaubert and the Real/Unreal." In *Jean-Paul Sartre: Contemporary Approaches to His Philosophy,* edited by Hugh J. Silverman and Frederick A. Ellison, 105–23. Pittsburgh: Duquesne University Press.

———. 1981. "Mediated Reciprocity and the Genius of the Third." In *The Philosophy of Jean-Paul Sartre,* edited by Paul Arthur Schilpp, 345–70. La Salle: Open Court.

———. 1984. *Sartre and Marxist Existentialism.* Chicago: The University of Chicago Press.

———. 1997. *Sartre, Foucault, and Historical Reason: Toward an Existentialist Theory of History. Volume 1.* Chicago: The University of Chicago Press.

———. 2014. *Sartre: A Philosophical Biography.* Cambridge University Press.

Freire, Paulo. 1992. *Pedagogy of the Oppressed.* Translated by Myra Bergman Ramos. New York: Continuum.

Freud, Sigmund. 1965. *The Psychopathology of Everyday Life.* Translated by James Strachey. New York: W. W. Norton & Company.

———. 1966. *Introductory Lectures on Psycho-Analysis.* Translated by James Strachey. New York: W. W. Norton & Company.

Giroux, Henry A. 2011. *On Critical Pedagogy.* Continuum.

Gordon, Haim. 1985. "Dialectical Reason and Education: Sartre's Fused Group." *Educational Theory* 35(1): 43–56.

Gordon, Mordechai. 2016. *Existential Philosophy and the Promise of Education.* New York: Peter Lang.

Gordon, Rivca, and Haim Gordon. 1995. "Seriality vs. Education: A Sartrean Perspective." *Social Philosophy Today* 11: 53–71.

———. 1997. "Sartre on the Curse of Modern Schools." *Sartre Studies International* 3(1): 66–81.

Greene, Maxine. 1988. *The Dialectic of Freedom.* New York: Teachers College Press.

———. 1995. *Releasing the Imagination: Essays on Education, the Arts, and Social Change.* San Francisco: Jossey-Bass Publishers.

———. 2001. *Variations on a Blue Guitar: The Lincoln Center Institute Lectures on Aesthetic Education.* New York: Teachers College Press.

Guerlac, Suzanne. 1997. *Literary Polemics: Bataille, Sartre, Valéry, Breton.* Stanford, California: Stanford University Press.

Gyllenhammer, Paul. 2015. "Progress and the Practico-Inert." *Sartre Studies International* 21(2): 3–12.

Hayim, Gila J. 1996. *Existentialism and Sociology.* New Brunswick: Transaction Publishers.

Hegel, G. W. F. 1942. *Hegel's Philosophy of Right.* Translated by T. M. Knox. Oxford: Clarendon Press.

Heidegger, Martin. 1962. *Being and Time.* Translated by John Macquarrie and Edward Robinson. New York: Harper and Row, publishers, Incorporated.

———. 1984. *The Metaphysical Foundations of Logic.* Translated by Michael Heim. Bloomington: Indiana University Press.

———. 1997. *Kant and the Problem of Metaphysics.* Translated by Richard Taft. Bloomington: Indiana University Press.

Hollier, Denis. 1986. *The Politics of Prose.* Minneapolis: University of Minnesota Press.

Horkheimer, Max. 1947. *Eclipse of Reason.* New York: Oxford University Press.

Horkheimer, Max, and Theodor Adorno. 2002. *Dialectic of Enlightenment.* Translated by Edmund Jephcott. Stanford, California: Stanford University Press.

Howells, Christina. 1979. *Sartre's Theory of Literature.* London: The Modern Humanities Research Association.

———. 1988. *Sartre: The Necessity of Freedom.* Cambridge: Cambridge University Press.

Husserl, Edmund. 1970. *The Crisis of the European Sciences and Transcendental Phenomenology: An Introduction to Phenomenological Philosophy.* Translated by David Carr. Evanston: Northwestern University Press.

———. 1973. *Experience and Judgment: Investigations in a Genealogy of Logic.* Translated by James S. Churchill and Karl Ameriks. Northwestern University Press.

———. 1991. *On the Phenomenology of the Consciousness of Internal Time (1893–1917).* Translated by John Brough. Dordrecht: Kluwer Academic Publishers.

———. 1995. *Cartesian Meditations: An Introduction to Phenomenology.* Translated by Dorion Cairns. Kluwer Academic Publishers.

———. 1998. *Ideas Pertaining to a Pure Phenomenology and to a Phenomenological Philosophy: First Book: General Introduction to a Pure Phenomenology.* Translated by F. Kersten. Dordrecht: Kluwer Academic Publishers.

———. 2001a. *Husserliana,* Band XXXIII. *Die "Bernauer Manuskripte" über das Zeitbewusstsein (1917/1918).* Dordrecht: Kluwer Academic Publishers.

———. 2001b. *Logical Investigations. Volume 1.* Translated by J. N. Findlay. New York: Routledge.

Jaeger, Werner. 1945. *Paideia: The Ideals of Greek Culture;: Archaic Greece: The Mind of Athens. Volume 1.* Translated by Gilbert Highet. New York: Oxford University Press.

Kaelin, E. F. 1966. "The Existential Ground for Aesthetic Education." *Philosophy of Education: Proceedings of the Annual Meeting of the Philosophy of Education Society* 11: 170–77.

Kant, Immanuel. 1987. *Critique of Judgment.* Translated by Werner S. Pluhar. Indianapolis: Hackett Publishing Company.

———. 1998. *Critique of Pure Reason.* Translated by Paul Guyer and Allen W. Wood. Cambridge University Press.

Keefe, Terry, and Rosanna Keefe. 2001. "The Concept of 'Ignorance' in Jean-Paul Sartre's *Notebooks for an Ethics* and *Truth and Existence." Journal of the British Society for Phenomenology* 32(1): 66–80.

Kern, Iso. 1977. "The Three Ways to the Transcendental Phenomenological Reduction in the Philosophy of Edmund Husserl." In *Husserl: Expositions and Appraisals,* edited by Frederick A. Elliston and Peter McCcormick, 126–49. Notre Dame: University of Notre Dame Press.

Kierkegaard, Søren. 1946. *A Kierkegaard Anthology.* Edited by Robert Bretall. Princeton: Princeton University Press.

Kneller, George F. 1958. *Existentialism and Education.* New York: Wiley.

Marrou, H. I. 1956. *A History of Education in Antiquity.* Translated by George Lamb. The New American Library.

Martinot, Steve. 2005. "The Sartrean Account of the Look as a Theory of Dialogue." *Sartre Studies International* 11(1/2): 43–61.

May, Rollo. 1969. "The Emergence of Existential Psychology." *Existential Psychology,* edited by Rollo May, 1–48. New York: McGraw-Hill, Inc.

McInerney, Peter K. 1991. *Time and Experience.* Temple University Press.

Merleau-Ponty, Maurice. 1964. "Metaphysics and the Novel." In *Sense and Non-Sense,* edited by John Wild et al., 26–40. Northwestern University Press.

Mill, John Stuart. 1909. *Autobiography.* New York: P. F. Collier & Son Company.

———. 2011. "Utilitarianism." *From Plato to Derrida,* edited by Forrest E. Baird, 923–61. Boston: Prentice Hall.

Morris, Van Cleve. 1966. *Existentialism in Education: What it Means.* New York: Harper and Row.

Newman, John Henry. 1982. *The Idea of a University.* Notre Dame: University of Notre Dame Press.

Nietzsche, Friedrich. 1997. *Daybreak.* Translated by R. J. Hollingdale. Cambridge University Press.

Papastephanou, Marianna. 2009. "Method, Philosophy of Education and the Sphere of the Practico-Inert." *Journal of Philosophy of Education* 43(3): 451–70.

Plank, William. 1981. *Sartre and Surrealism.* Umi Research Press.

Plato. 1968. *The Republic.* Translated by Allan Bloom. Basic Books.

Poster, Mark. 1975. *Existential Marxism in Postwar France: From Sartre to Althusser.* Princeton: Princeton University Press.

Pucciani, Oreste F. 1981. "Sartre and Flaubert as Dialectic." In *The Philosophy of Jean-Paul Sartre,* edited by Paul Arthur Schilpp, 495–538. La Salle: Open Court.

Ricoeur, Paul. 1981. "Sartre and Ryle on the Imagination." In *The Philosophy of Jean-Paul Sartre,* edited by Paul Arthur Schilp, 167–78. La Salle: Open Court.

Rybalka, Michel, Oreste F. Pucciani, and Susan Gruenheck. 1981. "An Interview with Jean-Paul Sartre." In *The Philosophy of Jean-Paul Sartre,* edited by Paul Arthur Schilpp, 5–51. La Salle: Open Court.

Sartre, Jean-Paul. 1943. *L'être et le néant: Essai d'ontologie phénoménologique.* Gallimard.

———. 1947. *Situations, I.* Gallimard.

———. 1955. "On *The Sound and the Fury:* Time in the Work of Faulkner." In *Literary and Philosophical Essays.* 84–93. Translated by Annette Michelson. New York: Collier Books.

———. 1960a. *Critique de la raison dialectique (précédé de Question de méthode). Tome I: Théorie des ensembles pratiques.* Paris: Gallimard.

———. 1960b. *The Transcendence of the Ego: An Existentialist Theory of Consciousness.* Translated by Forrest Williams and Robert Kirkpatrick. New York: Hill and Wang.

———. 1964. *Nausea.* Translated by Lloyd Alexander. New Directions Publishing Corporation.

———. 1968. *Search for a Method.* Translated by Hazel E. Barnes. New York: Vintage Books.

———. 1971a. *L'Idiot de la famille. Livre I.* Gallimard.

———. 1971b. *L'Idiot de la famille. Livre II.* Gallimard.

———. 1972. *L'Idiot de la famille. Livre III.* Gallimard.

———. 1974. *Between Existentialism and Marxism.* Translated by John Matthews. New York: Pantheon Books.

———. 1981. *The Family Idiot. Volume 1.* Translated by Carol Cosman. Chicago: The University of Chicago Press.

———. 1984. *Being and Nothingness.* Translated by Hazel E. Barnes. Washington Square Press.

———. 1987. *The Family Idiot. Volume 2.* Translated by Carol Cosman. Chicago: The University of Chicago Press.

———. 1988. *What Is Literature? and Other Essays.* Cambridge: Harvard University Press.

———. 1989. *The Family Idiot. Volume 3.* Translated by Carol Cosman. Chicago: The University of Chicago Press.

———. 1991. *The Family Idiot. Volume 4.* Translated by Carol Cosman. Chicago: The University of Chicago Press.

———. 1992. *Truth and Existence.* Translated by Adrian van den Hoven. Chicago: The University of Chicago Press.

———. 1993. *The Family Idiot. Volume 5.* Translated by Carol Cosman. Chicago: The University of Chicago Press.

———. 2004a. *Critique of Dialectical Reason: Theory of Practical Ensembles. Volume 1.* Translated by Alan Sheridan-Smith. New York: Verso.

———. 2004b. *The Imaginary: A Phenomenological Psychology of the Imagination.* Translated by Jonathan Webber. Routledge.

———. 2007. *Existentialism Is a Humanism.* Translated by Carol Macomber. New Haven: Yale University Press.

———. 2010. *Critical Essays (Situations I).* Translated by Chris Turner. London: Seagull Books.

Somerlatte, Curtis. 2020. "It's About that Time: Sartre's Theory of Temporality." In *The Sartrean Mind,* edited by Matthew C. Eshleman and Constance L. Mui. 198–211. London: Routledge.

Turgenev, Ivan. 2009. *Fathers and Children.* Translated by Michael R. Katz. New York: W. W. Norton & Company.

Warnock, Mary. 1976. *Imagination.* Berkeley: University of California Press.

———. 1977. "Educating the Imagination." *Royal Institute of Philosophy Lectures* 11: 44–60.

Williford, Kenneth. 2020. "Sartrean Reflection: Pure and Impure." In *The Sartrean Mind,* edited by Matthew C. Eshleman and Constance L. Mui. 89–103. London: Routledge.

Index

adequatio (relationship), 157n15; definition of, 68n19; between teachers and students, 64, 68n19
Adorno, Theodor, 186n5
aesthetics: education and, 42n9; existentialism and, 42n9
analoga, 85
apocalyptic moment, for groups, 2
Aristotle, 33, 187n10, 187n12
assimilation, 1
a-synchronous nature, of committed education, 62
authors: conscience of, 89; dialogue readers and, 93
The Autobiography of John Stuart Mill (Mill), 195

bad faith, as concept, 187n15, 200n2
Being and Nothingness (Sartre), 29, 42n13, 131n17; collective imagination in, 89; institutionalized teachers in, 119; *Mitsein* in, 47; phenomenology in, 45; temporality in, 66n1; us-object in, 156n6
Being and Time (Heidegger), 68n18
Bentham, Jeremy, 196
bounded images, public imaginary and, 77
bracketing: by committed teachers, 34; by institutionalized teachers, 123

"The Cartesian Way," 43n19
collective depersonalization, 175–86
collective imagination, 163–64; in *Being and Nothingness,* 89; committed literature and, 88–95; group renewal through, 89
collective personalization, committed literature as, 87–98
collective reductions, of institutionalized teachers, 122–23
committed education: analysis of, 190; a-synchronous nature of, 62; diachronic temporalization of, 46–55; educational thirds and, 54–55; historicization of location in, 62; historicization of students in, 53; imaginative content of, 63; imaginative-temporal process of, 62; Institutionalized Education and, 109; intersubjective temporalization of, 62–66; potentiality for conflict within, 65; practico-inert of, 46–47; presence-absence in, 61; synchronic temporalization of, 55–62; temporal dialogue in, 63; temporal transcendence-immanence

tension and, 62–63; totalization of knowledge in, 54–55
committed literature: collective images and, 87–88; collective imagination and, 88–95; as collective personalization, 87–98; committed act of reading and, 91–92, 94; *communis imaginans* and, 94; community of readers for, 92; conscience of author, 89; in *Critique of Dialectical Reason,* 72; derealization of, 92; diachronic past in, 97–98; as dialectic of time, 98; dialogue between author and reader, 93; educational purpose of, 88; eidetic variations in, 93; the future in, 95–96; group conscience and, 89; group forms of, 88; imaginary of, 98; imaginative modification of, 92; immanence and, 94; institutionalized reading of, 178; Kant and, 93; meaning in, 90–91; memory and, 98; pedagogical role in, 91; perception and, 98; perceptual-imaginative relation to, 92–93; praxis and, 87–98; synchronic demands of, 96–97; syntax in, 100n14; *temporal a priori* of, 90; temporal demands of, 97; temporality of, 95–98; transcendence and, 94; truth in, 91; in *What Is Literature?,* 72
committed students: binary of teacher and, 37–38; conscious relations among, 37–38; demands of, 36–37; dialogue with teachers, 39; educational relations among, 37–38; epistemological relations among, 38; as full group members, 35; functions and tasks of, 36; imaginative epoché of, 35, 38; knowledge for, 38; past selves for, 37; personalization process for, 39–40; reciprocity between, 37–39; synthesis of relations between, 37–38; totalization of, 37–38, 40–41; transcendence-immanence tension and, 35; truth for, 38; as unique third, 37, 40–41
committed teachers, 35; arch-function of, 29; bracketing by, 34; common objectives of, 29; as concept, 22; empathy and, 31; empirical reduction and, 34; existential orientation of, 32; forms of teaching for, 31; imaginative reduction and, 34; knowledge of students, 31–32; orientation of, 22; pedagogical task of, 30, 32; personalization of, 31; the present for, 29–31; reciprocity and, 28–30; role of, 22; the third and, 28–30, 32; transcendence-immanence tension and, 29–30, 33
communis imaginans, 7–8; committed literature and, 94
conflict. *See Mitsein*
conscience: of authors, 89; group, 89; of readers, 89
Contat, Michel, 6–7
continuity, 187n12
creation. *See* imposed creation; passive creation
creative imagination, dialectic and, 8
creative imperative, of groups, 26
“A Crisis in my Mental History” (Mill), 197
Critique of Dialectical Reason (Sartre), 3; committed literature and, 72; conflict of rationalities in, 8; diachronic dimension in, 45; education in, 15; group forms in, 1–2, 10n7, 16; individual in, 1–2; Institutionalized Education and, 138–39; practico-inert in, 47–48; reciprocity in, 28–30; regressive elements of, 6; the third in, 28–30; transcendental imagination in, 41n5
Critique of Pure Reason (Kant), 41n5; as committed literature, 93

Daybreak (Nietzsche), 68nn15–16

degraded Organizations, 3–4
Democritus, 67n13
depersonalization: collective, 175–86; definition of, 109–10; in Institutionalized Education, 138, 141; institutionalized reading and, 181; of institutionalized students, 126–27, 129; of institutionalized teachers, 118; intersubjective process of, 113; as negation, 110; personalization as process of, 7; reflection and, 111; of students, 151; of teachers, 109–15; temporal dimensions of, 112–13
derealization: of committed literature, 92; imagination and, 165; of objects, 85
detemporalization: imaginative-temporal repetition, 183–84; of Institutionalized Education, 154; of institutionalized literature, 182–86
determinate past, 97
detotalization: of education, 11n11; personalization and, 6
diachronic dimension: in committed literature, 97–98; in *Critique of Dialectical Reason,* 45; in *The Family Idiot,* 45, 67n2; of the Organization, 49; of past generations, 60; synchronic temporalization conflict with, 59
diachronic temporalization: of committed education, 46–55; generational elements of, 50–51; generations and, 55; of groups, 52–53; of Institutionalized Education, 134–44, 152; limits of, 51; macrocosmic character of, 136; microcosmic character of, 136; multi-dimensional, 135–36; personalization of education in, 48–49; practico-inert in, 47–48, 50; primary processes of, 135; secondary processes of, 135; teachers and, 146
Dialectic of Enlightenment (Adorno and Horkheimer), 186n5
dialectic of time, committed literature as, 98
dialectic reason: creative imagination and, 8; definition of, 3; imagination and, 9; public imaginary and, 80. *See also* institutionalized dialectic; temporal dialectic
Dostoevsky, Fyodor, 201n12

education, educational systems and: aesthetics and, 42n9; apparatuses of, 23–24; arch-task of, 29; character of, 17; committed, 46–55; through committed literature, 88; concrete objectives of, 15; in *Critique of Dialectical Reason,* 4–5, 15; definition of, 25; detotalization of, 11n11; diachronic temporalization and, 48–49; existentialist theories of, 10n6, 42n9; as form of generational conflict, 50–51; as form of resistance, 5, 28; in France, 9n3; of group members, 19; groups as influence on, 6; historical grounding as element of, 24–25; of imagination, 193; imagination in, 42n9, 103; institutionalized tasks of, 105–9; lived-experience of time in, 46; lived-time for students, 64; Marxism and, 5; methodological approach to, 104–5; oppressive theories of, 103–5; personalization of, 11n11, 22, 48–49; pre-temporalization of, 150; purpose of, 4; reinterpretation of, 4; retotalization of, 11n11; spontaneity of, 103; synchronic dimension of, 55; task of, 17–21; temporal limits of, 61; in *What is Literature?,* 4. *See also* Institutionalized Education; students; teachers
educational objects, 82
eidetic reductions, Husserl on, 33, 42n17, 93

empathy: committed teachers and, 31; of groups, 22; towards individuals, 22; of institutionalized teachers, 121
empirical reduction, 34
epoché, 194; of committed students, 35, 38; imaginative, 35, 38; phenomenological, 189–90; students outside of, 33
existentialism: aesthetics and, 42n9; of committed teachers, 32; education and, 10n6, 42n9; of institutionalized teachers, 121; Marxism and, 104; psychoanalysis of, 22

The Family Idiot (Sartre), 10n6, 41n3; diachrony in, 45, 67n2; group theory in, 16; imagination in, 186n1; "objective neurosis" in, 72, 160; Objective Spirit in, 48, 51–52; personalization in, 6; practico-inert in, 47–48; public imaginary in, 78; real/unreal distinction in, 42n10; synchrony in, 67n2
Fathers and Children (Turgenev), 201n12
Faulkner, William, 10n8
Flaubert, Gustave: Mill compared to, 191, 195–200; oracular character of, 162; psychoanalysis of, 32; public imaginary and, 74; Sartre on, 1, 6–7, 9n2, 11n11, 161–62
France, educational system in, 9n3
freedom: literature and, 20; pedagogical, 24–25; Sartre on, 106; transcendental, 115
Freud, Sigmund, 187n11, 187n13
the future: in committed literature, 95–96; dual future of teachers, 60; in *The Imaginary,* 95, 172–73; for teachers, 21–22, 24, 110–11, 145–46. *See also* the past; the present
future-past, for teachers, 145–46
future teachers, 110–11
generational temporality, 47–48; education and, 50–51; historical sequences of, 51
generations: diachronic dimension of, 60; diachronic temporalization and, 55; within the Organization, 49–50, 57–58; public imaginary of, 75
Giroux, Henry, 41n4
Greene, Maxine, 42n9
groups: apocalyptic moment for, 2; collective imagination of, 89; committed students as members of, 35; common objectives of, 3, 8; as *communis imaginans,* 7–8; conscience for, 89; creative imperative of, 26; in *Critique of Dialectical Reason,* 1–2, 10n7, 16; diachronic temporalization of, 52–53; dissolution into seriality for, 2–3; distribution and reciprocity of tasks within, 18–19; educational effects of, 6; education of members, 19; empathy towards individuals, 22; empirical tasks for, 81–82; failure of imagination for, 7; in *The Family Idiot,* 16; forms of, 3; hierarchies in, 18, 20; literary, 21; long-term goals of, 17; Organization and, 15; pedagogical freedom of, 24–25; pedagogical imagination and, 26; personalization of, 6; *praxis,* 7; prefabricated inertia of, 8; public imaginary by, 73–74; reciprocity between members, 83; recruitment for, 18; reflection of, 15–16; restrictions of, 23; Sartre theory on, 6; short-term goals of, 17; social imaginary of, 78; specialized apparatuses of, 18–19; statutory, 15; synchronic temporalization of, 52–53; totalization of members in, 16–17

Hegel, Georg Wilhelm Friedrich, 100n22

Heidegger, Martin, 11n13, 68n18
hierarchies: of group tasks, 18, 20; among institutionalized students, 125
historical time, synchronic temporalization of, 55
Horkheimer, Max, 186n5
Husserl, Edmund, 9n1, 157n16; on assimilation, 1; on eidetic reductions, 33, 42n17, 93; *Ideas I,* 41n8; on intentionality, 1; phenomenological reduction of, 33, 131n19, 132n20; on retention of teachers, 60; Sartre's critique of, 131n19, 132n20; on temporal objects, 68n17

Ideas I (Husserl), 41n8
images: bounded, 77; in committed literature, 87–88; false images of, 11n14; in *The Imaginary,* 71–72; in institutionalized literature, 175; in institutionalized reading, 176; language through, 20; perception through, 84–85; public imaginary and, 77; of reality, 115; in *What is Literature?,* 26
imaginary: of committed literature, 98; conflict of, 8; institutionalized teachers and, 115, 121–22; pedagogical, 76; public, 72–81; teachers and, 27
The Imaginary (Sartre), 7; future in, 95, 172–73; imagination in, 186n1, 191; individual image in, 71–72; institutionalized literature, 184
imaginary teachers, 27
imagination: actuality of, 194; collective nature of, 88–95, 163–64; in committed education, 63; in committed literature, 88–95; creative, 8; in *Critique of Dialectical Reason,* 41n5; derealization and, 165; dialectical reason and, 9; in education, 42n9, 103; education of, 193; epoché and, 35; in *The Family Idiot,* 186n1; of groups, 7; in *The Imaginary,* 186n1, 191; institutionalized, 164–65; institutionalized dialectic of, 167–75; of Institutionalized Education, 8–9; instrumentalization of, 114–15, 167–68; limitations of, 172; memory and, 187n16; object dimensions and, 171; pedagogical, 26; perception and, 166, 187n8; phenomenologies of, 191–95; potentiality of, 194; repetition as component of, 166–67; reproductive, 8–9; Sartre on, 2, 42n10, 99n1; of students, 26–27; of teachers, 22; temporal dialectic of, 81–87; transcendental, 41n5
imaginative *analoga,* 85
imaginative reductions, 33–34
imaginative-temporal repetition, 183–84
immanence: collective, 182; committed literature and, 94; institutionalized reading and, 182; of institutionalized students, 125; of students, 118–19, 125. *See also* transcendence-immanence tension
immanent reflection, 17
immediate past, 97
imposed creation, 178
individuals, individuality and: in *Critique of Dialectical Reason,* 1–2; empathy towards, 22; in Institutionalized Education, 104; relations to objects for, 83; restrictions of, 23; synchronic temporalization of, 57
inertia. *See* prefabricated inertia
Institution. *See* Institutionalized Education
institutionalized dialectic: asymmetrical symmetry in, 169; group harmony and, 170; of imagination, 167–75; of perception, 167–75
Institutionalized Education (Institution): as anti-dialectical, 130n4; committed education and, 109; *Critique of Dialectical*

Reason and, 138–39; as degraded Organizations, 3–4, 139; depersonalization in, 138, 141; detemporalization of, 154; diachronic temporalization of, 134–44, 152; discontinuity of, 148; educational *praxis* and, 136, 138; imaginary and, 160–67; individuals in, 104; linearity of, 148; mechanisms of, 148; methodological approach to, 2–9; microtemporalization of, 133–34; need as element of, 110; as negation of transcendence, 107–8; Objective Spirit and, 138; objective time in, 144; oracular nature of, 160–67; as perpetual space, 121; personalization in, 137–39, 141; practico-inert and, 110, 135–36, 145; purpose of, 5; reflection in, 105–6; reproductive imagination of, 8–9; as responsibility, 108; scarcity and, 110; serialized temporalization of, 151–56; sovereignty in, 106–7, 110–11, 134–35; synchronic temporalization of, 140–42, 144–51; tasks of, 105–9; temporal dimensions and rhythms of, 149–50, 154–55; totalization in, 134; transcendence-immanence tension and, 141, 151–52, 155; transformation of, 8; "une education-à-faire," 136–37; "une éducation-faite," 136–37. *See also* institutionalized teachers; students; teachers

institutionalized imagination, 164–65

institutionalized literature: as collective depersonalization, 175–86; collective temporalization, 185; detemporalization of, 182–86; images in, 175; *The Imaginary,* 184; imaginative-temporal repetition, 183–84; institutionalized reading, 176–82; as oppressive, 175–76; reality and, 184–85

institutionalized perception, 163

institutionalized reading: collective immanence, 182; of committed literature, 178; depersonalization and, 181; images in, 176; isolation of literature and, 181–82; literary demands of, 179–80; noetic-moematic correlations in, 177; pedagogical functions of, 178; sovereignty and, 177–78, 180–82; structure of consciousness in, 176–77; transcendence-immanence tension and, 182; truths in, 178; *What is Literature?,* 178–81

institutionalized students: analysis by, 127–28; collective perceptions of, 129–30; demands of, 126; depersonalization of, 126–27, 129; educational *praxis* and, 128; hierarchical culture of, 125; identification of, 127; immanence of, 125; isolation of, 128; mediation between, 128; passivity of, 124, 126; pedagogical regulation of teachers and, 127; reciprocity between, 126, 128; sovereignty of teachers and, 125, 129–30; synthesis by, 127–28; as third parties, 124–26; totalization of teachers and, 125, 128–30; transcendence of, 125

institutionalized teachers, 124; in *Being and Nothingness,* 119; bracketing by, 123; collective perceiving of, 121; collective reduction of, 122–23; degraded form of presence for, 120; depersonalization of, 118; empathy of, 121; empirical reduction and, 123; existentialism of, 121; imagination and, 115, 121–22; immanence of students and, 118–19; pedagogy of, 115, 119; perception and, 115, 121–22; personalization of, 115; reciprocity and, 117; reflection of, 116–17; role of, 117, 119; sovereignty of, 116; ternary relations and, 117; as third, 117–19,

131n13; transcendence-immanence tension and, 118–19; transcendental character of, 118
intentionality, Husserl on, 1
intersubjective temporalization: of committed education, 62–66; plurality of dimension in, 65

Kant, Immanuel, 41n5, 93, 166, 186n5
Kant and the Problem of Metaphysics (Heidegger), 11n13
Kern, Iso, 43n19
Kierkegaard, Søren, on teaching, 27
knowledge: for committed students, 38; digestive theories of, 1; of the past, 21–22; synchronic temporalization and, 61; totalization of, 54–55; transcendence through, 30–31

literary groups, 21
literature: freedom and, 20; institutionalized, 176–82; isolation of, 181–82; metaphysics and, 10n8. *See also* committed literature; reading

Marxism: education and, 5; existentialism and, 104
meaning, in committed literature, 90–91
memory: committed literature and, 98; imagination and, 187n16
Merleau-Ponty, Maurice, 99n3
The Metaphysical Foundations of Logic (Heidegger), 68n18
Metaphysics (Aristotle), 187n10
microtemporalization, 173, 199; of Institutionalized Education, 133–34
Mill, John Stuart: Flaubert compared to, 191, 195–200; microtemporalization and, 199; oracular character of, 200; personalization and, 199; *Utilitarianism,* 201n12
mimetic imperative, 114
Mitsein (conflict), 47
multi-dimensional diachronic temporalization, 135–36

Nausea (Sartre), 104
need: Institutionalized Education and, 110; Sartre on, 5
Nietzsche, Friedrich, 68n15
noetic-moematic correlations, in institutionalized reading, 177
Notes from Underground (Dostoevsky), 201n12

"objective neurosis," in *The Family Idiot,* 72, 160
Objective Spirit, in *The Family Idiot,* 48, 51–52, 138
objective-subjective time, 61, 68n18
objects: derealization of, 85; individuals' relationship to, 83; temporalization of truth and, 85; in *What is Literature?,* 84
"On *The Sound and the Fury*" (Sartre), 10n8
oracle: Flaubert as, 162; imaginary and, 160–67; Institutionalized Education and, 160–67; Mills as, 200
the Organization: definition of, 3; degraded Organizations, 3–4, 139; diachronic dimension of, 49; distribution of tasks within, 82; as form of self-reflection, 16; generations within, 49–50, 57–58; as permanent reorganization, 39; personalization in, 16; *praxis* and, 16; public imaginary for, 75; as reflection of statutory group, 15; relation between past and present and, 50–51; Sartre on, 17; synchronic dimension of, 49; synchronic temporalization of, 57–58; system of relations, 17; temporal rhythm of, 57. *See also* Institutionalized Education

passive creation, 178

the past: in committed literature, 97–98; determinate past, 97; diachronic, 97–98; dual past of teachers, 60; immediate past, 97; knowledge of, 21–22; the Organization and, 50–51; for teachers, 21–22; teaching influenced by, 148–49. *See also* the future; the present
past-future, for teachers, 145–46
pedagogical imaginary, public imaginary and, 76
pedagogy: committed literature and, 91; freedom of groups and, 24–25; imagination and, 26; institutionalized reading and, 178; institutionalized students and, 127; regulation of, 127; revisions of, 25–26; of teachers, 25–26, 115, 119
perception: collective, 129–30; committed literature and, 98; image as primary mode of access, 84–85; imagination and, 166, 187n8; institutionalized, 163; institutionalized dialectic of, 167–75; of institutionalized students, 129–30; institutionalized teachers and, 115, 121–22; object dimensions and, 171; origins in, 165–66; public imaginary and, 79; temporal dialectic of, 81–87; in *What is Literature?,* 115
personalization: collective, 87–98; committed literature and, 87–98; for committed students, 39–40; of committed teachers, 31; de-personalization process and, 7; detotalization and, 6; of education, 11n11, 22, 48–49; in *The Family Idiot,* 6; of groups, 6; in Institutionalized Education, 137–39, 141; of institutionalized teachers, 115; Mill and, 199; through the Organization, 16; plurality of, 22; as process, 23; public imaginary and, 74, 76; retotalization and, 6; synchronic temporalization and, 61; of teachers, 21–28, 113–14; temporalization and, 87. *See also* depersonalization
phenomenology: in *Being and Nothingness,* 45; "The Cartesian Way" and, 43n19; epoché and, 189–90; Husserl on, 33; of imagination, 191–95; Sartre on, 43n19
Philosophy from Plato to Derrida, 201n12
Philosophy of Right (Hegel), 100n22
Plato, 11n14
positive creative imperative, 114
practico-inert, 156n3; of committed education, 46–47; in *Critique of Dialectical Reason,* 47–48; in diachronic temporalization, 47–48, 50; in *The Family Idiot,* 47–48; Institutionalized Education and, 110, 135–36, 145; positive character of, 156n4; of public imaginary, 78; synchronic temporalization as, 58
praxis: committed literature and, 87–98; group, 7; Institutionalized Education and, 136, 138; institutionalized students and, 128; the Organization and, 16; public imaginary and, 79
prefabricated inertia, of group, 8
presence-absence, in committed education, 61
the present: for committed teachers, 29–31; the Organization and, 50–51; for public imaginary, 75; teachers and, 21–22; teaching and, 148–49. *See also* the future; the past
public imaginary, 72; bounded images and, 77; as constantly changing, 76–77, 80; content of life and, 74–75; cultural context for students and, 73; dialectical development of, 80; establishment of, 73; in *The Family Idiot,* 78; Flaubert and, 74; by groups, 73–74; modification of reality and, 79; new forms of, 77; as objective transcendental

condition, 77; oracular character of, 74–75; for the Organization, 75; of past generations, 75; pedagogical imaginary and, 76; perception and, 79; personalization process and, 74, 76; practico-inert of, 78; *praxis* and, 79; present forms of, 75; in public life, 73; repetition in, 80–81; social element of, 78; student style and, 73, 75; in *What is Literature?,* 73

reading, act of: committed literature and, 91–92, 94; community of readers, 92; conscience of readers, 89; definition of, 20; institutionalized, 176–82
reality: images of, 115; institutionalized literature and, 184–85; modification of, 79; public imaginary and, 79. *See also* derealization
reciprocity: between committed students, 37–39; committed teachers and, 28–30; in *Critique of Dialectical Reason,* 28–30; fixed, 39; between group members, 83; of group tasks, 18; between institutionalized students, 126, 128; institutionalized teachers and, 117; mediated, 3; Sartre on, 28, 38–39; for the third, 3
reductions, 194; collective, 122–23; conceptual development of, 189–90; eidetic, 33; empirical, 34, 123; imaginative, 33–34; of institutionalized teachers, 122–23; phenomenological, 33, 131n19, 132n20
reflection: depersonalization and, 111; of groups, 15–16; immanent, 17; in Institutionalized Education, 105–6; of institutionalized teachers, 116–17; Sartre on, 2; totalization of, 105–6. *See also* self-reflection
relationship. *See adequatio*
re-personalization, as permanent, 39
repetition: imagination and, 166–67; imaginative-temporal, 183–84; in public imaginary, 80–81
reproductive imagination, 8–9
resistance: as "negative" concept, 46; by teachers, 28, 56
retotalization: of education, 11n11; personalization and, 6
Romanticism, 199
Rybalka, Michel, 6–7

Sartre, Jean-Paul: critique of Husserl, 131n19, 132n20; on dialectic reason, 3, 8–9; on educational objects, 82; on Flaubert, 1, 6–7, 9n2, 11n11, 161–62; on freedom, 106; on groups, 6; on imagination, 42n10; the look for, 2; *Nausea,* 104; on need, 5; on "objective neurosis," 72, 160; "On *The Sound and the Fury,*" 10n8; on the Organization, 17; on phenomenology, 43n19; on public imaginary, 72–81; on reciprocity, 28, 38–39; on reflection, 2; on scarcity, 5; *Search for a Method,* 5, 104; on social image, 72; social imaginary and, 78, 99n4; on synchronic temporalization, 45–46; as teacher, 9n4; on temporality, 2; the third and, 2; on transcendence-immanence tension, 29–30. *See also Being and Nothingness*; *Critique of Dialectical Reason*; existentialism; *The Family Idiot*; *The Imaginary*; *What Is Literature?*; *specific topics*
scarcity: Institutionalized Education and, 110; Sartre on, 5
schema, 41n5
schematism, 186n5
screen memories, 187n11
Search for a Method (Sartre), 5, 104
self-reflection, the Organization as form of, 16
seriality, group dissolution into, 2–3

serialized temporalization, of Institutionalized Education, 151–56
social image, 72, 99n4
social imaginary, 99n4; of groups, 78
sovereignty: culture of, 162–63; definition of, 106–7; in Institutionalized Education, 106–7, 110–11, 134–35; institutionalized reading and, 177–78, 180–82; institutionalized students and, 125, 129–30; of institutionalized teachers, 116, 125, 129–30; totalization of, 107
statutory groups, 15
students: committed, 35–41; committed teachers' knowledge of, 31–32; as dependent thirds, 66; depersonalization of, 151; as historical thirds, 143–44; historicization of, 53; imagination of, 26–27; institutionalized, 124–30; lived-time for education of, 64; outside epoché, 33; passive totalization of, 152; public imaginary for, 73, 75; serialized temporalization and, 151–56; synchronic education of, 55; temporal adequation with teachers, 64, 68n19; temporal dialogue with teachers, 63; temporal transcendence-immanence tension of, 62–63, 151–52; transcendence-immanence tension, 35, 62–63, 151–52
surrealism, critique of, 186n7
synchronic dimension: in committed literature, 96–97; of education, 55; in *The Family Idiot,* 67n2; of the Organization, 49; students and, 55
synchronic temporalization: of collective, 57; of committed education, 55–62; communication of knowledge and, 61; diachronic conflict in, 59; of groups, 52–53; of historical time, 55; of individual, 57; of Institutionalized Education, 140–42, 144–51; limits of, 61; objective-subjective time and, 61; of the Organization, 57–58; personalization as element of, 61; as practico-inert, 58; Sartre on, 45–46; of teachers, 55–62; teachers and, 146–47
synchronic totalization, 46
syntax, in committed literature, 100n14

teachers: adaptability of, 25; anticipation of future, 21–22, 24; committed, 22, 28–35; committed students and, 37–39; cultural rhythm of, 56; curricula development by, 26; depersonalization of, 109–15; diachronic temporalization and, 146; dual past/future of, 60; educational apparatuses of, 23–24; as educational third, 40, 54; elements of teaching, 25; future, 110–11, 145–46; future-past for, 145–46; Husserl on, 60; ignorance of, 22; imaginary and, 27; imagination of, 22; institutionalized, 115–24; knowledge of past and, 21–22; lived-time of, 150–51; mimetic imperative of, 114; past-future for, 145–46; pedagogical revisions by, 25–26; pedagogy of, 115, 119; personalization of, 21–28, 113–14; positive creative imperative and, 114; in present, 21–22; resistance by, 28, 56; retention of, 60; revolutionary rhythm of, 56–57; spontaneity of, 25; synchronic temporalization and, 146–47; temporal adequation with students, 64, 68n19; temporal dialogue with students, 63; temporal-imaginative acts of, 66; temporal rhythm of, 56; totalization of, 53; as transcendent-immanent third, 41
teaching: by committed teachers, 28–35; form of, 31; Kierkegaard on, 27; lived-time of, 150; the past as

influence on, 148–49; present act of, 148–49; spontaneity of, 150
temporal dialectic: of imagination, 81–87; of perception, 81–87
temporality: in *Being and Nothingness,* 66n1; of committed literature, 95–98; depersonalization and, 112–13; generational, 47–48; Husserl on, 68n17; Sartre on, 2. *See also* the future; the past; the present; synchronic temporalization
temporalization: collective, 185; intersubjective, 62–66; microtemporalization, 133–34, 173, 199; multiplicity of, 86, 173–74; personalization and, 87; re-orientation of, 86–87; serialized, 151–56; standardized, 173–74; of truth, 85. *See also* diachronic temporalization; synchronic temporalization
the third, as concept, 2; committed education and, 54–55; committed students as, 37, 40–41; committed teachers and, 28–30, 32; in *Critique of Dialectical Reason,* 28–30; institutionalized students as, 124–26; institutionalized teachers as, 117–19, 131n13; mediated reciprocity and, 3; students as dependent thirds, 66; students as historical thirds, 143–44; teachers as, 28–30, 32, 40, 54; transcendent-immanent, 41
totalization: of committed students, 37–38, 40–41; of group members, 16–17; in Institutionalized Education, 134; institutionalized students and, 125, 128–30; of knowledge, 54–55; of reflection, 105–6; of sovereignty, 107; of students, 152; synchronic, 46; of teachers, 53, 125, 128–30
transcendence: committed literature and, 94; freedom and, 115; genuine forms of, 157n13; Institutionalized Education as negation of, 107–8; of institutionalized students, 125; of institutionalized teachers, 118; through knowledge, 30–31
transcendence-immanence tension: committed students and, 35; committed teachers and, 29–30, 33; Institutionalized Education and, 141, 151–52, 155; institutionalized reading and, 182; institutionalized teachers and, 118–19; Sartre on, 29–30; of students, 35, 62–63, 151–52; teachers and, 41; temporal, 62–63, 151–52; the third and, 41
transcendental imagination, 41n5
truth: in committed literature, 91; for committed students, 38; in institutionalized reading, 178; temporalization of, 85
Turgenev, Ivan, 201n12

"une education-à-faire," 136–37
"une éducation-faite," 136–37
utilitarianism, 199
Utilitarianism (Mill), 201n12

What Is Literature? (Sartre), 5, 20, 99n12; committed literature and, 72; critique of surrealism, 186n7; education role in, 4; images in, 26; institutionalized reading and, 178–81; needs of perception in, 115; objects in, 84; public imaginary in, 73

About the Author

Cameron Bassiri is a senior professorial lecturer in the Department of Philosophy and Religion at American University, Washington, DC. His research interests include phenomenology, existentialism, nineteenth-century philosophy, and the philosophy of education. He has taught a variety of courses in the history of philosophy such as "Philosophy and Literature," "Phenomenology and the Social World," and "Philosophy and Psychoanalysis." His last book—*Ideas toward a Phenomenology of Interruptions*, on Edmund Husserl and the phenomenology of time—was published in 2018 by Lexington Books.